Beyond Diagnosis

For Vic Meyer, in Memoriam

Beyond Diagnosis

Case Formulation in Cognitive Behavioural Therapy

SECOND EDITION

Edited by

Michael Bruch

WILEY Blackwell

This edition first published 2015
© 2015 John Wiley & Sons, Ltd.

Registered Office
John Wiley & Sons, Ltd, The Atrium, Southern Gate, Chichester, West Sussex, PO19 8SQ, UK

Editorial Offices
350 Main Street, Malden, MA 02148-5020, USA
9600 Garsington Road, Oxford, OX4 2DQ, UK
The Atrium, Southern Gate, Chichester, West Sussex, PO19 8SQ, UK

For details of our global editorial offices, for customer services, and for information about
how to apply for permission to reuse the copyright material in this book please see our
website at www.wiley.com/wiley-blackwell.

Library of Congress Cataloging-in-Publication Data

Beyond diagnosis (Bruch)
Beyond diagnosis : case formulation in cognitive behavioural therapy / edited by Michael
Bruch. – Second edition.
    p. ; cm.
  Includes bibliographical references and index.
  ISBN 978-1-119-96076-8 (cloth) – ISBN 978-1-119-96075-1 (pbk.)
I. Bruch, Michael, editor.   II. Title.
[DNLM: 1. Cognitive Therapy–methods.   2. Anxiety Disorders–diagnosis.
3. Anxiety Disorders–therapy.   WM 425.5.C6]
  RC473.C37
  616.89′14–dc23
                                                                    2014026820

A catalogue record for this book is available from the British Library.

Cover image: Magnifying glass with finger print © kostsov/iStockphoto.
Fingerprint series © wh1600/iStockphoto

Set in 10/12pt Sabon by SPi Publisher Services, Pondicherry, India
Printed and bound in Malaysia by Vivar Printing Sdn Bhd

1   2015

Contents

List of Contributors

Michael Bruch — Research Department of Clinical, Educational and Health Psychology, University College London, London, UK

Richard S. Hallam — Department of Psychology, University of Greenwich, London, UK

Peter G. AuBuchon — Department of Psychiatry, Pennsylvania Hospital & University of Pennsylvania Health System, Philadelphia, PA, USA

Kieron O'Connor — Department of Psychiatry, University of Montreal, Montreal, Québec, Canada
and
OCD Spectrum Study Research Centre, Fernand-Seguin Research Centre, Louis-H. Lafontaine Hospital, Montreal, Quebec, Canada

Amélie Drolet-Marcoux — Clinical Psychology Service, Department of Psychoeducation and Psychology, University of Quebec at Outaouais, Gatineau, Quebec, Canada

Geneviève Larocque — Clinical Psychology Service, Department of Psychoeducation and Psychology, University of Quebec at Outaouais, Gatineau, Quebec, Canada

Karolan Gervais — Clinical Psychology Service, Department of Psychoeducation and Psychology, University of Quebec at Outaouais, Gatineau, Quebec, Canada

Samia Ezzamel   Department of Mental Health and Learning Disabilities, London South Bank University, London, UK

Marcantonio M. Spada   Department of Psychology, London South Bank University, London, UK

Ana V. Nikčević   Department of Psychology, Kingston University, London, UK

David A. Lane   Institute for Work Based Learning, Middlesex University, London, UK
and
Professional Development Foundation, London, UK

Sarah Corrie   Institute for Work Based Learning, Middlesex University, London, UK
and
The Central London CBT Centre, CNWL Foundation Trust & Royal Holloway University of London, London, UK

Foreword

During the days I trained doctoral students in clinical psychology, I would begin with a very simple instruction: *understand what you are dealing with before you do anything.* This statement reveals the core of any effective and durable approach to treating a psychological problem.

The genesis of this line of thinking has many roots, but the British Psychological Society in 2011 identified historically four 'influential clinicians' as such in their landmark issuance of the *Good Practice Guidelines on the Use of Psychological Formulation:* Hans J. Eysenck, Victor Meyer, Monte B. Shapiro and I. Putting my own contributions aside (Turkat, 2014), each of the others had a profound impact on the field, and in my opinion, the present text represents primarily the influence of the lesser known of the three: Vic Meyer.

Eysenck led the United Kingdom to develop clinical psychology as a profession of science and not conjecture and became one of the most highly cited intellectuals in the history of mankind.

Shapiro innovated brilliantly how to apply the experimental method to the individual case, taking our clinical responsibilities a step beyond the requisite reliance upon existing knowledge generated by basic scientific research.

Both are considered to be founding fathers of clinical psychology in the United Kingdom, and their contributions are felt worldwide. But it was Meyer who devised a fascinating approach to *formulating an individual case* that met the criteria set forth by Eysenck and Shapiro that clinical actions be grounded in the knowledge produced by scientific research and that the scientific method be applied to the individual case. In so doing, Vic Meyer developed highly creative, impactful, and long-lasting contributions to the field at the practice level, unmatched by the vast overwhelming majority of mental health practitioners of the past half-century. His approach has touched clinical minds in every continent, including many unaware of his influence.

According to Vic, there was no standard intervention that could be effective for all and thus he promoted the notion that treatment must always be based on the unique presentation of the individual. To get there, there were some obvious prior steps: examine the presenting behavioural problems in descriptive detail, carefully trace their history, develop a theory unique to those problems about why they came about and continue, and then subject your theory to evaluation.

Unlike some forms of therapy in which the clinician would never, infrequently, or minimally reveal one's thinking about the patient's psychopathology, Vic would explain his theory directly to the patient in detail, seek confirmatory and disconfirmatory evidence, and adapt accordingly.

Vic viewed the therapist as a detective – searching for clues to come to an understanding and then subjecting that understanding to the reality of the clinical data. Once an explanatory theory was devised that was consistent with *all* of the data and was verifiable, then, one would be forced to create a treatment based uniquely on that theory. In this way, not only was treatment guaranteed to be individualized, it made the entire process open to scrutiny and therefore, accountability. For in the end, whatever you did would either positively impact your patient's functioning or not, and that could be measured in an observable way.

The fruits of this approach were many and their presentation is beyond the space limitations I face here, but easily illustrated with Meyer's brilliant adaption of basic animal research to innovate a unique treatment for certain cases with significant history of treatment failure: those suffering from debilitating compulsive rituals. His development in the 1960s of treatment for obsessive–compulsive motor rituals by response prevention stemmed from this approach and remains today one of the most effective tools available for appropriately formulated cases.

This example of Vic's innovations brings us to a fundamental distinction raised by his work and debated among mental health professionals for decades: psychiatric diagnosis. I will leave this debate to other forums, but it is critical to understand that Vic would never advocate response prevention for all cases of motor rituals. Why? Because it is the formulation of the individual case that sets the groundwork for developing a uniquely designed treatment that may or may not borrow or improvise upon existing techniques. More simply: it is not the diagnosis that drives the treatment but the conceptualization of the idiosyncratic attributes of the presenting case. As such, one must go *beyond diagnosis* if the goal is to truly understand the psychopathology in front of your eyes in order to be in a position to provide the proper intervention.

With this distinction between formulation and diagnosis, the present volume highlights the former. And there is no person better suited to bring this approach to you today than Michael Bruch, who not only practices, teaches and supervises others along these lines in London and elsewhere, but has devoted his entire career to evolving Vic's approach to clinical phenomena.

The reader will find this second edition of *Beyond Diagnosis* to be a most welcome addition to the clinical psychology literature.

Ira Turkat

Reference

Turkat, I. D. (2014). An historical perspective on the impact of case formulation. *The Behavior Therapist*, 37, 180–188.

Preface

Since the first publication of *Beyond Diagnosis*, now 15 years ago, clinical as well as academic interest in case formulation has grown enormously. At the time researchers involved in developing cognitive–behavioural therapy (CBT) were mostly interested in treatment protocols and manuals whereas case formulation was largely ignored or undervalued by the academic community. For example, Beck (1976) stated that CBT developed without much explicit reference to case formulation, and Schulte and coworkers (1992) claimed that individualized tailored interventions offered no advantages over manualized treatment procedures.

The first edition of this book was enormously popular with clinicians and training institutions alike, and I believe that it had great influence in bringing case formulation to the attention of a wider audience. It is very gratifying to see that over the years, earlier attitudes have now changed considerably and there appears growing interest in paying more attention to clinical realities in a 'bottom up' approach as some may call it. This is evidenced by a growing body of literature on case formulation, especially for more complex cases. However, for some, this just seems to mean improving clinical outcomes whilst others have suggested much broader or eclectic definitions (e.g. Eels, 2007).

I also note that the British Psychological Society (2011), in their response to the latest DSM5 draft, is now expressing a strong commitment to case formulation–driven procedures in the assessment and treatment of behavioural disorders. This stance on formulation contrasts with the recent government initiative to improve access to psychological therapies (IAPT). Although this initiative has hugely transformed cognitive–behavioural psychotherapy services in the United Kingdom, from the case formulation point of view, there appears to be a renewed tendency to medicalize psychological problems and rely on manualized procedures rather than individually-tailored therapy.

As shall be detailed in Chapter 1, formulating cases on the basis of individualized assessments guided by learning principles and experimental psychology was originally proposed by Hans Eysenck. However, it was Victor Meyer, the *clinical* pioneer of individualized behaviour therapy, who delivered a viable procedure (now labelled, after several revisions, *cognitive–behavioural case formulation*). Meyer's work has inspired many academics and clinicians since, and some of those have developed this model further, providing enhanced conceptual clarity and more precise definitions.

Unlike the first edition of this book, the current text is exclusively dedicated to Meyer's pioneering work, also known as the 'Middlesex approach'.

What is unique to Meyer's model? Unlike many ideas and models coming out of academic 'ivory towers', Meyers's approach is closely linked to the complexity of clinical realities, in particular to complex cases, and was developed and refined gradually over many years. This was done predominantly to the benefit of the patient as opposed to the furthering of academic ambitions. Vic himself was a rather reluctant publicist and always a little suspicious of research conducted in academic writings by scientists who he thought rarely saw 'real patients'.

Perhaps because of this, Vic's seminal work did not receive the publicity and academic attention it should have had; however, he was greatly acknowledged by clinicians and students all over the world for his clinical and training skills.

In comparison to other developments in behaviour therapy, Meyer's approach was predominantly rooted in the psychiatric setting, where 'treatment as usual' was rarely effective or appropriate when treating the more severe and complex cases that were referred. From work with these complex cases, it appeared that an individual case formulation approach, guided by experimental psychology and based on learning principles, achieved better results with patients than did the more ubiquitous approach of matching patient symptoms to specific techniques (the mainstay of proponents of psychiatric diagnosis).

Why was such an approach more effective and helpful to patients (and therapists)? This is for mainly for two reasons: (1) even seemingly similar presenting complaints showed great individual variation regarding development, presentation and maintenance and (2) it was unsatisfactory if not impossible to understand and conceptualize more severe, complex problems according to diagnostic categories, particularly when either multiple or non-specific complaints were reported.

Unfortunately, since these pioneering days, clinical case formulation has remained very much a backwater as the interest of mostly academic psychologists shifted to developing standard protocols suited to randomised controlled trials (RCT) research methodologies and geared towards psychiatric disorders. The goal was to create evidence-based protocols to treat the 'symptoms' grouped within psychiatric syndromes.

However, the wheel has now turned full circle and it is back to basics with increasing interest in complex and challenging problems. Over the past two decades, case formulation has gradually gained more attention and recognition as a fitting solution to such problems. It is exciting to see that this trend has accelerated strongly since the publication of the first edition of this book, as can be testified by a growing number of publications, conference presentations and training activities.

I feel it is timely now to offer an update of the UCL model including new clinical case examples to illustrate this. The authors were mostly trained in this approach or have extensive experience of its clinical application. I also hope that the clinical–experimental procedures of this model have been described in more practical terms for the clinician and trainee alike. I believe these improvements are timely to satisfy the growing interest in CBT training and practice.

The exclusive focus on the 'Middlesex approach' in this edition, or as it is now labelled, the 'UCL Case Formulation Model', will allow better descriptions of process and procedures. This time I have tried to achieve more transparent and detailed explanation and commentary of the clinical–experimental process as well as have suggested step-by-step procedures. Also, in view of the growing popularity of the case formulation approach, it appears timely and necessary to remind students and clinicians alike of the basic principles of case formulation as a clinical–experimental process rather than as matching techniques to symptoms. There is some concern that other recent models, despite offering improvements in clinical practice, might still be oriented to psychiatric nosology and standardization of techniques modelled on group-based research trials. We also recognize that in some countries, notably North America, it is mandatory to arrive at a diagnosis for legal and remuneration purposes!

As before, this text is intended for clinical and health psychologists, psychiatrists, psychiatric nurses, social workers and other mental health practitioners who are interested in the application of cognitive–behavioural methods to psychological problems and psychiatric disorders. And of course, once again I anticipate this book to be very useful and popular for training courses and students of CBT.

In Chapter 1, I provide an overview of the history and development of individualized clinical–experimental approaches, now labelled 'case formulation', from the early beginnings of behaviour therapy. I shall focus on three related aspects which have inspired and promoted this undertaking: (1) complex disorders in the psychiatric setting, (2) purpose and limitations of the diagnostic model and (3) problems with the standardization of techniques. The need for a comprehensive understanding of individual problems (problem formulation) and individually tailored treatment interventions will be argued. In addition, some issues of divergence and similarity in recent case formulation models will be discussed briefly.

In Chapter 2, I provide an overview of conceptual issues in case formulation followed by a description of the clinical application and procedures as developed and practised within the UCL model. I discuss the role of the initial interview, suggested clinical-experimental procedures, the 'problem formulation', clinical measurement and evaluation procedures, the self-schema model for complex problems and the role of the therapeutic relationship.

In Chapter 3, Richard Hallam presents and discusses clinical–experimental methodology in case formulation with particular emphasis on how to generate clinically relevant hypotheses about presenting problems and how to turn these into relevant questions to be tested during the interview and beyond.

Peter AuBuchon (with V Malatesta) had already presented his ground-breaking formulation-guided model for the therapeutic relationship in the first edition of this text. In Chapter 4, he now provides an updated account of his approach as it has evolved since and matured in clinical practice. He explains how his extensive clinical work with difficult and complex cases has shaped his thinking on the subject since the first edition.

In particular, Peter has become concerned that present options for the therapist's style might be applied in a simplistic 'cook book' fashion. It is for these reasons that he now strongly recommends formulation-guided individualized support involving all aspects of the interaction between client and therapist. He believes such relationships should also be regarded as an integral part of an individually tailored treatment programme. A clinical demonstration of this approach is presented in Chapter 5 by the same author featuring a difficult and complex case involving problems with adherence and the therapeutic alliance.

In Chapters 5–8, four invited experts on case formulation, who apply the aforementioned UCL approach in their clinical practice, were asked to illustrate how the UCL case formulation approach operates in their clinical work.

In Chapter 5, Peter AuBuchon illustrates how a case formulation can guide and support the therapeutic relationship in long-term treatment, addressing motivation, adherence, priorities as well as a focus in the therapeutic objectives. His case study demonstrates how the therapeutic relationship becomes a driving force for the complete therapeutic process, clearly challenging any traditional view regarding the unimportance of the relationship in cognitive–behavioural psychotherapy.

In Chapter 6, Kieron O'Connor and his coworkers present three cases of generalized anxiety disorder and demonstrate how individualized assessments can lead to distinct problem formulations, suggesting quite different treatment strategies. This is indeed a convincing way of illustrating how inappropriate and misleading a psychiatric diagnosis might be for the development of an effective treatment strategy.

In Chapter 7, David Lane and Sarah Corrie present their therapeutic work with an adolescent boy. David Lane's work (see Chapter 1) has been very influential in the development of the UCL case formulation model. He has devoted most of his professional life as a therapist to working with the difficulties of children and adolescents. To begin, David and Sarah present their generic version of case formulation, the Purpose-Perspectives-Process model, and show how their clinical application labelled 'DEFINE' (see Chapter 1) is applied in their case illustration, leading to a 'rigorous, creative and effective approach'.

In addition, they offer general guidelines for this type of case formulation which provide clinicians with a comprehensive understanding and help in developing their own formulation skills. Finally, Lane and Corrie argue strongly for collaborative consensus in the individual approach and point out the inappropriateness of conceptualizations based on diagnosis.

Finally, in Chapter 8, Samia Ezzamel, Marcantonio Spada and Ana Nikčević present a complex case of social anxiety and substance misuse involving hallucinatory flashbacks related to LSD. At present, little is known if such problems can be treated with CBT and what procedures might be effective. They demonstrate that a comprehensive formulation suggests the careful selection and adaptation of established treatment methods and also tailor-made procedures that are carefully evaluated for this individual case, thus adding to knowledge.

Authors were encouraged to illustrate their own style of applying the model. In other words, clinicians were asked to demonstrate how their assessment leads to a comprehensive problem formulation and, subsequently, how the formulation guides a treatment strategy including selection, adjusting and/or modifying therapeutic techniques. Finally, each author indicates how the case formulation was verified during the course of therapy.

Overall, in this book there will be greater emphasis on illustrating therapeutic rationales and strategies rather than a detailed discussion of treatment methods and outcomes. Clearly, the conceptualization of the case is what matters and each author will show in detail how problem assessment is conducted and leads to a formulation, and how treatment strategies are derived logically and guided in this process.

To conclude, the primary purpose of this book is to outline clinical case formulation as an experimental method based on cognitive and behavioural principles. This is clinically demonstrated with four case illustrations. Each author concentrates on presenting a case formulation, thereby adding substance and sophistication to the theory and practice of cognitive–behavioural psychotherapy.

It is my hope that the development and use of such an approach will allow clinicians to understand and intervene directly at the psychological source of clients' problems and that this will enhance effectiveness help. At present, a majority of texts on psychotherapy still focus on interventions to deal with specific symptoms or syndromes, thus failing to address underlying problems that may continue to trouble patients and are likely to lead to further complaints.

I am grateful to all contributors who have provided excellent clinical illustrations of case formulation according to the UCL model. Victor Meyer, who has sadly passed away in the meantime, deserves a special tribute as the 'spiritual father' of the case formulation philosophy as I point out in Chapter 1. My own professional identity would have been unthinkable without his stimulation, guidance and support.

For the second edition, my thanks goes to Darren Reed, the senior commissioning editor, who showed great interest in our work and has provided constructive support to see it through and also to Karen Shield who enabled and guided the production process efficiently and with great care and understanding.

Michael Bruch
London, April 2014

References

Beck, A. T. (1976). *Cognitive therapy and the emotional disorders.* New York: International Universities Press.

British Psychological Society [BPS]. (2011). *Response to the American Psychiatric Association: DSM-5 Development.* Leicester: BPS

Eels, T. D. (2007). History and current status of psychotherapy case formulation. In T. D. Eels (Ed.), *Handbook of psychotherapy case formulation* (2nd ed.). New York: Guilford.

Schulte, D., Künzel, R., Pepping, G., & Schulte-Bahrenberg, T. (1992). Tailor-made versus standardised therapy of phobic patients. *Advances in Behaviour Research and Therapy 14,* 67–92.

1

The Development of Case Formulation Approaches

Michael Bruch

There is nothing as practical as a good theory.

Kurt Lewin

Case Formulation and Psychiatric Diagnosis

Beyond diagnosis? The title of this book may sound intriguing to the reader, especially as, at first glance, cognitive–behavioural psychotherapy and psychiatric classification appear to be quite well suited to each other as evidenced by not only research publications but also textbooks on therapeutic techniques mostly presented according to diagnostic categories.

Are there any limitations with the psychiatric model? How can we define a relationship between psychiatric diagnosis and case formulation? Does case formulation require a diagnosis? And what is really necessary to know when understanding a problem and making a treatment plan? To answer these questions, it seems appropriate to produce reasons and developmental conditions for case formulation as a clinical approach.

Traditionally, clinicians dealing with behavioural disorders, especially in the psychiatric setting, were mostly expected to define and organize their clinical work in terms of nosological categories.

The practical end result of this was mostly classification and medication. There was little room for psychotherapy, and novel approaches were usually not encouraged. When, in the 1950s, behaviour therapy (BT) arrived on the scene, there seemed little willingness on part of the psychiatric establishment to change this tradition (Eysenck, 1990).

Beyond Diagnosis: Case Formulation in Cognitive Behavioural Therapy, Second Edition. Edited by Michael Bruch.
© 2015 John Wiley & Sons, Ltd. Published 2015 by John Wiley & Sons, Ltd.

However, this attitude caused growing irritation and dissatisfaction among behaviour therapists, as hardly any instrumental value could be found in a classification system that aimed mainly at 'scientific' order and communication (often with dubious validity and reliability [British Psychological Society [BPS], 2011]), but appears less helpful or even intent in explaining mechanism and directing treatment of respective disorders.

What are the problems with psychiatric diagnosis?

Apart from being merely descriptive, there can be considerable overlap between categories. Despite considerable improvements and refinements over the last two decades (APA/DSM IV-TR, 2000), this is largely true to this day, as Turkat (1990) has pointed out in the case of personality disorders: For example, when clinicians were asked to sort the criteria for all disorders to the matching categories, they were only able to assign 66% of these correctly, indicating lack of validity and diagnostic overlap (Blashfield & Breen, 1989). They also found a tendency to assign presented problems to multiple categories to (six to eight in the case of personality disorders).

More recently, Sturmey (2009) has provided an excellent critique from the methodological point of view about the shortcomings of the psychodiagnostic approach according to the medical model. In the field of BT, the adoption of diagnostic criteria when selecting treatment procedures came about in the 60s, in tandem with the development of standardized techniques evaluated in randomized controlled trials (RCTs). Although this approach is presented in a very persuasive way by many professional bodies, mostly of a medical background, Sturmey points out the many limitations of this approach. Given the problems of validity and reliability of psychiatric diagnosis, it is questionable if homogenous groups for controlled trials can ever be constructed. Psychological processes in development are mostly ignored, and individualization of treatment is not encouraged.

Furthermore, any interaction between diagnosis and treatment is not contemplated in these designs as one treatment method is simply compared with another one, placebo or waiting list control, etc. Such a design does not allow us to determine whether a treatment effective for one diagnosis would also be effective for another diagnosis or whether it was the most effective treatment for a diagnosis. One might speculate that anxiety-based disorders associated with a range of symptoms might be best treated with a method addressing the mechanism of the disorder rather than focusing on individual complaints (symptoms), which are presumably the main focus of a diagnosis.

From a clinical standpoint, which deals with a unique patient, average improvement, as established in RCTs, does not make much sense – the average patient simply does not exist. Besides, significance in trials can be achieved with large size samples and sensitive measures. And usually, substantial number of individuals improve little or not at all. And even with those who do improve, the effective ingredient remains unclear and might include non-specific effects such as the therapeutic interaction.

Taking these points together, it seems highly questionable whether parametric statistical methods are appropriate in evaluating the efficacy of psychotherapeutic treatments. On the assumption that treatment should be individualized, single-case experimental design methodology might be used instead.

Sturmey (2009) points out further limitations of the diagnostic model: When medication is recommended, individual responses can be varied and often quite problematic in the long term. For example, if perceived effectiveness of treatment is seen to lie outside one's own resources, dependency on medication may occur and self-efficacy arising out of personal coping responses is not encouraged.

Standardized psychological treatments are equally problematic as the response to them is unpredictable, improvements are often not maintained or some problems remain unchanged.

For all these reasons, creative and experienced clinicians tend to reject the straightjacket of the diagnostic model and prefer an individualized approach.

Finally, reliability and validity issues are a continuous problem with ongoing DSM and ICD (World Health Organization, 2010) revisions. Research trials on these criteria are few and far between and are usually conducted after criteria have already been established. Sturmey also points out that clinicians tend to use their own methods and not the recommended structured assessment procedures that may achieve better reliability.

Unfortunately, over time, these developments did lead to an increasing medicalization in treating behavioural disorders – a far cry from what was originally intended by the pioneers of BT such as Eysenck, who preferred to focus on a learning principle-based analysis of individual cases. This was motivated by complex and difficult cases that were rejected by the established providers, usually psychiatry or dynamic psychotherapy (Eysenck, 1990).

As the latest revision towards DSM-5 clearly demonstrates, scientists and clinical experts still share many disagreements and, despite considerable non-medical input, there does not appear much progress regarding advice and guidance for non-medical treatments.

It is difficult to see how, after many controversial revisions, DSM-5 will ever deliver a classification system acceptable to clinicians and sufferers. The recent response by the BPS (2011) addresses these expected shortcomings:

> The Society recommends a revision of the way mental distress is thought about, starting with recognition of the overwhelming evidence that it is on a spectrum with 'normal' experience, and that psychosocial factors such as

poverty, unemployment and trauma are the most strongly-evidenced causal factors. Rather than applying preordained diagnostic categories to clinical populations, we believe that any classification system should begin from the bottom up – starting with specific experiences, problems or 'symptoms' or 'complaints'. Statistical analyses of problems from community samples show that they do not map onto past or current categories (Mirowsky, 1990; Mirowsky & Ross, 2003). We would like to see the base unit of measurement as specific problems (e.g. hearing voices, feelings of anxiety, etc.)? These would be more helpful too in terms of epidemiology.

While some clinicians find a name or a diagnostic label helpful, our contention is that this helpfulness results from a knowledge that their problems are recognised (in both senses of the word) understood, validated, explained (and explicable) and have some relief. Clients often, unfortunately, find that diagnosis offers only a spurious promise of such benefits. Since – for example – two people with a diagnosis of 'schizophrenia' or 'personality disorder' may possess no two symptoms in common, it is difficult to see what communicative benefit is served by using these diagnoses. We believe that a description of a person's real problems would suffice. Moncrieff and others have shown that diagnostic labels are less useful than a description of a person's problems for predicting treatment response, so again diagnoses seem positively unhelpful compared to the alternatives. There is ample evidence from psychological therapies that case formulations (whether from a single theoretical perspective or more integrative) are entirely possible to communicate to staff or clients.

Another problem with diagnosis is the lack of interest in understanding the underlying psychological mechanism of a disorder. Obviously, this is quite unacceptable from a behavioural-learning perspective. Grouping problems into categories cannot advance this search for causes as learning biographies are ignored. Thus, psychiatric diagnosis will not help us to explain onset, development and maintenance of a behavioural disorder. Such information, however, must be considered to be crucial for a comprehensive case formulation with explanatory power.

Finally, psychiatric classification is clearly linked with concepts of *mental illness* and *normality*. Such labels are frequently experienced as stigmatizing value judgements by clients and have been shown to be counterproductive for learning-oriented therapy (e.g. Szasz, 1961). Despite great efforts towards operationally defined categories in diagnosis, the issue remains contentious, especially for non-medical psychotherapists.

However, it seems surprising that only recently claims were made to the contrary, i.e. the suggestion that medicalization of behavioural problems might provide relief for the sufferer (Markowitz & Swartz, 2007). There appears no substantial clinical evidence for this; however, labelling may be preferred by some individuals as it allows evading personal responsibility in preference for medicated treatment over psychological therapy. I believe this to be a short cut likely to undermine a personal locus of control in the development of new resources and coping behaviours, thus preventing enhancement of self-efficacy processes (Bandura, 1977).

These comments on the recent development of psychiatric classification clearly demonstrate that not much has been achieved since the publication of the first edition of this classification. There are no signs for a 'bottom–up' approach based on information experienced by problem sufferers and conceptualized according to case formulation methodology. Nevertheless, the commentary report of the BPS on the development of DSM-5 must be welcomed as a reminder that new initiatives are needed.

Although mostly inspired by psychologists, early developments of BT usually took place in psychiatric settings. However, right from the start, there was a difference of opinion how this approach should be applied to behavioural disorders. While psychologists preferred an experimental learning–based approach, psychiatrists saw the 'symptom focus' of this new method compatible with the medical model and were hopeful of finding symptom-focused techniques. It is also noteworthy that clinical psychologists in those early days were working under psychiatrists and were given limited scope to conduct BT without medical supervision. Originally, this method was expected by psychiatrist to supplement, like psychometry, psychiatrists diagnosis! (Eysenck, 1990).

In view of this background, it is hardly surprising that, apart from the pioneering experimental work carried out mostly by psychologists, efforts to develop treatment methods were targeted on technologies designed to match a diagnosis. These efforts were motivated by a need to satisfy the requirements of psychotherapy outcome studies, rather than addressing the real needs of individual patients. More recently, advances in 'operationalized' diagnosis (e.g. DSM-IV-TR, 2000) have facilitated the development of more disorder-focused treatment manuals. These tend to be more sophisticated as most are developed in clinical settings (see Wilson, 1996, 1997 for a discussion). Despite such substantial improvements, there remain strong doubts as to whether or not treatment manuals will ever be able to address fully the complexity of individual problems (Hickling & Blanchard, 1997; Malatesta, 1995a, 1995b). That is not to say that manuals, as a product of technical expertise, may not be useful in clinical training and therapy (e.g. the acquisition of technical skills by trainees) provided adjustments to individual cases can be made (see discussion later in this text).

To conclude, it appears obvious that psychiatric diagnosis has not become a facilitating tool for the development of individual-focused BT. Considering ongoing problems with reliability, validity, prognostic value and co-morbidity, there must be considerable doubts (e.g. BPS, 2011) that any psychiatric classification system does fulfil such criteria in a satisfactory way.

Despite such concerns, psychiatric diagnosis continues to be a powerful and deeply rooted system in mental health services across the world that casts a long shadow over the provision of psychological psychotherapies. And there is another, slightly more mundane, reason why, especially in the United States, the home of DSM, psychiatric classification is not indispensible: Usually, clinicians cannot expect remuneration by health insurance companies unless an established psychiatric diagnosis is submitted, together with matching techniques (I. D. Turkat, personal communication, 2012)!

Given the diverse natures of case formulation and psychiatric diagnosis, it may seem contradictory that early attempts to experiment with applications of learning theory took place in psychiatric settings. However, this is easily explained, as these settings were usually the location for complex and difficult-to-understand disorders, not suited for psychiatric intervention and even less so for psychodynamic approaches that tend to be highly selective. It was mostly for these reasons that psychologists were encouraged to experiment with alternative approaches (Eysenck, 1990).

A Short History of Case Formulation

Individualized BT using experimental methodology goes back to the very roots of BT itself. Indeed, most pioneers (e.g. Lazarus, 1960; Meyer, 1960; Wolpe, 1960; Yates, 1960) started out by applying learning principles to the assessment and treatment of clinical cases. It is this body of work that can be considered as the foundation of case formulation. However, the current label arrived much later: Turkat (1985) introduced the term 'case formulation', which is now fairly consistently applied for this concept and practised in the field of behavioural and cognitive therapies and beyond (e.g. Eells, 2007; Sturmey, 2009). However, as case formulation has become fashionable in recent years, its definition and description has changed in a less precise and focused direction, moving away from the original intention of its pioneers (Eells, 2007; Sturmey, 2009; Tarrier, 2006). For some, it just indicates good clinical practice with greater concern and attention for the individual and the therapeutic relationship. For others, the term itself is regarded as controversial (e.g. Dryden, 1998), for allegedly 'objectifying' human beings as cases. Nothing could be further from the nature and intentions of case formulation. Given today's sensitivity regarding politically correct terms, this may not be the most fitting label although it should be the substance that matters most. In an earlier period, no distinctive label other than 'individualized' was used, nor did it appear necessary or fashionable in those days. The remainder of this chapter addresses the origins of this important and unique approach to analyzing psychological problems.

The Contribution of the Maudsley Group

The foundations for clinical–experimental work on the basis of learning principles, both for assessment and treatment, were laid by Hans Eysenck (1990) and his team in the early 50s at the Maudsley Hospital in London. Eysenck's critical account and now-famous paper on the effects on psychotherapy and spontaneous remission (Eysenck, 1952) had inspired new psychotherapeutic thinking, mainly guided by experimental and learning psychology. This approach to psychotherapy was subsequently labelled 'Behaviour Therapy'. It was timely that this therapeutic innovation coincided with the establishment of clinical psychology in England, also led by Eysenck: Both developments, the 'new profession' compatible with a 'new approach', formed the basis for strong synergistic effects for years to come.

In the early days, Eysenck strongly encouraged experimental investigation of single cases on the basis of learning principles. This task was taken up by Monte Shapiro (1955, 1957) (Shapiro & Nelson, 1955) who pioneered a suitable methodology that allowed assessment and conceptualization of psychiatric disorders in their clinical context. Its main assumption was that each patient constitutes a scientific problem of its own and that the skills of the clinical psychologist were used to solve this unique problem by applying general methods of experimental psychology in a special framework of learning theory.

To elaborate, Shapiro proceeded as follows: Patients were interviewed to achieve a precise description of their problem behaviour. Next, it was attempted to quantify these subjective reports with suitable individualized measures. Further, learning models were employed in an attempt to explain the problem under investigation, or new models were formulated on the basis of individual data and learning principles. From here predictions were made, which were subsequently tested in clinical experiments, in order to eliminate false hypotheses. Having conducted such rigorous procedure, Shapiro expected to arrive at a valid model of explanation in learning terms that could be subjected to further verification procedures. It is notable that in this way the clinician operates like a researcher in the clinical field, which necessitates a considerable amount of time and resources.

There can be no doubt that Shapiro's experimental method has enabled gathering of relevant information to facilitate behavioural treatments based on learning principles. For these reasons, it must be regarded as a pioneering implementation of the scientist–practitioner model (Boulder Conference on Graduate Education in Clinical Psychology, 1949), generally accepted as the most suitable procedure for BT. At the time, it seemed appropriate and necessary to carry out such detailed and meticulous work to further the fledgling BT in clinical settings.

However, in the process, a number of problems and limitations became increasingly obvious with Shapiro's approach. Shapiro himself was of the opinion that his method should be universally applied in clinical practice; however, such views proved misguided as it soon turned out that his rather academic aspirations proved quite unrealistic for clinical settings. Only a small number of clinicians (i.e. the Maudsley group) working in specialized research settings were sufficiently interested and trained to follow his recommendations and protocol in detail. Clinicians working in routine practice, even given strong interest, did not have the expertise, time, and necessary resources to develop explanatory models guided by learning principles and individually tailored treatment programmes according to Shapiro's demanding experimental procedure.

Other problems concerned appropriate operationalization and measurement of problem behaviours. It turned out that clinicians, if not specially trained, found it difficult to select or even develop suitable instruments for psychotherapeutic evaluation. Instead, there was a tendency to resort to old-style psychometry, which is more suited to the assessment of personality traits, diagnostic labelling, and statistical comparisons.

Furthermore, therapists were not prepared to subject their interview style or preferred treatment techniques to empirical scrutiny and would continue with procedures that were perceived as effective according to their own experience and convictions (Meyer & Chesser, 1970).

Finally, patients suffering acutely were looking for quick results and did not want to participate in what was seen as guinea pigs in long-winded experimental investigations. However, it is surprising that even academic research–oriented psychologists lost interest in this methodology as they were lured into the world of diagnostic labelling and treatment techniques. The research paradigm of the natural sciences was considered as more relevant and important.

To conclude, despite its creative inventiveness, high scientific standards and potential usefulness, especially for complex problems, Shapiro's method was never fully established as a clinical tool in the field of psychotherapy. Typical examples of early experimental work were published in two separate volumes (Eysenck, 1960, 1964). To this day, these creative experimental studies provide fascinating reading for the student of cognitive–behavioural psychotherapy, offering extensive insight into the pioneering work of the early behaviour therapists. It is surprising that this line of work was not further pursued by academic researchers who instead got increasingly involved in diagnostically orientated research: The goal was to define matching techniques that could be evaluated in RCTs – thus following an established research paradigm considered to be more scientific and powerful than single-case methodology.

The Contribution of Victor Meyer

Victor Meyer was one of Eysenck's early students who began practising as a clinical psychologist in 1955. Meyer was predominantly interested in developing workable clinical applications of this new approach to behavioural disorders. He soon began to realize that BT, with growing scientific ambitions, was moving away from single-case work and was not addressing itself to real clinical problems as research focus shifted to analogue group design. Describing this dilemma, he later stated (Meyer, 1975):

> The emphasis in the literature is on the experimental approach to various problems in the field, and the majority of textbooks on BT have been written by authors who have little or no experience in the clinical application of the principles of BT. As a result, the current literature deals mainly with various problems and issues for pure and applied research and prepares the reader only to become a research worker in the field. Clinical practice and training, and the problems involved in these aspects of BT, are relatively ignored...thus, would be behaviour therapists find very little help from the literature concerning the nature of their duties and the problems pertaining to their role as clinicians (p. 11).

Instead, Meyer suggested that basic clinical questions ought to be addressed to achieve best clinical practice and a *clinical* research strategy:

> *What treatment, by whom, is most effective for a particular individual, with a specific problem, under which set of circumstances, and how does it come about?*

Obviously, the intent was to create a 'scientist–practitioner' who investigates empirically but adapts to the clinical setting in a pragmatic way at the same time.

However, the mainstream development of BT went into a different direction. As academic psychologists and also psychiatrists became interested in BT, research endeavours became increasingly focused on developing standardized techniques developed through controlled research trials. It became obvious that BT was moving further and further away from its original clinical base. In fact, researchers even started preferring analogue settings, typically investigating students with small animal phobias who were easily accessible in university research departments. This practice culminated in the practice of 'symptom–technique matching', the idea being to select standard methods to match diagnostic categories. This greatly facilitated research but was otherwise providing poor clinical outcomes, especially with more complex disorders. For the clinician, if he was at all able to follow such academic aspirations, this process provided little guidance in dealing with the complexities of real clinical problems and raised more questions than it answered.

Meyer (1975) sums up the problems from the clinician's point of view:

> ...most of the writings on behaviour therapy by 'experts' are experimentally oriented and advocate a technological approach to treatment by giving 'scientific respectability' to the techniques that have been derived from learning principles and intensively investigated. This no doubt has an influence on the practice of behaviour therapy. It is not surprising, therefore, that many practising behaviour therapists apply certain prescribed techniques to certain psychiatric conditions. Also, psychologists and psychiatrists seeking training in behaviour therapy expect to be grilled in techniques and the range of their applicability. Originally, I did subscribe to this approach, but, after gaining wide clinical experience, I was struck by its considerable limitations and its inappropriateness in many cases (Meyer & Chesser, 1970). The problems of technology are twofold. First, not all patients sharing the same complaint respond to the procedural requirements of techniques. For example, in the case of systematic desensitisation, some patients find it difficult to relax, some fail to conjure up clear images of phobic scenes in relevant modalities, some do not report anxiety to clearly imagined phobic stimuli, and a proportion fail to generalise adequately to real-life situations.
>
> Second, and more important, one seldom finds cases with isolated complaints in psychiatric clinics. It is more likely that one is confronted with a number of complaints and problems that may or may not be directly related to the main complaint presented by the patient; or the main complaint may turn out, according to the therapist's assessment, to be other than what the patient himself believes it to be (p. 16).

Typically, the research-oriented behaviour therapist tends to ignore individual differences and is rather concerned about matching group designs to allow, e.g. comparison and evaluation of treatment techniques.

Meyer, on the other hand, was rooted firmly as a clinician in the psychiatric setting where he attempted to apply the fledgling BT to more severe and chronic problems, e.g. existential problems, personality disorders and obsessive–compulsive disorders. It was also seen as important to complement clinical work with research and training based in the same setting. In other words, research and training ought to be adjusted to clinical requirements and not the other way round. Meyer (1975) expands on this as follows:

> Thus, as a therapist, I attempt to guide all my activities in terms of learning principles, no matter whether the goal of treatment is to modify motor, autonomic, or cognitive aspects of disordered behaviour. For myself, behaviour therapy is an ongoing process during which observations are collected, hypotheses put forward to account for them, tests of hypotheses carried out,

adjustments to new observations made, and so on...the advantage of the approach advocated here is that the clinician would be able to formulate treatment programmes for every patient that would be flexible enough to meet the myriad problems and practical obstacles found when treating patients and would not be obliged to put technical straitjackets on his patients. It is not the technological approach but the application of the principles that has enabled behaviour therapy to be extended to virtually every type of psychiatric picture.

In my opinion, learning principles offer a distinct contribution in the attempt to understand aetiology and to design treatment for psychiatric disorders...I attempt to structure my approach explicitly and systematically in terms of learning principles (p. 21).

Further, Meyer (1975) pointed to the crucial role of initial interviewing in this approach. He was critical of standardized or over-comprehensive schemes (e.g. Kanfer & Saslow, 1969), which he thought were too distant or cumbersome. Instead of rigid adherence to one scheme, therapists should be encouraged to develop hypotheses about the nature of the complaint. Such an approach shapes the interview and makes it fluent and will also be helpful in establishing rapport with the patient. Sources for hypotheses can be contextual, knowledge of learning principles, and personal experience, as Meyer (1975) explains:

The importance of this is obvious, since decisions about the goal and choice of treatment depend on the kind of information elicited from the patient...The main sources of information are the patient's verbal report, nonverbal behaviour during the interview, and response to psychological tests. In addition, the therapist has at his disposal other means of gathering information, such as seeing the relatives of the patient, observing the patient in his own environment, or getting the patient to observe and record his own behaviour (p. 22).

On the basis of such information, a so-called 'problem formulation' is established, which attempts to integrate all relevant data into a meaningful picture. This is then discussed with the patient.

The patient is then given the formulation in simple terms, and the objective of treatment is discussed with him. The subject should give his consent concerning the goal of treatment. Close relatives should also be consulted about it, particularly when the target behaviour is social behaviour. The therapist should consider the patient's wishes within the context of his own formulation, and it should be his duty to attempt to adjust the patient to the environment to which he wishes to be discharged, if possible.

Following this, the patient is given a simple general outline of possible treatment procedures and the rationale underlying them. The therapist emphasises the tentative nature of his formulation, but he also indicates that the patient's responses early in treatment may demonstrate any necessary modifications. While motivating the patient to undertake treatment, the therapist at the same time attempts to give him a realistic expectation for outcome. In addition, the patient is told that he is expected to be an active participant in the treatment, and that as soon as possible he will be required to become his own therapist and to exert self-control. Understanding of every step undertaken in therapy is essential and will enable him to cooperate and participate actively (Meyer, 1975: p. 23).

In other words, great emphasis is placed on understanding the patient's problem, explaining the rationale, seeking cooperation and thus building resolve and motivation for the treatment programme.

Another important aspect of Meyer's approach was the development of the therapeutic relationship. At the time, this issue was more or less ignored in BT, partly as a (over)reaction to psychodynamic therapies, where relationship issues were seen as being too prominent and thus distractive regarding treatment goals. Meyer and Liddell (1975) explain their rationale as follows:

> The relationship between the behaviour therapist and his patient is conceptualised in terms of learning principles from the start of the behavioural analysis. The patient's life style will give some idea of what type of behaviour the therapist must show to become a potent reinforcer. For the behaviour therapist there should be almost as many types of relationships as he sees patients. This adaptability is more important in cases of interpersonal problems than with isolated phobias. The behaviour therapist aims at something approaching an instructor/trainee relationship; he tries to avoid to hide behind the therapeutic veil. In the ideal situation he hopes that the patient will gradually become his own therapist and their interaction should reflect this (p. 237).

According to Meyer, in most cases, the therapist should structure his behaviour so it serves as an effective social reinforcer. The type of relationship to be developed should precisely meet the needs of the individual patient. This is illustrated as follows:

> If, for instance, the basic problem presented is fear of authority, then the therapist will behave in such a way as to make it easier for his patient to learn skills appropriate when dealing with people in authority. On the other hand, the therapist who treats an isolated phobia will attempt to inspire confidence and to make his patients relax in his presence (Meyer & Liddell, 1975: p. 226).

Obviously, there should be limits in accommodating patient's needs as this may lead to over-involvement (pathological relationship) or unwanted shaping of patient's behaviour by means of verbal conditioning, etc. Also, for any intensive and supportive relationship to facilitate the therapeutic procedure, there needs to be a clearly defined exit strategy to prevent unintended long-term dependency.

Meyer's groundbreaking work eventually led to the establishment of the first Behaviour Therapy Unit at St. Luke's Woodside Hospital, London, and the first training course of BT based on the case formulation model at the Middlesex Hospital Medical School in London in 1970. Two years later, Vic Meyer became the founding father of the British Association of Behavioural Psychotherapy (BABP, now BABCP).

Further Developments Based on Meyer's Approach

Further developments on Meyer's case formulation approach were carried out by some of his students, who, for the first time, attempted to apply case formulation in other settings, e.g. outpatient services and behavioural medicine. In particular, Turkat's important contributions enabled the model to take root in the United States where the field at the time was dominated by concern with academic research. Luckily, this coincided with a growing interest in clinical issues and more complex problems, like personality disorders. This new emphasis was reflected in several meetings of the American Association for the Advancement of Behaviour Therapy in the early 80s. Critical analyses and recommendations regarding the nature and direction of BT were put forward by a number of distinguished behaviour therapists (e.g. Wilson, 1982).

In the present context, I shall focus on the salient contributions of two outstanding clinicians who provided conceptual frameworks for Vic Meyer's ideas and clinical practice.

The Contribution of Ira Turkat

Ira Turkat was a clinical psychologist and academic from the United States, who had done his clinical internship with Victor Meyer in the late 70s. He embraced the model, refined it and made it more accessible. In his work, Turkat was also greatly influenced by Henry Adams, Monte Shapiro and Joseph Wolpe, all of whom had also collaborated with Meyer at one time.

As Meyer was a rather reluctant publicist, Turkat's great achievement was to define and operationalize the 'Middlesex approach' in numerous publications, thus putting it 'on the map'. Most relevant in this respect were his two textbooks entitled 'Behavioural Case formulation' (Turkat, 1985) and 'The Personality Disorders' (Turkat, 1990). Initially, Turkat proposed the label 'Behaviour-Analytic Approach' (Meyer & Turkat, 1979) to emphasize the individual analysis of behaviour, but later he argued against this 'poor choice of a label' as he feared that it implied synthesis of behavioural and psycho-analytic approaches (Turkat, 1986). Eventually, the term 'Case Formulation' was finally adopted, making it more consistent with Meyer's original choice of words, which were 'behavioural formulation' or 'problem formulation'. However, there still appears to be some confusion about the concept as was recently documented in a debate in the 'Behaviour Therapist'. Adams (1996) has clarified this by pointing out that...

> '*case formulation* is not a treatment procedure. It is a method for understand-ing the patient and their problems that allows for the selection and design of treatment procedures based on the knowledge of their case' (p. 78).

To elaborate, Turkat emphasized the 'tripartite nature' of case formulation, consisting of the *initial interview, clinical experimentation* and *modification methodology.* Continuous hypothesis generation and testing was proposed as a logical link between these components, and it also allows for corrective feedback when hypotheses cannot be verified. Apart from these rules, the process should be adjusted to the individual case in a flexible manner.

The main function of the initial interview is to achieve a *problem formu-lation*, as opposed to a diagnosis, which Turkat mainly advocates as a tool for communication. Turkat also states that a diagnosis has no immediate value in achieving a valid problem formulation. The problem formulation itself comprises three elements:

(1) A hypothesis about the relationship among various problems of the individual; (2) Hypotheses about the aetiology of the aforementioned diffi-culties; (3) Predictions about the patient's future behaviour (Turkat, 1990: p. 17).

In other words, the formulation assumes the status of a personalized clini-cal theory to explain the nature and mechanism of the patient's problem. Although an experimental approach is adopted, Turkat (1990) points out that a clinical assessment can hardly have the rigour of a controlled research experiment. The main focus, in consideration on current limited knowledge on psychopathology, has to be on reasoned hypotheses and clinical data.

In conducting the initial interview, Turkat (e.g. 1990) makes a number of recommendations:

> The *initial interaction* should be closely monitored, as it can provide non-ver-bal cues regarding, for example, the appearance, mannerisms and motivations of the patient. However, Turkat cautions that hypotheses may be wrong and the temptation to seek consistent data should be resisted.
>
> Next, he recommends constructing a precise *problem specification* on the basis of information offered by the patient. This may involve a number of problems that are not always presented in order of priority by the patient or possibly not mentioned at all. To guide more detailed specification, Turkat has

proposed the behavioural analysis matrix (Turkat, 1979), which investigates components of behaviour in more detail, including antecedent and consequent conditions. This procedure shall be addressed in the next chapter.

The gathering of relevant data helps to generate hypotheses that in turn open the path for further information. Of great importance is what Turkat labels 'etiology inquiries', that are directed at identifying, predisposing, precipitating and maintaining factors. Aetiology inquiries are in essence a combination of assessment of individual learning history and functional analysis. Investigation into predisposing factors aims at identifying vulnerability factors arising from genetic, social, cultural, professional, religious backgrounds, etc. in interaction with learning processes. In contrast, precipitating factors refer to the immediate trigger and maintaining factors to reinforcing conditions of the problem behaviour.

The precise examination of all these variables, continuously guided by hypotheses, is seen as critical for the development of the formulation, which is discussed in great detail with the patient. For further verification of this *clinical theory,* Turkat proposes 'clinical experimentation', a quasi-experimental procedure. This serves two main functions: (1) to validate the formulation by making predictions that are subsequently evaluated and (2) to specify further relationships between independent and dependent variables. The design and measurements should fit individual requirements, i.e. simple and obvious problems may not require extensive testing whereas complex problem formulations may have to be examined in a more rigorous manner. Turkat (1990) notes:

> Given the tremendous range of variables that could be generated from the diverse nature of psychopathology presented by personality disorder cases as well as the infinite possibilities involved in formulation of those problems, it is impossible at present to articulate very specific step-by step guidelines for engaging in clinical experimentation. The notion is in its infancy and at present time its success in everyday clinical practice depends on the ingenuity and skill of the particular clinician involved (p. 28).

Once this process has resulted in an acceptable formulation, the 'modification methodology' is developed accordingly. In the first instance, agreement is sought with the patient regarding both the formulation and intervention hypotheses. The 'ideal plan' emerging from this is not always acceptable or practical, but any compromise must be supported by the formulation. On the other hand, a valid formulation should also enable the clinician to make predictions about obstacles that are likely to occur during the course of treatment. Another important aspect in the design of treatment is described as 'intervention sequencing', which is a formulation-based prioritizing of treatment targets, especially with complex cases comprising several complaints that may be interdependent. As Turkat (1990) points out, this is in stark contrast to 'technical' BT (symptom focused), where only the most obvious presenting complaint receives attention. Finally, the style of relationship is also developed on the basis of the formulation, thus rejecting standard enhancement techniques as, e.g. applied in the Rogerian approach.

These points will be elaborated further in the next chapter.

The Contribution of David Lane

I conclude this chapter with a brief introduction and evaluation of David Lane's work, also a former student of Vic Meyer, who has gone furthest in refining and operationalizing the case formulation approach. As his approach was predominantly developed in school settings working with children and adolescents, the label 'context-focused analysis' was proposed (Lane, 1990).

Lane has been developing his model over a span of two decades. It provides a particular challenge as it focuses on a particularly difficult-to-treat client group. In more detail, Lane suggested five phases for the complete individualized case formulation procedure. This was labelled as **DEFINE**:

> Define the problem or objective, Explore the factors of influence, Formulate an explanation of factors of influence, Intervene using an action plan based on the formulation, and Evaluate the outcome of the plan based on the formulation (p. 116).

In the *definition* phase, information is sought from those who are involved with a problem as help is not always requested by the sufferer (especially important in the context of children and adolescents). The goal is to identify a target problem:

> The process is one of growing awareness (p. 118).

In the *exploration* phase, expert-led gathering of relevant data proceeds to determine influencing factors for the presented problem according to principles of learning:

> The process is one of observation (p. 118).

In the *formulation* phase, observations are evaluated and integrated to achieve a model of explanation. Behavioural experiments are carried out to test the validity of explanations:

> The process is one of hypothesis testing (the pragmatic scientist) (p. 118).

In the *intervention* phase, a treatment strategy and plan is developed that builds logically on the formulation:

It will ideally specify the 'what, how, who and when' necessary for behaviour change. The process is one of structured practice (p. 119).

Finally, in the *evaluation* phase, problem- and goal-oriented measures are employed to assess gains and failures and determine new objectives, if necessary. Reinforcing feedback is provided throughout:

The process is one of monitored achievement (p. 119)

Lane's operationalized model has served as the blueprint for the current UCL model, which will be presented in the following chapter.

More recently, Corrie and Lane (2006, 2010) have further developed a generic framework for formulations labelled 'The Purpose–Perspectives–Process Model'. They define this ...as the construction of a narrative which provides a specific focus for a learning journey. This learning journey takes the client from where they are now to where they want to be, based on a process of negotiating appropriate goals. The task of formulation centres on the creation of a shared framework of understanding that has implications for change (see further elaboration of this approach in the chapter by Lane and Corrie of this volume).

Finally, there were substantial contributions by Victor Malatesta and Peter AuBuchon regarding formulation-guided therapeutic relationship in case formulation (AuBuchon & Malatesta, 1998; see also chapter by AuBuchon in this volume). Both were involved in the development of formulation-based inpatient programmes (Malatesta & AuBuchon, 1992) building in the main on Turkat's work. Their contributions seem especially important as they are clinically based and are providing strong evidence for successful outcomes, despite the restrictions and limitations in a routine service provision. Malatesta also contributed to the ongoing debate on formulation-guided versus manual-based treatment strategies (e.g. Malatesta, 1995a, 1995b). This issue was discussed in the first edition of this volume (Bond, 1998).

Overall, Ira Turkat's and David Lane's elaborations have been most influential for refinement of the UCL case formulation model. Ongoing collaboration led to further conceptual clarity and optimization of clinical operationalizations. The current model shall be presented in the next chapter.

Concluding Remarks

Since the publication of the first edition, there has been a growing number of publications on case formulation in the cognitive–behavioural framework and beyond.

It does not seem relevant in the present context to offer a comprehensive review of these developments; this has already been provided elsewhere (e.g. Eells, 2007; Sturmey, 2008, 2009; Tarrier, 2006). Some additional comments shall be offered here instead.

To begin with, there appears considerable disagreement about historical perspectives. For instance, where Eells (2007) and also Tarrier (2006) assert that case formulation is a recent development, Sturmey (2008, 2009) points to long tradition starting in the 1960s. It was already stated earlier that case formulation procedures following a scientist–practitioner approach were instrumental in developing BT in the first place.

It is also noticeable that the term 'case formulation' is now being applied with a much broader meaning than originally intended by the pioneers of this approach. Some definitions would no longer include individualized clinical–experimental procedures as a core aspect of case formulation. Instead, it may merely describe enhanced individualized clinical practice within the preferred model and often with reference to diagnostic classification. This can mean that many forms of assessment and analysis found in various theoretical approaches may be labelled as such. Is this a useful and logical way of proceeding?

For example, Kanfer's early work on learning theory–inspired functional analysis (Kanfer & Saslow, 1969) has been described as an early version of case formulation (Sturmey, 2009). It is also curious how (and why?) various case formulation models are grouped together into general categories. For example, the present UCL model with its traditional behavioural background, later expanded with cognitive concepts, is now listed by Sturmey as 'non-behavioural!' Obviously, on close inspection, one finds that case formulation models tend to be unique in promoting individualized procedures and might incorporate concepts from a number of theoretical frameworks. For these reasons, such classifications appear oversimplistic and unnecessary as they serve no purpose.

Sturmey and Eells also discuss case formulation models from other theoretical perspectives. In both volumes, clinical illustrations are provided and with Sturmey, for the first time, direct comparisons between models of common clinical problems derived from different theoretical orientations were made possible using a rather complex procedure. A detailed description of a case was given to two clinicians of different orientations to formulate. Thereafter, these case formulations were given to a third clinician of another orientation for comment. As this may be an intriguing way of comparing approaches, results obtained must be judged with caution as standardized transcripts rather than real patients were used. It also seems unclear what the real benefit of such comparisons is. We know already that different models might work with different clients using their own methods of evaluation. Sturmey's claim is to fill a gap as "…educators providing professional training in case formulation, students and practitioners lack resources to learn about these differences." (p. 13).

Another issue of debate refers to empirical validation of case formulation (e.g. Kuyken, 2006). How should the utility of case formulation approaches be evaluated? And is it appropriate to make comparisons with diagnostically led standardized treatments?

Eells (2009) finds it puzzling that, given increasing attention and popularity, there is very little research in evidence. But what kind of research might be suitable and appropriate given the experimental and dynamic methodology of case formulation? Current proposals are mostly designed to achieve a psychometric type validity and reliability assessment. Obviously, as Eells points out, "...reliability should not be achieved at the expense of producing generic 'one size fits all' formulations that might satisfy us psychometrically but not fit the person well..." (p. 294). It seems questionable whether these are suitable criteria for evaluation of case formulation.

Instead, preference should be given to individual evaluation of treatment utility. Obviously, a functional and experimentally guided case formulation process designed to investigate, select, interpret and verify or reject information from the very beginning of the interview can be regarded as a unique individualized research procedure (see also Chapter 2). For these reasons, any empirical validation of case formulation should be led by advanced methodology in single-case experimental design (Barlow & Hersen, 1984; Petermann & Müller, 2001). Petermann and Müller have made useful suggestions for such strategies; however, it has to be acknowledged that such methodology might pose an enormous challenge. And of course, this should include subjective evaluation by respective clients regarding both presenting complaints and general satisfaction with their lifestyles – after all the proof of the pudding would be in the eating.

As it is not recommended to compare apples with pears, RCTs to evaluate treatment utility of case formulation in comparison with standard procedures appear equally problematic and are hardly compatible with the rationale of case formulation. For example, the frequently cited Schulte study (Schulte and coworkers, 1992) did not find any significant differences between standard procedures and case formulation. However, on close inspection, serious flaws can be detected, i.e. case formulation therapists were rather inexperienced and in the standard condition treatments were individualized to some degree.

In clinical training, the therapist ought to be encouraged to provide a running commentary on his action to make his reflections as transparent as possible, for himself, for observers and of course for the client himself. In addition, the role of co-therapy and close supervision should assume special significance. In more detail, a co-therapist might monitor the process for comparing notes and critical discussion. The supervisor might scrutinize any transcript or videotape line by line, for instance, to investigate the process of generating hypotheses leading to testing questions (see also Chapters 2–4).

In reviewing recent developments in case formulation, it is also apparent that behavioural concepts, previously out of fashion and almost forgotten, appear to be staging a comeback as, e.g. demonstrated with Sturmey's Functional-Analytic Model (Sturmey, 2008, 2009). As a 'radical behaviourist', Sturmey rejects structuralism in preference to functionalism in psychotherapy. In his recent text (Sturmey, 2008), Sturmey offers a comprehensive overview of basic learning principles that had formed the bedrock for pioneering clinical–experimental work in the establishment of BT. Another example is Persons' (2008) recent expansion of her cognitive model (ironically originally inspired by Turkat's (1985) behavioural model [see discussion with Bruch, 1998]), which now incorporates traditional learning theories, clinical hypothesis testing and behavioural analysis procedures as well as emotional processing concepts. However, the model still relies strongly on diagnostic classification and associated assessment methods and also treatment protocols based on randomized controlled research trials – a square peg for a round hole?

Despite many remaining problems with case formulation, the surge of interest and activities has to be welcomed. This can be seen as evidence that both therapists have become increasingly dissatisfied with standard techniques according to the nosological model. And this seems especially relevant for complex and chronic problems labelled as personality and psychotic disorders. Recent advances in these fields owe much to experimental case formulation approaches (e.g. Turkat, 1985). At UCL, we began in the early eighties to treat such difficult clients in the experimental spirit of the early pioneers of BT. These patients were considered as little motivated and unresponsive to standard treatments; however, closer analysis did inspire new concepts of understanding as well as innovative ideas for treatment (e.g. schema-focused therapy; Bruch, 1988).

References

Adams, H. E. (1996). Further clarification on case formulation. *The Behaviour Therapist, 19*(5), 78.

American Psychiatric Association. (2000). *Diagnostic and statistical manual of mental disorders* (4th ed./text revision). Washington, DC: APA.

AuBuchon, P., & Malatesta, V. J. (1998). Managing the therapeutic relationship in behaviour therapy. In M. Bruch & F. W.Bond (Eds.), *Beyond diagnosis. Case formulation approaches in CBT*. Chichester, UK: Wiley.

Bandura, A. (1977). Self-efficacy: Toward a unifying theory of behavioural change. *Psychological Review, 84*(2), 191–215.

Barlow, D. H., & Hersen, M. (1984). *Single case experimental designs—Strategies for studying behaviour change* (2nd ed.). New York: Pergamon.

Blashfield, R. K., & Breen, N. J. (1989). Face validity of the DSM III R personality disorders. *American Journal of Psychiatry, 146*, 1575–1579.

Bond, F. W. (1998). Utilising case formulations in manual-based treatments. In M. Bruch & F. W.Bond (Eds.), *Beyond diagnosis. Case formulation approaches in CBT*. Chichester, UK: Wiley.

Boulder Conference on Graduate Education in Clinical Psychology. (1949). *The scientist-practitioner model*. American Psychological Association: http://en.wikipedia.org/wiki/Scientist–practitioner_model. Accessed on July 24, 2014.

British Psychological Society [BPS]. (2011). Response to the American Psychiatric Association: DSM-5 Development. Leicester: BPS.

Bruch, M. (1988). *The self-schema model of complex disorders*. Regensburg, Germany: S. Roederer.

Bruch, M. (1998). The development of case formulation approaches. In M. Bruch & F. W. Bond (Eds.), *Beyond diagnosis. Case formulation approaches in CBT*. Chichester, UK: Wiley.

Corrie, S., & Lane, D. A. (2006). Constructing stories about client's needs: Developing skills in formulation. In R. Bor & M. Watts (Eds.), *The trainee handbook. A guide for counselling and psychotherapy trainees* (2nd ed., pp. 68–90). London: Sage.

Corrie, S., & Lane, D. A. (2010). *Constructing stories, telling tales: A guide to practice in applied psychology*. London: Karnac.

Dryden, W. (1998). Understanding persons in the context of their problems: A rationale emotive therapy perspective. In M. Bruch & F. W. Bond (Eds.), *Beyond diagnosis. Case formulation approaches in CBT*. Chichester, UK: Wiley.

Eells, T. D. (2007). *Handbook of psychotherapy case formulation*. New York: Guilford Press.

Eells, T. D. (2009). Contemporary themes in case formulation. In P. Sturmey (Ed.), *Clinical case formulation. Varieties of approaches*. Chichester, UK: Wiley-Blackwell.

Eysenck, H. J. (1952). The effects of psychotherapy: An evaluation. *Journal of Consulting and Clinical Psychology, 16*, 319–324.

Eysenck, H. J. (1960). *Behaviour therapy and the neuroses*. Oxford, UK: Pergamon.

Eysenck, H. J. (1964). *Experiments in behaviour therapy*. Oxford, UK: Pergamon.

Eysenck, H. J. (1990). *Rebel with a cause. The autobiography of Hans Eysenck*. London: W. H. Allen.

Hickling, E. J., & Blanchard, E. B. (1997). The private practice psychologist and manual based treatments: Post-traumatic stress disorder secondary to motor vehicle accidents. *Behaviour, Research and Therapy, 33*(3), 191–203.

Kanfer, F. H., & Saslow, G. (1969). Behavioural diagnosis. In C. M. Franks (Ed.), *Behaviour therapy: Appraisal and status*. New York: McGraw-Hill.

Kuyken, W. (2006). Evidence-based case formulation. Is the emperor clothed? In N. Tarrier (Ed.), *Case formulation in cognitive behaviour therapy. The treatment of challenging and complex cases*. London: Routledge.

Lane, D. (1990). *The impossible child. Stoke on trent*. London: Trentham.

Lazarus, A. A. (1960). The elimination of children's phobias by deconditioning. In H. J. Eysenck (Ed.), *Behaviour therapy and the neuroses*. Oxford, UK: Pergamon.

Malatesta, V. J. (1995a). 'Technological' behaviour therapy for obsessive compulsive disorder: The need for adequate case formulation. *The Behaviour Therapist, 18,* 88–89.

Malatesta, V. J. (1995b). Case formulation enhances treatment effectiveness. *The Behaviour Therapist, 18,* 201–203.

Malatesta, V. J., & AuBuchon, P. G. (1992). Behaviour therapy in the private psychiatric hospital: Our experiences and a model of inpatient consultation. *The Behaviour Therapist, 15,* 43–46.

Markowitz, J. C., & Swartz, H. A. (2007). Case formulation in interpersonal psychotherapy of depression. In T. D. Eells (Ed.), *Handbook of psychotherapy case formulation* (2nd ed.). New York: Guilford.

Meyer, V. (1960). The treatment of two phobic patients on the basis of learning principles. In H. J. Eysenck (Ed.), *Behaviour therapy and the neuroses.* Oxford, UK: Pergamon.

Meyer, V. (1975). The impact of research on the clinical application of behaviour therapy. In R. I. Thompson & W. S. Dockens (Eds.), *Applications of behaviour modification.* New York: Academic Press.

Meyer, V., & Chesser, E. S. (1970). *Behaviour therapy in clinical psychiatry.* London: Penguin Books.

Meyer, V., & Liddell, A. (1975). Behaviour therapy. In D. Bannister (Ed.), *Issues and trends in psychological therapies.* London: Wiley.

Meyer, V., & Turkat, I. D. (1979) Behavioural analysis of clinical cases. *Journal of Behavioural Assessment, 1,* 259–269.

Persons, J. (2008). *The case formulation approach to cognitive-behavior therapy.* New York: Guilford.

Petermann, F., & Müller, J. M. (2001). *Clinical psychology and single-case evidence: A practical approach to treatment planning and evaluation.* Chichester, UK: Wiley.

Shapiro, M. B. (1955). Training of clinical psychologists at the institute of psychiatry. *Bulletin of the British Psychological Society, 8,* 1–6.

Shapiro, M. B. (1957). Experimental methods in the psychological description of the individual psychiatric patient. *International Journal of Social Psychiatry, 111,* 89–102.

Shapiro, M. B., & Nelson, E. H. (1955). An investigation of an abnormality of cognitive function in a cooperative young psychotic: An example of the application of the experimental method to the single case. *Journal of Clinical Psychology, 11,* 344–351.

Sturmey, P. (2008). *Behavioural case formulation and intervention. A functional analytic approach.* Chichester, UK: Wiley-Blackwell.

Sturmey, P. (2009). *Clinical case formulation. Varieties of approaches.* Chichester, UK: Wiley-Blackwell.

Szasz, T. S. (1961). *The myth of mental illness.* New York: Hoeber.

Tarrier, N. (2006). *Case formulation in cognitive behaviour therapy. The treatment of challenging and complex cases.* Hove, UK: Routledge.

Turkat, I. D. (1979). The behaviour analysis matrix. *Scandinavian Journal of Behaviour Therapy, 8,* 187–189.

Turkat, I. D. (1982). Behaviour-analytic considerations of alternative clinical approaches. In P. L. Wachtel (Ed.), *Resistance: Psychodynamic and behavioural approaches*. New York: Plenum.

Turkat, I. D. (1985). *Behavioural case formulation*. New York: Plenum.

Turkat, I. D. (1986). The behavioural Interview. In A. R. Ciminero, K. S. Calhoun, & H. E. Adams (Eds.), *Handbook of behavioural assessment* (2nd ed.). New York: Wiley-Interscience.

Turkat, I. D. (1990). *The personality disorders. A psychological approach to clinical management*. New York: Pergamon.

Wilson, G. T. (1982). Psychotherapy process and procedure: The behavioural mandate. *Behaviour Therapy, 13*, 291–312.

Wilson, G. T. (1996). Manual based treatments: The clinical application of research findings. *Behaviour, Research, and Therapy, 34*(4), 295–314.

Wilson, G. T. (1997). Treatment manuals in clinical practice. *Behaviour, Research, and Therapy, 34*(4), 295–314.

Wolpe, J. (1960). Reciprocal inhibition as the main basis of psychotherapeutic effects. In H. J. Eysenck (Ed.), *Behaviour therapy and the neuroses*. Oxford, UK: Pergamon.

World Health Organization. (2010). *International Classification of Diseases* (Version 10). Geneva, Switzerland: WHO.

Yates, A. J. (1960). The application of learning theory to the treatment of tics. In H. J. Eysenck (Ed.), *Behaviour therapy and the neuroses*. Oxford, UK: Pergamon.

2

The UCL Case Formulation Model
Clinical Process and Procedures

Michael Bruch

> *I have no data yet.*
> *It is a capital mistake to theorize before one has data.*
> *Insensibly one begins to twist facts to suit theories,*
> *instead of theories to suit facts.*
>
> Sherlock Holmes

This chapter will provide a description of the current status of the model as developed at the University College London (UCL). The current design draws predominantly on the work of Ira Turkat and David Lane, who were both associated with the Cognitive–Behavioural Psychotherapy unit at UCL and have made strong contributions to the model in recent years.

Unlike in psychiatry, where the interview is mainly guided by a categorical classification system (e.g. DSM; see previous chapter), case formulation is an experimental, hypothesis-driven procedure in pursuit of an explanatory model that subsequently assumes a guiding role for the ongoing therapeutic process. In addition to explaining acquisition and maintenance of a presented disorder, the problem formulation facilitates intervention hypotheses, leading to individually tailored treatment programmes.

As the initial interview is of central importance in this procedure, special attention shall be devoted to this aspect.

Beyond Diagnosis: Case Formulation in Cognitive Behavioural Therapy, Second Edition.
Edited by Michael Bruch.
© 2015 John Wiley & Sons, Ltd. Published 2015 by John Wiley & Sons, Ltd.

The Clinical Purpose

Case formulation is about developing a 'clinical theory' of an individual problem under investigation. This is done within the cognitive–behavioural framework. To achieve this, relevant information has to be obtained and suitable hypotheses developed and tested. As Vic Meyer would put it, the therapist acts like a Sherlock Holmes type of detective: Guided by cognitive–behavioural knowledge as well as personal life experience, he is observant and vigilant and picks up clues from appearance, behaviour, language and so on. Out of this process, hypotheses about the aetiology and nature of a problem can be generated, which in turn would inspire questions for the purpose of testing such hypotheses.

Such subjective experimental procedure appears appropriate if we accept the reality of individual differences, especially with complex and deeply rooted problems. Moreover, important decisions and interventions have to be made that involve long-term consequences for the client. Furthermore, it is expected that the quality and outcome of the interview will be crucial for building motivation and the patient's insight into the problem as well as being instrumental in establishing the beginnings of a constructive therapeutic relationship. Let us consider this model in some more detail.

The case formulation procedure is conducted in a dynamic and deterministic manner. It rests on the assumption that disordered behaviours can be understood according to established cognitive–behavioural knowledge when assisted by experimental principles of investigation. In this approach, the initial interview is of pre-eminent importance as we set out to achieve a plausible framework, the problem formulation, to account for the behaviour in question in terms of its causal history and maintaining factors. Such clinical theory is also expected to enable us to make predictions for target behaviours in specified situations and is expected to facilitate intervention hypotheses.

Another important aspect are *individual differences* in problem behaviours. Pioneering clinicians have always acknowledged this fact. Meyer's (e.g. 1957) original groundbreaking work focused on the *individualized analysis* of complex cases in the psychiatric setting as it became obvious that psychiatric diagnosis was not facilitating psychological treatment of individual patients. On the level of *labelling*, presenting complaints might appear similar; however, individual analysis often reveals discrepancies in terms of causal histories and mechanism of the disorder, thus suggesting different problem formulations. The case of social phobia may serve as an example: The underlying mechanism may relate, e.g. to either lack of social skills or fear of negative evaluation: each would suggest different treatment priorities and sequencing of treatment strategies.

Finally, the narrowness of classical and operant conditioning models merely focusing on functional analysis of presenting complaints has proved insufficient, especially for complex clinical cases. We consider it useful to keep an open mind concerning other knowledge concepts, both from within and outside the learning framework. Employing innovative and creative practice, we are keen to extend our scope and to improve our model for understanding, in order to match the complexity of human behaviour and abnormal behaviour in particular. In case formulation, we attempt to utilize any relevant knowledge from any discipline that can further the application of operationalized methods to effect behavioural changes. However, such knowledge concepts should be understood and applied according to the learning frame of reference involving experimental methodology. This is necessary to avoid conceptual confusion, which in our opinion would undermine the integration of 'new' ideas. As clinicians, we consequently intend to do this in view of clinical applications to the individual case. For example, Meyer (1970) has suggested such diverse fields as *social and cognitive experimental psychology, physiology, anatomy, neurophysiology, sociology, pharmacology,* and even *electronics* as suitable sources to broaden our methodology.

Foundations and Assumptions

The UCL case formulation model was originally pioneered by Meyer (1957). This was already outlined in the last chapter. Meyer preferred to apply established learning principles directly to clinical settings with psychiatric inpatients. He felt that learning theories were often too speculative and lacked empirical support. To facilitate this, the distinction between learning *principles* and learning *theories* seemed important to Meyer: Principles referred to observable phenomena that were experimentally verified but were not indicative of any theoretical explanation. Theories, on the other hand, were considered as highly speculative (especially in the 1950s) and thus neither valid nor useful for experimental assessments and the development of individually tailored treatment programmes. This issue has been critically discussed elsewhere (Meyer, 1975).

More recently, Turkat and Maisto (1985) have proposed case formulation as a 'scientific approach to the clinical case'. They emphasize both the process and the outcomes of science, the former referring to the experimental method requiring hypothesis generation and testing and the latter producing a method to modify the problem behaviour under investigation. This dual-aspect approach seems important, as it emphasizes the practical implications of a problem formulation, unlike psychiatric diagnosis that has rather limited relevance in guiding the therapeutic process.

The outcome achieved by this type of formulation process has been clinically demonstrated without any doubt. The fact that this approach began as a clinical effort using single cases highlights individual differences regarding the mechanism of presented problems.

In more detail, clinical–experimental analyses of seemingly similar complaints often reveal significant differences in structure, predisposing factors and learning histories. For example, one can usually detect complex interactions between presenting complaints and earlier learnt underlying maladaptive behaviours (e.g. schemas; Bruch, 1988). As the development of a problem in the biography of an individual can be highly idiographic, we suggest that assessment strategies should go beyond a description of the presenting complaint (as attempted in psychiatric classification) and subsequent treatment strategies should be designed accordingly. Such thinking was hardly fashionable in the early days of behaviour therapy, when clinical efforts were mostly directed at 'symptoms'.

The Initial Interview

The main purpose of the interview process is to collect *relevant* data, integrate these into an operationalized description for further expert analysis and eventually formulate a model for explanation and prediction covering all presented problems. This resulting 'clinical theory' will be provisional and subject to ongoing experimental scrutiny. Wolpe and Turkat (1985) have listed the critical questions to be answered as follows:

1. What are the problems the patient is experiencing?
2. Which of these are behavioural problems (i.e. are any of these psychologically based?)
3. If psychologically based, what are the functional relations between environment and behaviour?
4. Why have these developed and persisted?
5. What factors can produce change? (p. 7)

The style of interviewing is empathic but can also be directive when required. We do not regard direct questioning as 'unethical manipulation' as is sometimes suggested by dynamic or humanistic psychotherapists. With these approaches, to be directive is taboo and a scientific discussion of their 'golden rule' is not encouraged. Turkat (1986), on the other hand, has argued that, if logic prevails, the whole therapeutic procedure should follow directive principles: after all, it is the client who is looking for direction in order to cope better with his life problems. He further advances his case as follows:

> The directive style of interviewing as advocated here has often been the target of criticism. Such objections stem from theoretical notions that seem to have little scientific basis. For example, the author has seen many beginning therapists berated by their supervisors for being 'too directive'. Often, they are accused of being non-empathic and 'threatening the fragility' of the patient. These assertions deserve some comment. First, one cannot be empathic if one does not understand the specifics of a problem. It would seem that the most efficient way to understand is to ask direct questions. Second, the notion of a patient to be 'too fragile' to handle direct inquiry has little scientific support. Descriptively speaking, the patient encounters daily the problems he or she is purported to be 'too fragile' to discuss. The author finds that directness and openness seem highly valued by most patients. (p. 127)

At the start of the interview, a great amount of time is spent explaining the rationale and purpose to the patient. This involves clarification of his understanding and expectations of therapy, the procedure of cognitive–behavioural psychotherapy, the collaborative (team) approach and his participation in what is described as an 'active therapy'. Unlike in the classical psychiatric ward round, the patient becomes very much an active member of the group of professionals, who is invited to comment and contribute with his own questions or request further clarification and so on. A large white board is used to record all relevant information for all participants to refer to as much as possible.

When teaching the initial clinical interview, we prefer small group sessions with the patient and trainee therapist(s) present. In this way, every step is commented on and explained. For example, the supervisor might ask: What is the purpose of a particular question? Is there a relevant hypothesis being pursued? What conclusion can be drawn from any outcome? Does it make sense to the patient? and so on.

Typically, the interview will be started by an experienced clinician. From time to time – given the consent of the patient – trainees will be given the opportunity to put forward questions, however, on the condition that they can provide a clear rationale including a supporting hypothesis for the purpose of any question. Meyer likened this procedure with 'being a detective on a mission'. Above all, it is important to explain all processes and outcomes to the patient in a language that is as jargon free as possible.

Developing Hypotheses

To facilitate and develop a problem formulation, it is paramount to generate hypotheses of cause and maintenance of the problem behaviour under investigation. These will drive the interview strategy in order to test their validity.

This experimental procedure is mainly applied to phases 1–3. Whereas phases 1 and 2 are designed to identify, specify and describe problem behaviours, it is attempted in phase 3 to test and verify the problem formulation with clinical experiments. This shall be elaborated in more detail later on in this chapter.

The role of hypothesis generation in the interview is twofold: (1) Any information starting with the first contact should be utilized to develop hypotheses (2) which in turn form the basis for further questions designed to verify or reject adopted hypotheses. However, in a clinical context, experimental rigour, as was originally proposed by Shapiro (see Chapter 1), is normally neither possible nor desirable. As a compromise, Turkat (1985) suggested confirming or eliminating untenable hypotheses by means of systematic questioning. In fact, a similar strategy had already been practised and taught by Victor Meyer since the early 1960s.

As such a strategy can be influenced by the clinician's own personal (life) experience as well as expert knowledge of cognitive–behavioural principles, it is important for the clinician to review the process of hypothesis generation continuously. For further validation, it seems desirable to communicate this information to colleagues, trainees and patients in order to confirm its logical basis and achieve professional consensus. Obviously, this procedure must be described as 'pseudo-experimental' as it involves a rational appraisal of information instead of controlled experiments.

In consideration of the complexity of lifestyles and the idiosyncratic nature of problems, a high standard of clinical skills, (life) experience and therapist ingenuity are called for. In most cases, the clinician will have to perform a triple role: develop sensible hypotheses with the information provided, define suitable questions and evaluate the outcome of this process, all at the same time.

It is important that all information provided by the patient is accounted for. Discrepancies and contradictions need resolving, even if this means discarding otherwise suitable hypotheses and restarting the process.

Generating hypotheses begins at the very first contact with the client, i.e. the clinician may even use the initial impression to develop hypotheses as to what the problem may be. Turkat (1986) gives a fitting illustration:

> The clinician scrutinises the manner in which the patient speaks, such as tone, pitch, style, choice of words and phrases, intensity, latencies between words, sentences, questions, and replies, searching for a clue. The clinician…also scrutinises the patient's physical presentation such as hairstyle, clothing, posture, motor activity, and so forth.
> …An example will help to illustrate this point. If a young man in the clinic lobby whose physical presentation includes poorly matched, ill-fitting clothes, unstyled hair, thick-rimmed eyeglasses, and uneasy movements and facial expressions when introduced to the therapist, then a preliminary general

hypothesis of a social skills deficit is suggested. Depending on subsequent inquiry, one might hypothesise further certain consequences of this social skills deficit such as loneliness, depression, and so forth. (p. 121)

Any item of information provided by the client is treated in this way, which provides guidance throughout the interview. As we progress towards the problem formulation (detailed below), we collect information in a systematic and logical manner. Therapists are encouraged to base questions on reasoned hypotheses and reject questions that do not fit these criteria. This strategy will prevent the collection of too much and, especially, unnecessary information, a problem one often finds with inexperienced therapists who might continue the interview over many sessions. Typically, numerous topics might be covered and in the end a therapist might find it difficult to make sense of the accumulated information. Eventually, the elegance, simplicity and purposefulness of the experimental approach are in danger of being lost as an inexperienced therapist begins to 'drown' in a vast amount of data. (A typical question to the supervisor is 'what shall I do next?'). It is not recommended to jump from topic to topic in a random fashion as this tends to lead to disorientation or even confusion. Such interviewing styles are usually associated with inexperience, uncertainty and lack of knowledge. In these circumstances, close guidance and supervision is needed. By contrast, the discipline of the hypothesis-driven approach provides a sense of orientation and guidance throughout the interview.

Thus, it is useful to conduct teaching sessions to demonstrate interviewing in a transparent manner with both trainee therapist and patient present. Hypotheses are put forward and are commented upon and discussed until consensus can be achieved. It seems particularly important to encourage trainees to formulate hypotheses that can be supported by the cognitive–behavioural psychotherapy framework.

Furthermore, hypotheses may be derived from sources other than information provided by the patient. All aspects of the immediate environment may be relevant, including a patient's key relationships with others. Finally, it is important to recognize that hypotheses at all stages of the interview may be wrong and prove to be unsupported by data. To remedy wrong hypotheses, open mindedness and flexibility are called for. For example, highly experienced therapists may develop biases based on preferred models of explanation leading to matching hypotheses. This bias may subsequently lead to selective perception and direction in the interview and may even include shaping of the patient's verbal behaviour.

Clinical illustrations for hypothesis generation and testing can be found with Turkat (1985, 1987/see appendix). A more in-depth discussion regarding generation and testing of hypotheses in the context of the interview is given by Richard Hallam in the next chapter.

Practical Steps

To enhance the model's practicality, Lane (1990) has proposed five basic phases (see Chapter 1). This involved more precise definitions and clearer operationalization of the procedure, originally developed for the assessment and treatment of children and adolescents. This design allows for correcting feedback and continuous verification of the process by means of hypothesis generation and testing. An updated version of this stepwise procedure is detailed below in Table 2.1. The first three phases are covered during the initial interview. These steps shall be explained in more detail below.

Defining problems (Phase 1)

This phase is focussed on the individual narrative of the patient. The purpose is to explore the client's main problem(s), why he is seeking help at this point in time and what changes he may envisage? A detailed and personally meaningful description of present difficulties is sought to facilitate generation of reasoned hypotheses. We actively encourage clients to use their own 'language' and refrain from jargon or interpretations of other professionals acquired during the course of previous assessments or treatments. The patient's statement normally inspires a host of hypotheses that can be investigated further.

Already at this stage, the patient is encouraged to express his views and expectations regarding therapeutic change and outcome (to be reviewed later in the light of the problem formulation). In cases that involve relationship problems (e.g. marital or family issues), it may be appropriate to obtain statements and opinions of other individuals involved. Discrepancies and conflicting information might have important implications regarding both motivation and outcome of therapy.

Consider the case of a person with obsessions and compulsions who disrupts his marital life through repeated checking and cleaning rituals. As the situation becomes unbearable, his wife might threaten divorce if he refuses to be treated for his problems. In cases like this, a consensus about treatment motivation and goals has to be found before a modification programme can be envisaged. In other words, we support a process of increasing awareness to achieve a consensus for all individuals who may get involved in the therapeutic process.

How do we get started in the initial interview? Routinely, we begin by explaining to the client the purpose of the interview and may discuss briefly various options of approaching behavioural problems (e.g. emphasizing a psychological versus a psychiatric approach; or more specifically, emphasize and explain differences between various psychological approaches). Depending on a client's expectations and previous knowledge, we may also

Table 2.1   Phases in the Case Formulation Process.

Phase One: Definition of Problems

1   A narrative of the problem(s) from those involved is obtained.

2   Problems are described and specified on the basis of initial information provided by the client.

3   Initial objectives of the client are clarified.

Theme: A process of growing awareness aimed at a therapeutic consensus.

Phase Two: Exploration

4   Defined problems are conceptualized in cognitive–behavioural terms.

5   Multi-level cognitive–behavioural assessment is conducted.

6   Data are collected to test hypotheses.

Theme: The process is one of increasingly refined expert assessments.

Phase Three: Formulation

7   A problem formulation and intervention hypotheses are established.

8   Explanation and discussion with participants and redefinition of therapeutic objectives.

9   Clinical experiments to check and verify the problem formulation.

Theme: The process is one of summarizing and integrating gathered and tested information until an adequate explanation is available.

Phase Four: Intervention

10   The procedures to be used are selected and specified.

11   An intervention contract is established.

12   The agreed programme is enacted and monitored.

Theme: The process is one of structured practice.

Phase Five: Evaluation

13   Accomplished outcomes are evaluated.

14   Any gains made are supported and enhanced, the programme is optimized and further objectives, if suggested, are pursued.

15   Continuing evaluation and review. Generation of further ideas to consolidate progress.

Theme: The process is one of monitored achievement and support.

explain the rationale and practicalities of cognitive–behavioural psychotherapy: stressing active participation of the patient, frequency of sessions, a goal-oriented focus, continuous engagement and learning experience, 'homework' assignments, behavioural contracts and so on.

If this is a teaching session involving trainee therapists, one introduces each individual and facilitates adaptation to the situation. The patient is assured that he is a volunteer and is only expected to offer information that he feels comfortable with and that he may be able to talk to a therapist in private later on. Finally, the patient is actively encouraged to participate in the interview by asking questions and by making comments or suggestions, etc. Next, we may take some biographical details, e.g. age, sex, marital status, and profession.

An account of the way we start focusing on the presenting problem has been provided by Meyer and Turkat (1979):

> We begin typically by generating a list of all the behavioural difficulties the client is currently experiencing. Each problem is listed in general terms with the aim of generating an exhaustive list. The list of behavioural difficulties serves a variety of purposes such as structuring the clinical interview, specifying the range of problems the individual is experiencing, and, most importantly, providing the therapist with information for generating hypotheses. Preferably, the list of problems and subsequent information is recorded on a blackboard or some other medium which the client and therapist can visually refer to (as the wealth of information to be elicited is usually beyond memory capabilities). Visual inspection of the behaviour problem list often provides clues as to how the presenting complaints may be related and account for one another. If such relationships are discovered, then clinical efficiency is facilitated. For example, with a particular client it may be hypothesised that this person is depressed because he is sexually impotent. Consequently, for clinical expediency, sexual impotence will be examined first. In certain cases, the list of behaviour problems does not facilitate the formulation of such an hypothesis. Therefore, the most incapacitating behaviour difficulty is examined first. In either case, the next step in conducting the initial interview involves a developmental behaviour analysis of each individual problem the client is experiencing (p. 262).

In cases where it seems impossible to elicit a clear description of the main presenting complaint, it can be appropriate to ask the client to list all problems in session or as a homework task. Such list should be used to facilitate hypotheses regarding relationships between single complaints and might thus be helpful in detecting the underlying problem mechanism. Turkat (1986) provides an example for this:

> ...assume the following list of problems is generated: (1) Depression, (2) Lack of friends, (3) Excessive hand washing, (4) Inability to leave the house, (5)

Difficulty sleeping, (6) Excessive cleaning. The therapist attempts to find an explanatory hypothesis for all of these complaints. A striking hypothesis from the problems listed in this case is a *fear of contamination*. Such a hypothesis is derived from the following type of thinking: The patient probably *washes her hands* and *cleans her house* excessively to prevent possible contamination by dirt, germs, and so forth. Further, she *avoids leaving her home* in order to prevent exposure to more contaminating stimuli. This results in *social isolation*, rumination about her predicament at night (which produces sleep onset *insomnia*) and thus, *depression*. Other problems predicted from the general mechanism of 'fear of contamination' might include: avoidance of touching others, sexual problems, hosing down or vacuuming others when they enter her house(this is not as uncommon as it might sound), preventing others from entering her house, and so forth. (p. 123)

This style of reasoning is at variance with some 'case formulators' who prefer to focus on psychiatric diagnosis using standardized assessment procedures (e.g. Persons, 2008). In hypothesis-guided case formulation, the use of tests or questionnaire batteries and such like (as performed in search of a diagnosis) is not considered helpful as it would undermine the experimental–investigative rationale; however, it might be useful, when normal interviewing is not possible, to use screening or other hypothesis-inspired measures (e.g. behavioural observation) to facilitate the generation of appropriate hypotheses for further investigation. The impetus for such investigations should always be on the individual! Finally, additional interviewing of partners, family members or even friends might provide useful information for further investigation; however, full consent of the client would be of crucial importance.

Exploring problems (Phase 2)

Phase one concludes with a list of concretely described problem behaviours to be subjected to further analyses. It needs to be stressed that such analyses should not be a typical diagnostic or psychometric procedure but hypothesis-driven individualized assessments for all identified problem(s) answering all questions relevant toward a valid problem formulation. In our experience, most cases will require a *functional analysis* including *triple response system analysis* and a problem-focused *developmental analysis*. Further optional analyses (e.g. schema analysis) as suggested by hypotheses arising from clinical observations and initial interviewing may also be conducted.

Functional analysis   This analysis was originally suggested by Kanfer and co-workers as a core part of the learning equation model of behavioural analysis (e.g. Kanfer & Phillips, 1970). The principal goal is to investigate antecedent and consequent conditions of the problem behaviour. This analysis is still being recommended as a salient component in cognitive–behavioural investigations.

More recently, tripartite response system analysis has been incorporated into this design to allow the systematic study of individual response modalities. This seems appropriate as response systems have been shown to be highly interactive (e.g. Lang, 1979; Turkat, 1979). A graphic outline of the complete model is provided in Figure 2.1.

The clinician scrutinizes each presenting complaint according to these criteria. One attempts to identify relevant triggers regarding high (S+) and low (S−) probability. It is also important to determine whether stimulus generalization has occurred, i.e. is the behaviour triggered by a *single stimulus* or a *cluster of related stimuli* (which may be hierarchically organized).

Regarding organismic variables, it is useful to explore whether biological factors or related predispositions contribute to the expression of the investigated response. For example, an elevated level of habitual arousal has been shown to be of predictive value for anxiety patterns following stress (Lader & Wing, 1966).

Most salient in the functional analysis is the examination of response systems as illustrated in Figure 2.1. This follows Lang's (1971) influential model, which has proposed three related components of behaviour: *verbal–cognitive, autonomic–physiological and behavioural–motoric*. This conceptualization allows us to study the contents as well as the complex interactions between these responses. For example, it is useful to identify the primary and dominant response mode that may have causal impact on other response systems. Or, as in the case of anticipatory anxiety, we may detect a mutually enhancing interaction between cognitive and autonomic variables (Meyer & Reich, 1978). The study of such interactions can provide guidance for the design of suitable treatment method. Obviously, the importance of therapeutic aims would suggest tackling dominant and primary response systems first.

Further, it is of interest to know whether response systems are in a state of synchrony (high correlation) or desynchrony (low correlation) (Rachman & Hodgson, 1974). Such patterns can be highly individual suggesting different treatment options. For example, decoupling synchronous systems can be a

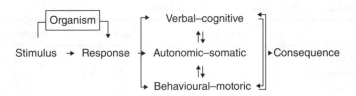

Figure 2.1   Functional analysis.

successful strategy to reduce anxiety by (cognitive) relabelling of autonomic cues. Also, the three systems should be assessed to determine whether there is a predisposed response mode in individuals as one can frequently detect primary 'cognitive' or 'autonomic' responders (e.g. Bandura, 1977; Bruch, 1988). Part of this investigation should focus on the sequence of events, i.e. in what way can response systems influence each other?

The mode of assessing response systems requires further consideration. We have found that self-report may differ significantly from direct measures in response to stress. For example, we have detected significant discrepancies regarding autonomic–somatic responses. To complicate things further, individuals tend to respond to stress in different modalities. For example, we found in one experiment using two physiological measures that some individuals showed an increase in 'heart rate' whereas others rather responded with increases in 'skin conductance'. This suggests that direct measures may vary independently. At the same time, it was found that subjective ratings of the same parameters showed significant correlations and increases in the expected direction. For clinical purposes, it seems of significance how physiological arousal is perceived, evaluated and labelled by the individual. For example, those who perceive an increase as positive activation would find that this facilitates a stressful task whereas quite the opposite would be true when the perception is negative (Bruch, 1988).

To conclude, an analysis investigating response primary and sequences should provide important clues for understanding the problem mechanism. For example, an anxiety response that is initiated and dominated by the verbal–cognitive system may require a different therapeutic focus (e.g. cognitive restructuring) as compared with a strong autonomic reaction (e.g. biofeedback). The arrows in Figure 2.1 indicate possible interactions.

Additional relevant parameters of each response system such as intensity, frequency and duration may also be studied to gain deeper understanding of the presenting complaint. This process is assisted by the *behaviour analysis matrix* (Table 2.2), which recommends additional assessment of cognitive, autonomic and motoric components under antecedent and consequent conditions. These can be either behaviours or environmental events. A fuller discussion can be found in Turkat (1979).

Table 2.2   The Behaviour Analysis Matrix.

	Antecedent	*Behaviour*	*Consequence*
Cognitive	X	X	X
Autonomic	X	X	X
Motoric	X	X	X
Environmental	X		X

The assessment of consequences in the functional analysis is designed to clarify the operant maintaining factors of the problem behaviour under investigation. It is important to identify whether there are conflicting short-term versus long-term consequences. For example, a social phobic might be able to reduce social anxiety by means of withdrawal and avoidance, which in the long run may to lead to complete isolation and subsequent depression. The balance between short-term and long-term consequences can also shed light on the level of self-control. (Maladaptive self-regulation is operating when immediate reinforcement is preferred to long-term gratification, i.e. reduction of anxiety by means of substance abuse.)

Lane (1990) has suggested a variety of additional strategies that can be employed in the exploration phase if suggested by appropriate hypotheses or in the event that the functional analysis is inadequate. Any assessment method outside the traditional cognitive–behavioural methodology should be supported by a hypothesis with a clear rationale and only in pursuit of a clearly defined goal. For example, it may be appropriate to activate a deeply seated and avoided schema by means of emotive techniques (Young, 1990).

It is also important to observe that any analysis of behaviours is not treated as an isolated 'snapshot'. As behaviour is continuous, a functional analysis should be conceptualized as part of a wider loop. Responses may become stimuli for subsequent behaviours and so on. The Behaviour Analysis Matrix (Turkat, 1979) provides a useful conceptualization for such assessments.

As already discussed above, we do not recommend standardized, often very detailed and seemingly over-inclusive schemes of analysis (e.g. Kanfer & Phillips, 1970). Consistent with the case formulation model, the selection and focus on problem areas should be determined by hypotheses, as the potential number of investigations can be otherwise limitless. Apart from being time-consuming, this may create an unmanageable and sometimes confusing array of data that may become a distraction when attempting a problem formulation. In the worst case scenario, the purposeful, dynamic flow of the interview may get substituted by an over-concentration on 'correct' categorization. It has proved to be more useful to collect additional data at a later stage during assessment and treatment if and when relevant hypotheses suggest so and point to apparent information gaps.

Developmental analysis The usefulness of a developmental assessment has been the subject of controversy among behaviour therapists and was treated with suspicion by early learning theorists (who preferred a 'here' and 'now' focus, e.g. Stuart, 1970). They sensed a backsliding towards psychodynamic positions.

It has to be emphasized that in case formulation such analysis should not be general but precisely focused on individual complaints. Turkat (1986) has summarized the main arguments for the usefulness of a developmental aetiologic analysis:

> First, there is sufficient scientific and clinical evidence that one of the best overall predictors of future behaviour is previous behaviour. Second, in order to change a behaviour in a meaningful way, one must know the potential causal and maintaining variables. Finally, one cannot prevent future behavioural problems unless one knows what the etiologic determinants are. In the initial interview, etiologic enquiry usually serves to either identify antecedents and consequences of relevance or to validate predictions from the hypothesised mechanism of disorder. In the former case, etiologic enquiry is used to *develop* an hypothesis about the mechanism of disorder. In the latter case, the clinician *predicts* what the history of the presenting problems are. In either case, every behavioural problem is examined from its very first occurrence through all changes in its development to the present. (p. 124)

Historical information is usually also the main source for generating hypotheses about predisposing factors like biological vulnerabilities and earlier learned, deeply seated behaviours, etc. Turkat (1985) illustrates this for the case of a 'socially inept individual':

> ...he is likely to have had parental models for such behaviour (i.e. vicarious conditioning), promoting a lack of opportunity to acquire appropriate skills (operant conditioning) and, perhaps, traumatic consequences such as social rejection resulting in the present social anxiety (classical conditioning) problem. (p. 30)

In case formulation, the developmental analysis attempts to construct a focused timeline for each identified problem behaviour. We start with an assessment of the onset circumstances involving predisposing and precipitating factors that may have contributed to vulnerability for onset of these complaints. Thereafter, all significant further occurrences until the present date are carefully recorded, including any changes in manifestation of identified problems and their maintenance mechanism (antecedent and consequent conditions). Such changes can have implications for the intervention hypothesis (as suggested by the problem formulation; see below). For example, a phobia may be established through classical conditioning but over time increasingly maintained by operant factors such as a protective partner.

Possible interactions between different problem areas (if in evidence) are also carefully investigated. This might provide clues as to what the main and central problem might be and thus be useful information for the construction of the problem formulation.

Particularly when working with complex cases, we have often found evidence for early established maladaptive schemas being closely related to cognitive–behavioural problems. Schemas were hypothesized to promote behavioural disorders in general. We have conceptualized this mechanism as deficient self-regulation (Bruch, 1988). Hypotheses arising from such observations have inspired an optional *schema analysis,* which shall be addressed in the next section.

Schema analysis Case formulations and related clinical research with complex and difficult problems have evidenced early learned maladaptive schemas that are strongly related to dysfunctional cognitive processing styles and interpersonal behaviours (Bruch, 1988). In more detail, we have found a cluster of excessive negative and pessimistic thinking, distorted attribution, low self-efficacy, social isolation and depression. This cluster of behaviours was shown to be strongly related to self-ideal discrepancy, negative self-image and low self-esteem. We have described such a scenario as deficient self-regulation, usually resulting in deeply seated self-perpetuating vicious cycles creating a complex pattern of multiple, often interrelated, problems (as typically found with personality disorders). In therapy, it is mainly the deficient self-regulation that can undermine all previous therapeutic efforts and achievements. The main underlying mechanisms appear to be maladaptive cognitive styles that prevent the correct processing and appraisal of therapeutic progress and outcomes. As a consequence, the building of positive self-schema structures is prevented.

In clinical practice, such complications are not always obvious and are sometimes difficult to explore, as schemas may operate in a *non-conscious* mode. As well as promoting schema-consistent cognitive biases and behavioural complaints, clients are often unaware of their automatic and continuously operating nature. In the long term, negative schemas may lead to maladaptive 'personal theories' that are often responsible for maintenance of these problems and also resistant to treatment. It is also common that sufferers deny or suppress negative schemas because of the painful evidence they provide as well as the feelings of hopelessness and helplessness they may cause (Bruch, 1988; Young, 1990). In the long term, this leads to an avoidant, insecure, anxiety-prone and increasingly depressive lifestyle. Also, clients suffering from this condition tend to lack motivation and adherence in treatment.

It is for these reasons that relevant schemas should be investigated very carefully in order to obtain full cooperation of the client. It also helps to explain the rationale of schema focus therapy and pointing out of possible treatment options.

According to the self-schema model (Bruch, 1988), we have proposed that the pervasive maladaptive cognitive and behavioural patterns underlying presenting complaints should receive more attention. Obviously, the need for this arises in the context of evidence gained in the initial interview. For example, in analyzing client's early history, hypotheses regarding basic anxieties and conflicts can be generated.

Common basic anxieties include those associated with having to achieve in response to high standards or those associated with becoming independent from overprotective parents, etc. In terms of conflicts, it may be hypothesized that the client is in an *approach–avoidance* conflict when basic anxieties associated with taking responsibility conflict with the consequences of avoiding responsibility (e.g. parental, social or self-disapproval). A dysfunctional lifestyle often develops in response to such basic anxieties and conflicts. A schema analysis usually aids the explanation of the onset and development of problem behaviours. This is especially true for complex cases, where a lack of traumatic conditioning events renders explanations based on a principle of conditioning inadequate. Furthermore, a conceptualization of problem behaviours that involves self-schemas and lifestyle can have predictive value with regards to 'high-risk' situations where exacerbation of problem behaviours or relapse might occur.

This analysis is highlighted here as a typical creation arising from the case formulation approach with complex problems – clearly a far cry from symptom–technique matching technology.

Additional issues   Finally, we are keen to establish knowledge about the assets and potentials of patients. This prevents us from falling into a one-dimensional understanding of problems and may also provide important clues for involvement of the patient in treatment. For this purpose, we assess areas of positive adjustment with particular emphasis on self-control skills. It may also be of interest to find out whether clients can cope with their problems under certain circumstances or have done so previously and for whatever reasons.

This enumeration of procedures for the initial interview cannot be considered complete. There are no limits for inventiveness as long as the general experimental strategy is followed. In principle, we try to keep assessment routines to a minimum and adopt a flexible, hypothesis-led approach. This avoids the collection of unnecessary information, which can muddy the waters when attempting a plausible problem formulation.

Although the client is regarded as the principal source of information, we might also consider it appropriate to use other sources, such as direct observation in the natural environment or interviewing partners, friends or family members. Information that is not consistent with prevailing hypotheses during the interview must always be accounted for. This may be due to a wrong hypothesis, insufficient interview technique or even manipulative behaviour of the client. It is recommended not to cling to hypotheses that cannot be supported. Also, the interview procedure should carefully avoid the confirmation of favoured hypotheses. Should there be justifiable doubts about the client's account, one might consider interviewing other individuals who know the client well, provided full consent has been given.

The problem formulation (Phase 3)

The problem formulation assumes a central role as the locus of data integration from which all further therapeutic steps should logically evolve. Meyer and Turkat (1979) have defined the problem formulation as a clinical theory which...

> ...(1) relates all the client's complaints to one another, (2) explains why the individual developed these difficulties, and (3) provides predictions concerning the client's behaviour given any stimulus conditions. (p. 261)

Meyer has argued against reductionism in behaviour therapy (Meyer & Liddell, 1977) and has pointed out that functional analysis or other singular assessment tools cannot be regarded as sufficient for a full understanding of behavioural problems – instead a conceptual system is preferred that approaches the whole person in cognitive–behavioural terms. The ultimate questions in cognitive–behavioural analysis that ideally have to be answered are as follows: *Why has this individual at a particular point of time acquired this specific presenting complaint? How did the problem develop? Which (underlying) conditions (if any) were instrumental? And what is the functional value of the problem for his life in general?*

Such an analysis should also clarify any predisposing factors that may explain why a patient tends to behave in a particular way in a given situation or why a specific situation is more influential than another one and so on.

By integrating all relevant data gathered in the initial interview, we hope to arrive at such a comprehensive formulation to explain aetiology and maintenance of problem behaviours that should enable us to make predictions for specified situations. Subsequently, it is important to present and discuss the formulation with the client. In so doing, we are not just seeking approval but are trying to make the assessment and conclusions as transparent as possible, thus hoping to motivate the client for active participation in the subsequent treatment programme. However, any criticism or even rejection by the client is also considered as helpful as this may point to lack of information, faulty conclusions or other inconsistencies that might require clarification. Turkat (1986) has recommended a checklist for this procedure:

1. Informing the patient that the clinician's formulation of the problem will be presented and that he or she should comment on its accuracy
2. Stating what the presenting problems are
3. What the general mechanism of disorder is
4. Illustrating how this mechanism is causing all the presenting problems

5. Explaining why these problems developed, using examples provided by the patient
6. Emphasising how these are (potentially) learned responses
7. Outlining the range of treatment options
8. Discussing all positive and negative consequences expected from each treatment option
9. Predicting obstacles to successful intervention
10. Stating whether or not the therapist can treat the patient, and if not, why not
11. Asking the patient to comment on all that has been said
12. Asking the patient what he or she believes would be the best option to follow
13. Encouraging the patient to spend a week or so contemplating the formulation, its indications and treatment options
14. Answering any questions the patient asks. (p. 125)

The other important purpose of a problem formulation is to provide guidance for all further therapeutic steps, i.e. to enable the therapist to decide on appropriate treatment strategies, determine priorities and sequencing, develop or select suitable techniques and so on. For example, this should clarify whether the main complaint is isolated or is supported by other underlying problem behaviours acting as independent variables. We should also be able to explain why the individual has been vulnerable to stressful conditions leading to a variety of complaints whereas another might appear immune.

We believe that problem formulations based on such multi-level analysis guided by individual clinical hypotheses are best suited for understanding the underlying mechanism of individual problems. Problem formulations should allow predictions of target behaviours and enable intervention hypotheses (see below). It is difficult to see how a diagnosis or psychometric procedure could provide equally relevant information.

To conclude, factors that contribute to a valid problem formulation include (a) recognition of individual specificity, (b) multi-level analysis guided by cognitive–behavioural principles and (c) the relation of complaints to underlying conditions (e.g. schemas). The experimental method applied throughout this analysis serves as a guiding and integrating factor. In rare cases where a formulation cannot be achieved (when information is insufficient or unobtainable), one adopts a more pragmatic approach. Obviously, this can be expected to reduce therapeutic effectiveness greatly, especially when complaints are treated in an isolated fashion.

Clinical experimentation   To validate the problem formulation, i.e. its explaining and predictive power, suitable behavioural tests and measurements should be employed in relevant clinical settings. Precise hypotheses should be delineated and tested with in vivo experiments set under relevant stimulus conditions. The selection of procedures will depend on client variables, nature of hypotheses as suggested by the formulation and inventiveness of the clinician.

In practical terms, the clinician should provide stimulation across all response modalities and select appropriate measures covering all response systems. As outlined earlier, this can be useful for investigating response patterns, e.g. to determine discrepancies between verbal reports and motoric behaviours or to determine the dominant response mode that may react first and have impact on the others.

Distorted perception and dysfunctional labelling of physiological arousal is also a common aspect of response system interactions. For example, an actress who perceives physiological activation before or during a performance as negative and debilitating is likely to label the outcome as stage fright.

At other times, physiological cues may get exaggerated, which is likely to promote the vicious cycle of *anticipatory anxiety* (operationalized as enhancing interaction of cognitive and autonomic variables).

Another issue that may need to be investigated is a possible discrepancy between verbal reports and actual behaviours as assessed in vivo. For example, this can occur when phobic situations have been avoided for long periods of time.

Some other relevant measures might also be appropriate. These could pertain to information provided by other individuals involved, in vivo observations, self-monitoring data or even questionnaire measures, which should be carefully selected to be relevant to the hypothesized problem. Naturally, converging evidence of multiple measures covering several dimensions will provide strong support for the problem formulation. The clinician continues to conduct 'experiments' to verify or eliminate untenable hypotheses as new information arises. Finally, the most plausible explanatory formulation is tested for its generality with further clinical experiments.

In some cases, it may not be possible to verify a problem formulation. This can be caused by several factors including faulty information, a 'weak' formulation, inappropriate hypotheses or unsuitable measures. In some circumstances, reformulation of problem behaviours becomes necessary and clinical experimentation has to be repeated. If this does not solve the problem, additional information sources may be consulted or otherwise a pragmatic approach to treatment is adopted, e.g. to focus on the most salient complaint. Such an approach may also provide new information for a revised formulation.

Observations arising from clinical experimentation might also suggest prototypic therapeutic techniques (e.g. in vivo exposure) including measurements for baseline and change during intervention and follow-up.

Obviously, rigorous clinical experimentation might not be required as a routine measure, especially with simple problems that are formulated unambiguously and are generally agreed.

Unexpected surprises may also occur when clinical experiments assume a treatment effect. For example, a client with a reported travel phobia (result-ing from traumatic conditioning) had avoided travel for many years. She reported mild anticipatory anxiety before a clinical approach/exposure experiment. However, once confronted with the fearful situation, spontane-ous immediate habituation took place. No further treatment was required.

Finally, we like to emphasize that this experimental and hypothesis-guided procedure should not be confused with standardized psychometric test batteries, which we consider as inappropriate in a psychotherapeutic context where the focus should be on individual change processes. Any selected measure should serve a purpose within this rationale. Typical examples for clinical experimentation have been provided by Turkat and Carlson (1984) and Turkat and Maisto (1985). A more detailed discussion of the method can be found in Carey, Flasher, Maisto, and Turkat (1984).

Intervention hypothesis   A plausible and verified problem formulation explaining the underlying mechanism of the problem(s) should enable the clinician to make reasoned proposals for treatment goals, strategies and prototypical methods of intervention.

Regarding goals, we carefully review the patient's original statement (as obtained in phase one) in the light of the formulation. Any major discrep-ancies should be fully explored and discussed with the client so that acceptable agreement can be found jointly. Obviously, this process is greatly facilitated when the patient comprehensively understands and accepts the problem formulation. Hopefully, full consent for any modifications, refine-ments or revisions of the previously stated goals can subsequently be achieved. Only in rare cases of disagreement must the therapist decide whether he can adopt a pragmatic compromise or rather disengage from the treatment process.

Understanding the underlying mechanism of a disorder in terms of learning, cognitive or additional theoretical principles is the key source for intervention hypotheses and proposals. Obviously, the therapist is expected to have sound knowledge of cognitive–behavioural methodology based on single case–based and group-based research. Handbooks on techniques and quality manuals might also be useful in providing technical expertise about methods but should be adapted to the individual case. Finally, we find that clinical experiments in problem-relevant settings can be highly instrumental for designing specific treatment methods. For example, the knowledge that a phobic reaction is started with catastrophic thoughts would point to a matching treatment strategy.

Baselines and measures of change In addition to clinical experiments, the predictive power of the problem formulation can be further tested using self-report measures that can be subsequently used to establish baselines and to evaluate change during therapy as well as for outcome and follow-up. Suitable measures may range from questionnaire-type to rating scale–type assessments. All measures should be individualized and as meaningful as possible. In case formulation, we reject standardized psychometric test approaches based on trait personality conceptualization as inappropriate as clinicians should predominantly be concerned about evaluating the therapeutic change process rather than a comparison with normative groups. In training and supervision, we do encourage therapists to develop personal questionnaires or rating scales using statements in the personal language of patients. For example, such work led to a "dog phobia questionnaire" (Tuomisto, 1994), which was subsequently used as a prototype for similar problems but required adjustment for each new case.

For comprehensive evaluation, we recommend a multidimensional approach: *client/therapist (or team); global/specific; short-term/long-term.* To state this in more detail, any changes or outcomes ought to be evaluated *independently* by both patients and therapists; measurements should be directed to both specific *problems* as well as *overall life adjustment* and, finally, *short-term changes* (e.g. response to an exposure session) as well as *long-term changes* (e.g. rating of severity of problems) should be considered.

Furthermore, it is desirable to conduct a long-term follow-up for realistic assessment of therapeutic achievements. Obviously, multidimensional assessments may yield contradictory results that need to be addressed in an overall clinical evaluation. For example, our own data suggest strong pre-treatment agreement between the client and therapist, whereas strong discrepancies tend to be more typical for the follow-up stages (Bruch, 1988). This appears especially true for global long-term measures like life adjustment, indicating the need for greater processing and generalization of treatment achievements. These issues ought to be discussed fully and disagreements need to be reconciled. Lane (1990) has provided some examples for suitable measurement techniques.

Phases one to three pertain to the initial interview and are considered to be the most salient and instrumental elements in the case formulation procedure. The intervention and evaluation phases in case formulation are in principle not distinct from best standard cognitive–behavioural psychotherapy practice. However, apart from formulation-guided design or selection of a treatment model, there will be a strong emphasis on the individual tailoring of all applied methods, be it adjustment of established techniques or the creation of innovative methods. Another important element in case formulation is close monitoring of the efficacy of any applied method in order to be able to provide corrective feedback to the formulation phase in case the programme does not work as expected. This may require revision of earlier phases where mistakes were possibly made or important information was overlooked.

Intervention (Phase 4)

Formulation-guided intervention is designed to produce general options for the modification of problem behaviours. This would include all response systems as outlined earlier.

1. Increase of appropriate behaviours that occur infrequently, are of low intensity, or occur on 'wrong' occasions.
2. Decrease of inappropriate behaviours that occur too frequently and are of high intensity.
3. Instil new behaviours, i.e. building/shaping desired behaviours from scratch.

Any chosen procedures should be specified in detail and explained and discussed with the client. For example, is it clear which (and how) behaviours are to be increased, decreased or instilled? Have the techniques to be used been clearly explained to the participants? (in brief: Who, What, When, Where and How?). Does the treatment procedure follow the logic of the formulation and subsequent discussion with the client and is it consistent with treatment objectives?

This discussion can be followed by an intervention contract that provides an agreed description of the programme including the therapist's role and the tasks to be carried by the client, etc.

Finally, the agreed programme is enacted and monitored in a structured way. This should involve a suitable environment and active participation of the client according to the treatment contract.

The course of treatment should be designed as a continuous learning process. There is no good reason why therapy should take place once a week in a consulting room. This means that, after the initial interview and formulation, scheduling of sessions should be designed to foster continuous learning with increasing engagement of the client and therapist-led session should increasingly focus on review and corrective feedback. Generally, from the start of therapy, we encourage self-regulation processes in the application of treatment methods. The intervals between sessions should be flexibly adjusted to therapeutic progress. Typically, the frequency of sessions should be reduced gradually when self-control of the client and subsequent consolidation as well as generalization of treatment effects improve.

Evaluation (Phase 5)

How and why should accomplished outcomes be monitored and evaluated? We have already suggested some suitable dimensions for measurement. It seems equally important to employ a broad range of modalities, e.g. involving clinical judgement, behavioural observation, diaries (thoughts, feelings, behaviours), self-ratings and questionnaires. Such a range of measures might be helpful in detecting inconsistencies in outcome evaluation, whereas strongly converging measures across all modalities might provide convincing evidence for accomplished outcomes.

If the programme has worked well, the ultimate confirmation of the problem formulation can be concluded and one can proceed to the follow-up phase. If success is only partial, we recommend a review of the formulation to detect possible errors, omissions, etc. If the programme proves a complete failure, the initial definition of problem(s) and treatment targets should be looked at.

Apart from the academic and clinical interest of the 'scientist–practitioner', we also advocate substantial involvement of the client.

The interface between active treatment and follow-up should seek to refine and consolidate achievements, enhance and generalize treatment gains and guide/supervise a client's self-regulation processes.

A number of questions might help the therapist to optimize the intervention process further: Have new objectives arisen that require clarification and action? Have the implications of the 'new behaviours' for all involved been considered? Has a programme to maintain gains and/or meet the new objectives been introduced? Has a post-intervention contract been established so that each participant is aware of his/her role in maintaining gains and taking necessary action in the event of difficulties or further new objectives arising?

For the follow-up, we recommend continuing review of both therapy goals and measurement. To provide continuous feedback and enhance processing of therapeutic experiences, patients should be encouraged to keep behavioural diaries to strengthen mindfulness and resourcefulness of newly acquired behaviours, such as coping with anxiety or activation of alternative behaviours when depressed.

Finally, regarding follow-up, we recommend an open end that should be determined by the patient as judged by his progress and help needed. Short and unsupported follow-up has shown in clinical practice to be rather counterproductive for enhancement and consolidation processes, whereas open-ended arrangements appear to instil confidence and paradoxically are rarely needed by a client over a prolonged period.

At the end of follow-up, a number of further questions may be asked:

Have the gains been maintained?
What changes have taken place?
What can be learned from follow-up data relevant to future programmes?

Which areas need to be rethought and which can be consolidated? What information can be usefully fed back to participants?

The therapeutic relationship Curiously, in the early 60s, when behaviour therapy became more technique orientated, little attention was paid to relationship issues in the therapeutic process. This was perhaps appropriate when dealing with rather simple monosymptomatic problems where the focus was mostly directed at the diagnosis and a prescribed technique. Another explanation might point to an overreaction to a perceived indulgence of psychodynamic therapies with relationship issues.

However, with growing interest in complex and difficult cases in the last two decades, often involving low motivation and poor adherence as well as deficient self-regulation, it became increasingly obvious that a formulation-guided therapeutic relationship should be given more attention.

Clearly, the virtues of a positive therapeutic relationship hardly need to be recommended; however, we would like to emphasize some issues that appear particularly important in the context of *case formulation*.

In principal, we conceptualize the therapeutic relationship as an integral part of the whole treatment process and we recommend that this aspect should not be treated in an isolated manner. Thus, emphasis and direction of such relationships should be guided by the individual problem formulation and subsequent treatment requirements. Turkat and co-workers (e.g. Turkat & Brantley, 1981; Turkat & Meyer, 1982) have argued against standard relationship enhancement techniques according to Rogerian principles (i.e. to indicate *understanding* and to demonstrate *empathy*), which appear to be endorsed by most clinicians (e.g. Goldfried, 1982). They may be incompatible with individual problem formulations as Wolpe and Turkat (1985) have illustrated previously:

> "Unquestionably, one must be able to empathise with the patient if one is to be able to formulate the case. However, the question as to what demonstrable empathy is remains the basis of difference. We would argue that *accurate empathy is demonstrated when the therapist can accurately predict the patient's behaviour.* This difference in demonstrating empathy can be seen in the following example:
>
> PATIENT: I get very nervous when I leave the house by myself, I just feel as if I were going to pass out.
> ROGERIAN: BEHAVIOURAL INTERVIEWER It must be upsetting when this happens.
> PATIENT: Oh yes, I just want to run away.

Here, the clinician has 'demonstrated empathy' by providing a summary statement of how the patient must have felt during this situation. This can be compared with the response of the skilled behaviour analytic interviewer.

PATIENT: I get very nervous when I leave the house by myself, I just feel as if I were going to pass out.

CASE FORMULATION INTERVIEWER: Do you also get this feeling of passing out in aeroplanes? (patient nods), trains? (patient nods), elevators? (patient nods), crowds? (patient nods), and if you can make it to a movie, you sit in the last row, the seat closest to the exit?

PATIENT: That's me, all right.

Here, the interviewer is testing hypotheses the validity of which demonstrates more accurate empathy than a simple pseudo-expression of understanding as advocated in Rogerian approaches. In this regard, for the case formulation clinician, the relationship to the patient is a means to an end; a good relationship exists if the clinician has created an environment for the patient which enables him to get the information he needs to make accurate predictions (p. 10).

The general conduct of our interview is open and natural. We try to avoid professional jargon that often makes clients feel uncomfortable. Clients are encouraged to intervene and ask questions if proceedings become unclear or confusing or if they feel they have misunderstood. The atmosphere is kept generally relaxed and there is also room for jokes that can have pleasant, counter-conditioning effects on apprehension or even tension in clients. Perhaps more than other therapeutic schools, we prefer an active and motivated client who is treated as a partner in achieving the behavioural analysis, problem formulation and treatment programme. This entails discussion of each significant step with the client and only proceeding if full agreement has been reached. Also, we consider it important to take the patient's point of view into account. Foremost, this includes discussion of the formulation that has to be presented to the client in an understandable manner. Subsequently, before treatment commences, clients are explained the rationale of their programme and, at an intermediate stage, they are usually encouraged or even challenged to design and carry out their own treatments.

In other words, the therapeutic relationship is conceptualized to enable such active involvement. It seems crucial that the patient feels fully understood and supported with his problems. The way we can motivate and involve the patient will depend on his needs and competence, i.e. we may at times attempt a complimentary relationship (e.g. acting as a primary reinforcer with a socially withdrawn and depressed patient) to achieve the desired behaviour.

The initial interview must be regarded as an important phase for the facilitation of a relationship that seeks to involve and motivate the client. In view of individual differences, the role of the therapist is best guided by the problem formulation (e.g. when deciding whether a non-directive or directive style should be adopted). Options and selection of therapeutic styles have been previously presented and discussed by AuBuchon and Malatesta (1998) in the first edition of this text. Peter AuBuchon will provide an update on these issues in a separate chapter of this volume.

Summary

To conclude, the *case formulation approach* is a dynamic, innovative and goal-oriented process. It involves continuous collection of information and hypothesis testing and is guided at all times by principles of experimental psychology in general and cognitive–behavioural principles in relation to specific problems.

It is important to note that above-described phases are not distinct or separate from each other – together they form a process of collaborative cooperation between the client and therapist aiming at comprehensive understanding and subsequent modification of individual problems.

This chapter has provided an introduction to the UCL model that is rooted in the pioneering work of Hans Eysenck, Monte Shapiro and Victor Meyer. In all, we are aware that human behaviour is incredibly complex and that any psychological model will have severe limitations in explaining and predicting specific behaviours, such as clinical problems. Nevertheless, we claim that this approach has been established as a useful clinical method with heuristic value. In fact, it formed the basis of the first behaviour therapy training course in the United Kingdom established by Vic Meyer and Ted Chesser at the Middlesex Hospital Medical School in 1970. Since then it has been presented and taught at numerous conferences worldwide and is part of many current training courses in cognitive–behavioural psychotherapy.

Detailed clinical transcripts of the initial interview can be found elsewhere (e.g. Bruch, Bond, & Hudson, 1995; Meyer & Liddell, 1977; Turkat, 1986).

References

AuBuchon, P. G., & Malatesta, V. J. (1998). Managing the therapeutic relationship in behaviour therapy: The need for a case formulation. In M. Bruch & F. W. Bond (Eds.), *Beyond diagnosis. Case formulation approaches in CBT*. Chichester, UK: Wiley.

Bandura, A. (1977). Self-efficacy: Toward a unifying theory of behavioural change. *Psychological Review, 84*(2), 191–215.

Bruch, M. (1988). *The self-schema model of complex disorders*. Regensburg, Germany: S Roederer.

Bruch, M., Bond, F. W., & Hudson, R. (1995). *Videotape of the initial interview of an obsessive-compulsive disorder*. Audio-visual unit, University College London, London, UK.

Carey, M. P., Flasher, L. V., Maisto, S. A., & Turkat, I. D. (1984). The a priori approach to psychological assessment. *Professional Psychology, 15*, 519–527.

Goldfried, M. (1982). Resistance and clinical behavior therapy. In P. L. Wachtel (Ed.), *Resistance: Psychodynamic and behavioural approaches*. New York: Plenum.

Kanfer, F. H., & Phillips, J. S. (1970). *Learning foundations of behaviour therapy.* New York: Wiley.

Lader, M. H., & Wing, L. (1966). *Physiological measures, sedative drugs and morbid anxiety.* London: Oxford University Press.

Lane, D. (1990). *The impossible child. Stoke on trent.* London: Trentham.

Lang, P. J. (1971). The application of psychophysiological methods to the study of psychotherapy and behaviour modification. In A. Bergin & S. Garfield (Eds.), *Handbook of psychotherapy and behaviour change.* New York: Wiley.

Lang, P. J. (1979). A bio-informational theory of emotional imagery. *Psychophysiology, 16*, 495–512.

Meyer, V. (1957). The treatment of two phobic patients on the basis of learning principles. *Journal of Abnormal Psychology, 55*, 261.

Meyer, V. (1970). Comments on Yates: Misconceptions about behaviour therapy: A point of view. *Behaviour Therapy, 1*, 108–112.

Meyer, V. (1975). The impact of research on the clinical application of behaviour therapy. In R. I. Thompson & W. S. Dockens (Eds.), *Applications of behaviour modification.* New York: Academic Press.

Meyer, V., & Liddell, A. (1977). Behavioural interviews. In A. R. Ciminero, K. S. Calhoun, & H. E. Adams (Eds.), *Handbook of behavioural assessment.* New York: Wiley.

Meyer, V., & Reich, B. (1978). Anxiety management – The marriage of physiological and cognitive variables. *Behaviour, Research and Therapy, 16*, 177–182.

Meyer, V., & Turkat, I. D. (1979). Behavioural analysis of clinical cases. *Journal of Behavioural Assessment, 1*, 259–269.

Persons, J. (2008). *The case formulation approach to cognitive-behavior therapy.* New York: Guilford.

Rachman, S., & Hodgson, R. (1974). I. Synchrony and desynchrony in fear and avoidance. *Behaviour Research and Therapy, 12*, 311–318.

Stuart, R. B. (1970). *Trick or treatment: How or when psychotherapy fails.* Champaign, IL: Research.

Tuomisto, T. M. (1994). Case Formulation of a dog phobia. Unpublished Case Dissertation, Cognitive-Behavioural Psychotherapy Unit, Dept of Psychiatry & Behavioural Sciences, University College London.

Turkat, I. D. (1979). The behaviour analysis matrix. *Scandinavian Journal of Behaviour Therapy, 8*, 187–189.

Turkat, I. D. (1985). *Behavioural case formulation.* New York: Plenum.

Turkat, I. D. (1986). The behavioural interview. In A. R. Ciminero, K. S. Calhoun, & H. E. Adams (Eds.), *Handbook of behavioural assessment* (2nd ed.). New York: Wiley-Interscience.

Turkat, I. D. (1987). Invited case transcript: The initial clinical hypothesis. *Journal of Behaviour Therapy and Experimental Psychiatry, 18*(4), 349–356.

Turkat, I. D., & Brantley, P. J. (1981). On the therapeutic relationship in behaviour therapy. *The Behaviour Therapist, 4*(3), 16–17.

Turkat, I. D., & Carlson, C. R. (1984). Symptomatic versus data based formulation of treatment: The case of a dependent personality. *Journal of Behaviour Therapy and Experimental Psychiatry, 15*, 153–160.

Turkat, I. D., & Maisto, S. A. (1985). Application of the experimental method to the formulation and modification of personality disorders. In D. H. Barlow (Ed.), *Clinical handbook of psychological disorders.* New York: Guilford.

Turkat, I. D., & Meyer, V. (1982). The behaviour-analytic approach. In P. Wachtel (Ed.), *Resistance: Psychodynamic and behavioural approaches.* New York: Plenum.

Wolpe, J., & Turkat, I. D. (1985). Behavioural formulation of clinical cases. In I. D. Turkat (Ed.), *Behavioural case formulation.* New York: Plenum.

Young, J. E. (1990). *Cognitive therapy for personality disorders: A schema-focused approach.* Sarasota, FL: Professional Resource Exchange.

3

Case Formulation
A Hypothesis-Testing Process

Richard S. Hallam

Individual case formulation (ICF) has a long history within psychological therapy (see Chapters 1 and 2 by Bruch in this volume). This chapter discusses case formulation as a process that draws upon scientific knowledge and experimental reasoning but, as I hope to show, this is only part of a mix that includes knowledge of culture and practical wisdom. In other words, case formulation (and therapy in general) cannot simply be a matter of applying science in a manner comparable with engineering. Scientific methodology is a component of a therapist's expertise in the sense that it contributes to a systematic analysis of problems and provides guiding principles that draw upon well-validated psychological processes.

Within the general field of applied psychology, ICF is distinctive because it takes an idiographic approach to the task of applying expertise. It differs from the mainstream nomothetic view that expertise is based on (a) theoretical models that have been developed to explain a type of problem (e.g. depression, anxiety and obsessions) and (b) techniques and methods that have been shown in controlled trials to 'work' in ameliorating a certain kind of problem. According to the nomothetic approach, a therapist's expertise consists in knowing which theoretical model to use to understand a problem and knowing what the evidence shows in terms of the techniques likely to resolve it. In current jargon, it is 'evidence-based'.

The idiographic approach to applying knowledge in formulation places more emphasis on a therapist's ability to build a 'unique theory' to make sense of a client's problem. The difference is only one of emphasis because both nomothetic and idiographic approaches draw upon 'bottom–up' and 'top–down' reasoning. A 'bottom–up' process can be defined as one that is

Beyond Diagnosis: Case Formulation in Cognitive Behavioural Therapy, Second Edition.
Edited by Michael Bruch.
© 2015 John Wiley & Sons, Ltd. Published 2015 by John Wiley & Sons, Ltd.

driven by data or observations, while a 'top–down' process involves searching for certain kinds of data within the presenting problem, guided by theoretical principles or a general model. The reason for preferring an emphasis on bottom–up processes in ICF is scepticism about the assumption that any problem falls neatly into a type for which there is an adequate theoretical model or set of treatment guidelines. The ICF therapist is more likely to draw upon a variety of theoretical principles and knowledge resources. Consequently, in order to formulate systematically, she or he has to be more reliant on disciplined procedures for collecting and evaluating the observations that are made. The final case formulation may not resemble anything that has been produced in any previous case analysis.

As already noted, nomothetic and idiographic approaches lie on a continuum. It would be foolish for an ICF therapist to ignore evidence that has accumulated in outcome studies even if it relates to rather rigidly defined problem categories. Moreover, theoretical models that have been produced to account for specific 'disorders' (i.e. problems diagnosed as expressions of a psychiatric disorder) have been developed on the basis of research evidence and are always worth considering. Contrariwise, it is also necessarily true that therapists who follow a nomothetic approach have to be sensitive to the individual circumstances of their clients. A manual that follows a disorder-specific theoretical model cannot be allowed to become a bed of Procrustes to which a client is fitted regardless of their unique needs.

A criticism often meted out to the ICF idiographic approach is that it is 'subjective', meaning that it is biased by untested assumptions or simply that it is too 'intuitive'. In this chapter, I will stress that the process of case formulation needs to be systematic and aware of its potential biases. No one, I believe, wishes to advocate 'on the hoof' inspired guesswork. The model of applied science put forward by detractors of ICF is also open to criticism. It has followed the argument of Paul Meehl (1954) for a more 'objective' actuarial approach in applied psychology. He showed that a clinician's intuitive judgement about what to do is often inferior to using a set of objective or operational procedures when the outcomes (e.g. a diagnosis or a therapeutic outcome) could be specified in advance. Once the desired outcome is known, the predictive accuracy of the objective measure or procedure can be gradually improved over time, based on empirical research and 'hard data'. This, broadly speaking, has been the mainstream approach for adding to knowledge about 'what works for whom' in the field of psychological therapy.

This approach to applied science works well when input and output (e.g. type of problem and desired outcome) can be specified in a way that satisfies all concerned. In the area of social epidemiology, a great deal has been learned about the phenomenology of common problems by systematically studying the relationship between well-defined variables (e.g. a history of childhood sexual abuse and a later diagnosis of schizophrenia). All of this knowledge can contribute to a therapist's expertise. However, clients' problems and the goals they aspire to reach are largely defined by clients, not by the experts treating them. Problems are typically obstacles, compulsive habits or deficits of some kind that interfere with the attainment of an aspiration. They are rarely, as in medicine, problems that the patient wishes to have diagnosed as a treatable disorder. This means that nomothetic knowledge of the kind that technique X is the best treatment for disorder Y is less relevant in psychological therapy.

Meehl's approach is, of course, valuable in many technical fields. As technology develops, there is less need to rely on the judgement of an expert. The early pioneers of flight had to assess all the variables that kept the plane in the air, whereas modern pilots can leave most of the decisions to computers. Rather like one of the pioneers of flight, an early conception of an expert in applied psychology was a person trained as a scientist who heroically investigated and solved whatever problem was thrown at them. This was understandable given that the old paradigms of medicine and psychoanalysis were obviously failing, and psychologists took it upon themselves to make a fresh start using empirical and experimental methods.

One model of the expert in ICF remains that of the so-called scientist–practitioner (Raimy, 1950). Do we still have need of them? Subject to the cautions expressed earlier about fitting clients to models and methods rather than vice versa and with regard to research and development, the answer is obviously yes, just as we still need test pilots to see how a newly designed plane performs. I believe that the answer is also a qualified yes in the sense that every client presents a practitioner with a novel and unique problem to solve. A therapist has to be a general problem-solver, and part of this expertise is grounded in an experimental style of reasoning originally developed for scientific purposes.

It should not be controversial to assert that there are novel, unique and impossible to categorize aspects of any individual client's problem. There is often no well-validated model or technique to turn to, even if one wished to follow that path. Consequently, it is necessary to fall back on principles of problem generation and behaviour modification in general, rather than categories of problem and specific techniques. An analogous situation might be presented to a geologist who attempts to explain the combination of natural forces that have led to a particular rock formation. By virtue of historical accident, the formation is unique. The equivalent of Meehl's equations might not be available.

In fact, when attempting to understand a client's problem, the situation is not one of prediction (by filling in the values of an established formula) but of making coherent sense of all the prevailing aspects of a client's life taken together. A knowledge of general principles should, of course, give rise to particular hypotheses – which in a sense are predictions – but they have to be tested by collecting further data from the client. A prediction could take the form that if a client continues to do X, an undesirable consequence, Y, will follow. A number of such predictions could be made. However, it will still be necessary to weigh up these predictions and put them in the balance. Perhaps, doing Z would lead to even worse consequences, and the client is limited to a choice between X and Z. The point I am making is that resolving a problem involves pragmatic choices and practical wisdom. Perhaps, it has not occurred to the client that doing W is worthy of consideration. There is always an element of choice in how a problem is solved because a problem is a manifestation of unique cultural–historical circumstances. Problems do not always have obvious solutions. The sense that has to be made of any problem also has to be owned by the client and accepted as valid. However, clients also seek out therapists on the basis of their acknowledged expertise. A therapist must make sense of a set of observations, notwithstanding the fact that this creative leap of the imagination must be tempered by knowledge of what is possible and feasible. Included in this set of limits is the influence of unbending universal psychological processes. For instance, are a client's choices limited by their capacity to learn?

The creative element is held in considerable suspicion by some writers on case formulation. Haynes and O'Brien (2000: p. 59) express a bias against 'subjectivity' when they state: 'There are few empirically-based guidelines for making data-based clinical judgments and almost no guidelines for designing intervention programs. The dearth of guidelines has encouraged the use of purely intuitive approaches to clinical judgment.' Haynes and O'Brien are certainly in favour of an individual approach to formulation but they seem unwilling to go the further step of accepting that the basis of clinical judgement cannot be purely quantitative. There simply are limits to the use of algorithms.

Scientific Reasoning in Case Formulation

An approach to studying individual phenomena that emphasizes the reasoning processes of the scientist has an illustrious history. For instance, there is still a great deal to be learned from the writings of Claude Bernard (1813–1878), a famous French physiologist, who wrote about his experimental method (Bernard, 1957). Of course, Bernard was interested in establishing the validity of universal generalizations – a nomothetic enterprise – but he experimented on single animals. His subject was the internal environment of the body, an area of study that was complicated enough, but psychological therapists are faced with a far more unwieldy set of variables. These interact dynamically from week to week and include a number of unpredictable environmental events as well as a client's reflexive awareness of any changes that are occurring within their own life and sense of well-being. And unlike Bernard's animal subjects, clients react to the methods used by therapists to investigate their problem. For instance, a client may 'know' what a therapist is up to when following a certain line of questioning. Case formulation is necessarily a collaborative process. A therapist is not attempting to establish universal generalizations (as in Bernard's case), but there are still certain lessons we can take from him; these are lessons connected with the way causal inferences are made from observations.

1. He feels it important to separate the act of observation from the act of reasoning. 'The observer listens to nature: the experimenter questions and forces her to unveil herself' (Bernard, 1957: p. 6). This separation is suggested on the basis of a methodological caution: there are, of course, two phases in the experimental method. The aim of the experimenter is to induce new observations and, having done so, he or she reverts to observing without prejudice. Bernard also notes that this separation is hard to achieve because the initial facts may be viewed selectively according to preconceptions and the new 'induced' facts may not be perceived with an open-minded attitude that allows the information they convey to truly answer the question posed by the experimenter.

2. The observed 'facts' must be accurate to begin with. The observer might be unaware of the reasoning that she/he brings to the facts, and one aim of the experimental method is to bring these to light. Reasoning deals with two facts – comparing or relating the observed fact and the induced fact.

3. Bernard therefore stresses that 'Pile up facts or observations as we may, we shall be none the wiser' (1957: p. 16). He refers to the induced facts as controls in the reasoning process.

4. Inducing a new fact always involves an idea (or a hypothesis) that comes from intuition. Bernard, with his background knowledge, was not, of course, pulling rabbits out of a hat. But even he admitted that it was sometimes necessary to go fishing in 'groping experiments' (1957: p. 21).

5. While stressing that observation should be unbiased, the stage of reasoning involves an active, questioning mind according to 'various hypotheses that suggest themselves' (p. 22). However, the experimenter then reverts back to observing the induced facts without preconception. He or she must be ready to abandon the idea that inspired the experiment. The experimenter is always sceptical, and hypotheses are always provisional.

6. Bernard was suspicious of generalizations that gathered in a range of facts. 'Scientific generalizations must proceed from particular facts to principles, and principles are the more stable as they rest on deeper details.'

7. An experiment is a supposition about the causes of perceived activity, and then measures are taken 'to make facts appear' (p. 32), which logically inform the experimenter that the supposition is confirmed or negated. The supposition must of course be of a kind that is potentially verifiable or refutable. Bernard does not think that there are any rules for thinking up a good idea. In some cases, this is just a rare creative talent, but hopefully, among therapists, experience and training can make a contribution as well. Ultimately, it is good method, not creativity alone, that promotes lasting scientific developments.

8. Bernard was well aware of the dangers of his method. Nevertheless, for him, '… it is better to know nothing than to keep in mind fixed ideas based on theories whose confirmation we constantly seek, neglecting meanwhile everything that fails to agree with them' (p. 37).

Bernard seems very much aware of what we would now term biases in information processing (Kahneman & Tversky, 1973; Ross, 1976; Turk & Salovey, 1988). He also stresses the process of thinking creatively about a collection of related observations and bringing them together in a synthesis. This is now referred to as 'abductive reasoning' (Evers & Wu, 2006). Before expanding on the processes involved in bringing the facts together in a coherent and productive formulation, I will examine how Bernard's style of single-case experimentation was taken forward in psychology.

Single-Case Methodology

One example of this approach comes from the group of researchers associated with M. B. Shapiro at the Institute of Psychiatry in London. Victor Meyer was part of this group, and he later developed his own model of formulation at the Middlesex Hospital (see Bruch, Chapters 1 and 2). In the late 1950s and early 1960s, therapists began to see themselves as both scientists and practitioners and used single-case experimental methods to investigate a client's problem with the aim of developing a theoretically based intervention. The general approach is described by Shapiro (1961) who underlined the importance of (a) devising measures that are geared to the unique nature of a client's problem (b) establishing experimental control over a phenomenon of interest, meaning that a therapist comes to understand what produces it or removes it, and (c) ensuring that relationships observed between variables found in a single client can be replicated again in the same client or in other clients with a similar problem. The underlying rationale was to work out the parameters and determinants of a problem with the aim of discovering an individually tailored solution.

Another very important development in single-case investigation took place in North America, influenced by B. F. Skinner's methods and concepts. The origins of this method were not therapeutic although they came to be applied in clinical settings (e.g. Lindsley, 1959). Over time, a sub-field of research methodology developed, now known as single-case experimental design.

Although single-case methodology of this type is still alive and well, most therapists find a commitment to this experimental method too demanding in routine practice environments. It proves time-consuming to carry out thoroughly, even assuming that the parameters of a problem can be identified with the level of precision required. Nevertheless, the early examples of this approach created a new emphasis on causal relationships and exerted a strong influence in a less rigorous form, shaping the style of work of some of the early pioneers of behaviour therapy. For instance, in a functional analysis of a client's problem, data are collected in a 'baseline period' by an observer or by the client herself or himself between sessions. A change of conditions is then introduced, and data collection continues. The conditions may then be changed back to baseline. With the help of these experimental designs, inferences about potential causal relationships (i.e. what produces or removes a behaviour) can be taken to a highly sophisticated level (see Barlow, Nock, & Hersen, 2008).

The spirit of hypothesis generation and testing, in a more clinician-friendly form, was carried forward by Meyer and also by Joseph Wolpe and Ira Turkat. Wolpe describes his interviewing approach in a book edited with Turkat, who had worked previously with Meyer (Wolpe & Turkat, 1985). These early pioneers focused on the concrete details of a problem, and their interview method involved a process of testing hypotheses about its underlying causal determinants. They demonstrated that even without the benefit of precise measurement and the experimental manipulation of conditions, a practitioner could reach sound conclusions with implications for selecting a successful intervention. An account of the interviewing style developed by Meyer and Wolpe now follows.

The Hypothesis-Testing Interview

This style of interview is very much in keeping with Bernard's experimental philosophy. Taking our cue from Bernard, we can ask what is a 'fact' and what is an 'induced fact'? What kinds of knowledge does the therapist draw upon? At what level of complexity (theoretical principles, comprehensiveness or scope, integration or coherence) should a hypothesis be framed? If we regard a case formulation as a kind of synthesis that results from the hypothesis-testing interview, how should it be expressed – in words, symbols, diagrams, etc.?

The style of interviewing advocated by Wolpe focuses on specific lines of inquiry and is motivated by the testing of hypotheses (see Wolpe & Turkat, 1985, for a transcript of this type of interview). In the course of inquiry, descriptive observations are sought, and continue to be sought, in order to test whether a hypothesis has any credibility. Typically, there are a number of competing hypotheses to explain the same observations. The general aim is to entertain several hypotheses at the same time until one or more of them are well supported and others are discarded. An inquiry into a particular hypothesis is continued until it has produced a result, even if it turns out to be a dead end. At this point, the inquiry may proceed down a different route. Although hypothesis testing constitutes the framework for the interview, there is no need to proceed in a rigid manner. If urgent issues come up, or a client happens to reveal new material of interest, a hypothesis can be 'put on the shelf' for later investigation. Other considerations, such as strengthening a relationship, building trust or correcting a false impression, may take precedence over hypothesis testing and determine the flow of an interview at any one moment. The interview style is in strong contrast to one that amasses a pile of facts and leaves it until later to analyze their significance.

An important characteristic is that there should be no wasted questions. Evidence is gathered until it eventually favours some hypotheses over others. Occasionally, a question is completely open-ended (How can I be of help? What's your problem?), while at other times it is closed (Do you mean this or that?). Occasionally, a client drops in a 'lead' to a new line of inquiry. A therapist persists when a client has difficulty describing something and may offer a choice of examples with which to compare the experience, based on predictions from current hypotheses. A therapist notes any discrepancies in the account provided. A therapist may frankly admit to not knowing how to make sense of a discrepancy in the evidence and ask a client to explain it. A hypothesis is only abandoned when disconfirming evidence builds up to a critical point. When a therapist is reasonably sure that a hypothesis is being confirmed, it may be presented as an interpretation and the client is invited to respond. Alternatively, a different tactic at this stage is to test out a prediction by asking, say, 'How do you feel in situation X, or with person Y', bearing in mind an expected answer. It should be clear from this description that the style of interaction is collaborative. A client's own understanding of a problem begins to be shaped up by the interview itself. Although therapists following different theoretical models are unlikely to follow similar lines of questioning, the hypothesis-testing interview should be self-correcting if carried out with Bernard's advice in mind.

Take the example of a 30-year-old woman who was brought up by a violent father and anxious mother. She was very shy until her mid-twenties when she responded well to psychological therapy, including assertiveness training. She now has a number of close friends and lives happily with her partner. However, in general, she still expects that others will demonstrate a lack of respect and will 'overlook' her point of view. She has frequent episodes of a depressed, angry mood in which she feels fully justified in wallowing in her anger. She is currently in dispute with a health practitioner who she claims gave poor advice and she has made a formal complaint to his professional body. She also tends to nurse other grievances, and since a confrontation with her parents 15 years ago, in which they dismissed her complaints against them, she has had no further contact, not knowing whether they are alive or dead. One feature of her resentment is that 'it eats away at her' and she 'cannot let it go'. However, her anger problem seems to be almost entirely dependent on her mood, for which few triggers can be found. A negative mood triggers past resentments, and her mood spirals down into anger. However, events that *actually* justify resentment can be dismissed when she is in a good mood, and if distracted by a work obligation or a friendly social interaction, her mood can change rapidly for the better. This was demonstrated within one assessment session that began in a depressed and ruminative way but was quickly turned around by the problem-solving attitude of the therapist.

This brief description illustrates the point that it is possible to entertain a variety of hypotheses about the causes of this woman's problem. There is unlikely to be just one good explanation that accounts for all the facts: (a) It is clear there is 'unfinished business' regarding her family's treatment of her. Given her history, her tendency to expect a lack of respect and to be ignored is understandable. However, she is not willing to re-engage with her past and feels it is too easy to blame all her problems on that. (b) Regarding present cues for anger, it could be argued that she has not learned how to cope assertively when she feels that others show disrespect. Assertiveness training helped considerably in the past and perhaps her skills in this regard need to be consolidated. However, there was little evidence that she fails to cope assertively in a number of situations, especially when her mood is good. Her problem seems to be that of letting go of resentment after she has done what any reasonable and assertive person would have done. (c) Another viable hypothesis relates to the way she copes with the spiral of low mood, resentful thoughts and increasing anger. She readily admits to a trait in her personality that makes it difficult for her to let go of a problem that has not been solved to her satisfaction. She then tries to fight her frustration by trying to be productive or to distract herself. Similarly, if waking up in low mood, she feels that the day is 'doomed' for her and that nothing she does will help. Her strategy of distraction rarely works unless she is completely taken up with a new activity or swept up into a new social situation.

It is likely that all three hypotheses could be supported by further evidence collected through interview, fantasy re-enactment or diary recording.

As already hinted, the approach taken has to be consistent with her own preferred way of approaching the problem. In the course of the assessment, she became persuaded by the idea that she was perpetuating her negative moods and accompanying resentments by the way she coped with them. In particular, her rapid shifts of mood that seemed to depend on changes in her own thinking (or were influenced by social interactions that changed her thinking) convinced her of this. The instruction to accept her negative thoughts and moods and not to fight them or do anything (apart from passing the time in a pleasant way) led to a rapid change in the way she saw her 'problem'. She reinforced this new strategy by attending a course in mindfulness meditation.

This brief case history illustrates the point that a problem can generate a number of viable hypotheses. Attempts were made to obtain evidence for and against each one (details omitted here for the sake of brevity). The client's conceptualization of her own problem and her preferred way of dealing with its likely causes were also a vital part of the formulation. It is highly likely that her problem could be traced to childhood physical abuse and her decision to have nothing more to do with her family. However, she did not wish to be reconciled with this history by exploring it, and she decided instead to change the way she responded to her own negative thoughts and feelings. This was the solution that appealed to her most at this point in time. It is possible that she will see the situation differently at some future time.

It is of course rather difficult to remain open-minded and faithful to phenomena as a client reveals them. There is a strong tendency to fall back on tried and tested formulae. A requirement for the success of this interviewing style is to reach consensus on the questions being addressed and the outcomes that are generally desired. Without these in place, there is a risk of formulation degenerating into an idiosyncratic process no better than divination. For instance, early attempts to compare the effectiveness of psychoanalysis with that of behaviour therapy broke down because there was no consensus on any of the criteria for selecting participants or for defining therapeutic outcomes. Despite many obstacles, there is now a much greater chance of therapists of different theoretical persuasions reaching agreement about the formulation process without resort to a medical model of disorder (see below).

The hypothesis-testing style of interview is not applied science but it is a disciplined form of inquiry. There remain a number of knotty conceptual issues to consider and a discussion of some of them follows. In large part, these issues call for a pragmatic response that combines scientific knowledge and expertise with a 'good-enough' set of procedures that avoid subjectivity and do not consume too much time. They are the procedures that define a 'process of formulation' (Hallam, 2013).

Observations versus hypotheses

As regards the description of what is to count as a problem, there would seem to be no alternative but to use a refinement of commonly understood everyday language (e.g. Jose & Goldfried, 2008). The psychoanalyst and behaviourist might recognize social anxiety in an everyday sense when they see it but they might interpret or explain the phenomenon very differently. Consensus at the descriptive level can be ensured by striving to use terms that are understood by all concerned, especially by the client who is attempting to frame the problem conceptually as well. Each might induce new facts to confirm their own conceptual understanding. The therapist does this by asking a question (that should yield an answer consistent with or contradictory to his/her conceptualization), by conducting a behavioural experiment or by doing something (such as applying a technique) that is designed to change the parameters of a problem. In fact, feedback can be obtained in a variety of ways, such as by trying to resolve a contradiction in the existing evidence. As far as the therapist is concerned, feedback needs to be experienced and processed, in accordance with Bernard's advice, in as unprejudiced a manner as possible. The intervention (even if only a question) produces a response that casts some light on the idea that provoked it.

If the concept of hypothesis testing is to have credibility in the context of assessment, it seems essential to distinguish observation and hypothesis in the formulation process. This permits the same observation to have a similar meaning but to be susceptible to a different interpretation, and this is a fundamental necessity for any productive dialogue. In the case example just provided, it was important to attend to the sequence of events that occurred when the client woke up with a negative mood and angry thoughts and what she did to change the situation. These were observations rather than hypotheses. They could have been interpreted as signs of the activation of a maladaptive childhood schema (which they may have been), but they were interpreted instead as an example of a self-defeating coping strategy.

Formulation versus hypothesis

Some texts on case formulation reserve the term hypothesis for a set of concepts that make theoretical sense of all the observations. It is seen as a 'unifying hypothesis' or 'theoretical model'. I prefer to use the term 'case formulation' or 'case conceptualization' for this unifying framework. The final summary understanding of a problem is not a grand hypothesis that derives from a theory (or a disorder-specific theoretical model) but simply a means by which a therapist grasps all the relevant facts and puts them together, usually in a manner that is unique for each individual. The facts referred to here are those that are relevant to the problem as the client and therapist jointly understand it (or provisionally agree to view it). This joint understanding is not an attempt to produce a global analysis of a client's entire life – clearly an impossible task. Typically, a therapist only formulates problematic areas of a client's life, and if there is more than one problem area, several formulations may be needed, which may or may not interrelate. For instance, a fear of flying may or may not relate to a problem within a marriage.

Hypotheses versus everyday assumptions (degrees of inference)

In an everyday sense, the term hypothesis has a fairly imprecise meaning, signifying only a proposed explanation made on the basis of limited evidence. It is a starting point for further investigation. This is the sense in which I will use it in the context of case formulation. In a scientific context, a hypothesis is often put forward on much stronger grounds of pre-existing theory. In fact, a hypothesis in a scientific experiment may be worded very carefully so that it can be disproved if a prediction based on the hypothesis is not confirmed or the experiment produces results that contradict it. Scientific experiments rarely confirm theories but they may produce results for which a better explanation other than a proposed theory cannot be found. This is the situation also in case formulation. It is the best 'theory' available even though it cannot be shown definitely to be true. And in so far as the formulation is merely suggestive of a solution to a problem, that solution is normally based on a number of imponderable elements that cannot be precisely calculated. The formulation could invite a variety of potential solutions, each with its own costs and benefits and advantages and disadvantages. In fact, a therapist might put forward several options to a client for solving their problem. The validation of a formulation rests ultimately on its pragmatic utility, and so it is not validated in the same way as a scientific theory. Clients are seeking practical wisdom rather than objective truth.

A hypothesis might be grounded in assumptions about the world that therapist and client understand in a common way, even though the assumptions are questionable. They are not normally questioned because to do so would shatter the everyday construction of reality. For instance, it is assumed that therapist and client will remain alive during the course of therapy, although on one occasion the author was asked by a client to promise not to die.

The normal perception of reality therefore depends on inferential processes, but the common sense descriptive level typically involves only a low level of inference. The hypothetical level in case formulation makes more assumptions and is best referred to as 'high inference'. The process of therapy, at least with consenting participants, has to begin with a collaborative understanding at a low inference level. In some cases, a therapist may be engaged in challenging a client's common sense interpretation of the causes of a problem, in which case a client's interpretation becomes an additional problem to solve (a problem for the therapist rather than the client). A client's positive attitude towards solving a problem is a relevant observation that enters the formulation, even though a client may not see it as an aspect of the problem scenario. When the attitude is negative, a therapist might have to generate a number of hypotheses to understand it, e.g. as an aspect of the main problem, as based on a lack of information/ understanding, as based on fear of change, as a therapy-interfering behaviour and so forth.

It follows that a case formulation is primarily a therapist's perspective on what is causing a problem and maintaining it in a form that a client cannot resolve. So, even though a formulation is developed collaboratively, it is not a compromise position between two opinions. It would make no sense to modify a formulation on the basis that a client might not like it (which they might not). In this situation, a therapist would simply aim for what is achievable within the scope of an agreement about the formulation as she or he conceives it. It is, of course, the client who puts forward the goals of therapy, but even in this sphere, a therapist is unlikely to go along with a goal that is unachievable according to the formulation.

For the reasons just stated, a therapist has to be seen as an 'expert'; it is assumed that she or he possesses skills and knowledge and that a formulation is a judgement about all the factors that it are necessary to consider in order to help a client move on. Given the possibility of a difference of opinion in the way a problem is understood, there is always an adversarial element in the relationship, which should be openly admitted if it is likely to prove an obstacle to therapy. This is the prime reason for sharing a formulation – to ensure that it is acceptable, so that any differences of approach can be resolved at an early stage. Although clients present problems as they see them and have reasonably clear ideas about their ultimate objectives, this is not always the case. A client may seek to have their goals delineated as well. This means that assessment, formulation, goal setting and choice of a therapeutic intervention are not independent processes. The process of case formulation is only one element in a multitasking encounter. All of the tasks evolve together and may change substantially at a later stage of therapy, e.g. the task may be to ensure that any resolution of a problem will be maintained.

'Depth' or 'level' of a formulation

A final case conceptualization (or case formulation) of a single client's problem has also been conceptualized at different *levels*. For instance, assuming there is no undetected pathophysiology, the physiological level need not be theorized at all unless it produces phenomena that enter the 'psychological level', such as pain, dizziness, memory loss, etc. The sociocultural level could also be conceptualized separately for some purposes. However, in general, a formulation has to be an integrated analysis of a client's personal world. Consequently, a formulation refers to whatever phenomena compose that world, or cause it to be the way it is, regardless of their source at different levels of analysis. A therapist may draw up hypotheses at any theoretical level. For instance, it is very frequently the case that there is an interaction between psychological and medical causes of a problem, including medical pathology of which the client may be entirely unaware except in terms of its negative personal impact.

Current versus historical causation

A distinction that is commonly made is between an analysis of factors that currently maintain a problem and an analysis of developmental (historical) events and processes that have contributed significantly to the presentation of the problem in its current form in the current situation. This can be a useful distinction if the current problem (e.g. a fear of flying) does not require the developmental factors to be addressed even when they are assumed to be present. In the case of a marital problem, it may not be possible to ignore a client's developmental history or, as might be the case, to do so would severely lessen the probability of a good outcome. In the case illustration presented above, it was decided to ignore the developmental causes. A client might be given the option of working on a current problem or a 'deeper' problem that requires a developmental analysis and probably a longer period of therapy. The problems could also be formulated and worked on in sequence.

However, there seems to be no good reason for separating developmental and current causal factors when the formulation of a problem demands it. If progress cannot be made without incorporating developmental/historical issues, there are no grounds for omitting them, apart from the fact that the necessary resources (in terms of time and skill) may not be available. In one sense, all causes of a problem are 'current', although many of them represent the residue of earlier learning or unprocessed memories. Another good reason for treating the developmental perspective as central is that current problems only make sense in terms of a client's life goals, stage of life and opportunities for developing in new directions. A problem is something that interferes with a client's self-concept or life narrative. It is for this reason that one essential part of a case formulation is to list those positive resources and skills that enable a client to overcome the problem in a new way, consistent with the overall direction of their life story.

The summative process or 'case conceptualization'

The end product of the process of formulation is a provisional account that links together all the relevant observational elements and identifies causal links between them, some which are likely to be amenable to change. The formulation, if it is soundly constructed on the basis of principles relevant to therapeutic change, will lead naturally into the intervention phase. In fact, as Wolpe and Turkat (1985) observe, the hypothesis-testing style of interview is a collaborative one that shapes a client's understanding. The reasoning that persuades the therapist should also be persuasive to a client. The formulation is often drawn out in the form of a visual diagram, and this is commonly shared and discussed with a client. Naturally, it is to be expected that the formulation will change as new information comes in after the initial intervention has commenced. It is probably unwise to attempt any intervention until a provisional formulation that gives good grounds for intervening has already been developed. There may be moments of 'groping around in the dark', but they should be few. The initial assessment phase may have to be extended until a provisional formulation has been arrived at.

Types of hypothesis

Consistent with a loose definition of a hypothesis, it seems reasonable to include any kind of speculation, inference, hunch, interpretation or any product of inductive or deductive reasoning. The significance of an item of information usually depends on a hidden reasoning process. The descriptive terms used by a client (or statement of the 'facts') have a logical meaning from which certain conclusions can be deduced. If a client refers to her father, the meaning may not be clear without further inquiry. The inquiry could be framed as a hypothesis that can be answered by further questions: for instance, whether this is a male who raised her or her biological father (whom she might never have met). Of course, a deduction is only valid if the client is reporting the facts honestly in the first place.

Other hypotheses are based on a process of inductive reasoning. The client uses long words and has a refined manner of speaking. The hypothesis might be that the client has received an extended education: in fact, the client might be self-taught and an avid reader. Note that the replacement interpretation is also an inductive inference grounded in a therapist's cultural knowledge. Hypotheses based on shared cultural knowledge may work smoothly when client and therapist share the same cultural background but it is often advisable to confirm even the most obvious of inductive inferences. When the cultural background is not shared, this process of checking back is even more important. A therapist may have to research independently a religion, a cultural practice, etc., or simply ask for it to be explained. For example, if a client has been brought up by a family belonging to a strict fundamentalist religious sect, the therapist might want to inquire exactly what that meant in terms of family life.

The process of reasoning that is involved when drawing upon technical or theoretical knowledge is not always a transparent and explicit process: in fact, it is often opaque and sometimes intuitive. Perhaps based on long experience of a range of problems and psychiatric phenomena, a therapist will be alerted to a fairly rare pattern of presenting facts. Further questioning will then support or disconfirm the intuition. Of course, the fact that a problem falls into a recognizable pattern does not mean that it has been explained. For instance, a client may show many of the features of a primary depressed mood but this is only a starting point for exploring, say, a history of previous episodes of depressed mood, typical eliciting events, causes of variations in mood from one day to another, the account a client can put forward to explain their depressed mood, etc.

The importance of identifying empirical patterns of relationship

Therapists following different theoretical models will focus on the factors they consider to be most relevant to the presenting problem. In a functional and causal approach to formulation, a great deal can be discovered about the eliciting and maintaining conditions of a behaviour without having to produce high-inference hypotheses. For instance, having discovered what a client means by a state of social anxiety, hypotheses can be generated about the eliciting conditions – whether the problem exists in one-to-one or in public situations; whether the age, gender and relative power of social actors are significant, and whether the problem occurs mainly at work, at home or in leisure situations.

A functional analysis attends to the impact of both the presence (A) and the absence (not A) of a critical event, situation or response. The importance of the double-sided nature of an empirical contingency is sometimes forgotten in an eagerness to show that one element in a formulation is associated with another. A critical event, situation or response may or may not be followed by another critical event (i.e. B or not B). Consequently, a therapist might be interested in the following types of contingency: A–B, A–not B, not A–B and not A–not B. It is rare that a critical element is connected with another critical element with 100% certainty, in the way, say, that a puff of air to the eye always produces a blink. Novices in formulation frequently do not investigate all the possibilities just outlined, where the situation is not an either/or one, such as blinking to a puff of air (Godoy & Gavino, 2003). To give a simple illustration, the four possibilities could be as follows: drinking coffee–not sleeping, drinking coffee–sleeping, not drinking coffee–sleeping and not drinking coffee–not sleeping. The information that can be extracted from this pattern of information could include whether insomnia is relatively more likely after drinking coffee late at night than after not drinking coffee. Clients and also therapists might jump to conclusions without exploring these relationships systematically and comparing them. It may turn out that drinking coffee is (or is not) a probable contributory factor to the insomnia. It may require a lengthy period of data collection (e.g. client diary recordings) before firm conclusions can be reached.

This kind of functional analysis provides a more accurate description of what is happening than relying on more casual methods. However, contingent relationships still require theoretical explanation. A hypothesis might be put forward on the basis of familiar learning theory paradigms but a psychodynamic theorist might put forward an equally cogent hypothesis. In the case of coffee and insomnia, the hypothesis might concern central nervous system arousal related to the effects of caffeine. The next stage in the formulation process, following Bernard's advice, is to induce new facts and observe them impartially.

For instance, in the case of anxiety in social situations, a cognitive therapist might be particularly interested in a client's own thinking processes and their perceptions of the social actors (i.e. what a client assumes them to be thinking). Attention might be given to hypotheses about cognitive mediating processes, based on the cognitive theory that the therapist happens to endorse. Information that casts light on these hypotheses might be derived from homework tasks that consist of behavioural experiments (Bennett-Levy, Butler, Fennell, Hackman, Mueller, & Westbrook, 2004), role-play or tasks involving fantasy explorations (Hackmann, Bennett-Levy, & Holmes, 2011). By asking a client to vary their behaviour and the assumptions on which it is based, a test of a hypothesis yields information that confirms or disconfirms it. Behavioural therapists are more inclined to accompany a client to a situation in which the problem arises, in order to make observations, but the purpose is the same.

A therapist herself or himself is also a measuring instrument for making observations. In this instance, a therapist attends to how the client makes her or him feel – perhaps optimistic, worried, perplexed, drained of energy, etc. This might provide limited evidence for a hypothesis that can be tested more systematically. Is this feeling connected to a therapist's own issues (perhaps a recent disappointment, a hangover, frustration with a client) or is it a feeling that is more telling of a client's own difficulties? A therapist also pays attention to a client's non-verbal behaviour – strain or emotion in the voice, signs of muscular tension, an odd speech habit, posture, breathing pattern, etc. These additional observations may support or fail to support a hypothesis or provide clues for generating new ones.

Representation of observations and hypotheses in a formulation diagram

There is a large literature on how to construct a case formulation diagram that will not be reviewed here. The conventions used to symbolize observations and hypotheses differ but there seems to be general agreement that a visual diagram has advantages over a purely verbal summary of a case formulation. In particular, causal and non-causal relationships between observations can be depicted by different symbols. Virtuous and vicious circles are made more apparent when it can be shown visually how one critical component of a problem leads to another, reinforcing or weakening it. The strength of a causal relationship can also be indicated. For examples of different conventions, see Hallam (2013), Haynes and O'Brien (2000), Kuyken, Padesky, and Dudley (2009), Muller (2011) and Nezu, Nezu, and Lombardo (2004).

The author's preference is to make it quite clear that a therapist's hypotheses are not causes, and so when they are introduced into a formulation diagram they are distinguished from the descriptive elements, i.e. the 'facts' or observations that they are intended to explain. However, a hypothesis is linked to some observations and not to others (or to contingent relationships between descriptive elements). It therefore makes sense to indicate this connection in a way that shows it as a labelling procedure and not a causal link.

This manner of representing the formulation differs from the way disorder-specific theoretical models are employed. The boxes in these models are theoretical components (e.g. avoidance, attention, core belief and emotion), and the tendency is therefore to fill in the boxes with observations. This 'painting by numbers' approach is in direct contradiction with Bernard's experimental method. He advocates a bottom–up (observations → hypotheses) method rather than a top–down (hypotheses → observations) orientation. Although bottom–up and top–down are two phases of a single process, Bernard stresses the importance of perceiving induced facts with fresh eyes.

Bringing It All Together: Abductive Reasoning

To reason abductively means making a best guess at the most likely explanation given all the facts under consideration. Evers and Wu (2006) define it as 'inference to the best explanation' or justifying a generalization by relying on 'the fact that it explains the observed empirical data and no other alternative hypothesis offers a better explanation of what has been observed'. It is, perhaps, what we expect when asking someone for their considered opinion.

This kind of reasoning is typical of case formulation where information is often incomplete and highly contextual in nature. The information or 'facts of the case' may relate to a single client or to a subset of the data that has been collected. The latter point is important because it is very unlikely that a single explanatory hypothesis could explain all of the facts about a person's life. In fact, in everyday situations, we are rarely so ambitious in our opinions. There is usually a choice between several possible explanations because the facts 'do not speak for themselves' and, indeed, the facts may look very different from the perspective of, say, the client's partner or a different therapist. This underlines the importance of starting out with low-inference observations that do not prejudge the final synthesis.

Although it is always possible to add to the stock of facts, at some point a decision or judgement has to be made. In a scientific context, abductive reasoning can be highly creative – a leap from the facts to a completely new interpretation of what the facts tell us. The new speculative theory leads to predictions that can then be tested out rigorously through experiment. The therapeutic situation is not unlike this. A case formulation that does not seem to lead anywhere might be completely replaced by a new way of integrating the facts. It then becomes obvious what further data collection (or intervention) will prove or disprove the new conceptualization.

Evers and Wu (2006: p. 523) portray the process as follows. A favoured theory implies a pattern of expectations or, over time, a succession of patterns. An exact matching of patterns and theory is unlikely, so there has to be a persistent matching of feed-forward patterns of expectation with feedback patterns of experience. In the case of inevitable mismatches, either the theory can be amended or the investigator looks to the next most-favoured theory as a source of feed-forward patterns. Both strategies can be pursued simultaneously and 'through the process of iterated theory revision and theory competition, the task is to come up with the most coherent theory that can account for the case, subject to the pattern matching constraint' (Evers & Wu, 2006: p. 524).

As noted earlier, there is always the risk of selective attention to confirmatory evidence and *ad hoc* adjustments to theory. The criteria to apply as a way of avoiding premature acceptance of a case formulation are to appeal to its simplicity as an explanation, its comprehensiveness in explaining all the facts, its explanatory unity, its ability to generate secondary explanations and possible interventions and its coherence with other established bodies of knowledge.

Meyer's original paper concerning his therapeutic approach to compulsive rituals illustrates very clearly the kind of reasoning that enters into a creative adaptation of theory to a real-world problem (Meyer, 1966). Fifty years ago, a person with obsessional thoughts and compulsive rituals was very unlikely to receive benefit from psychological therapy. Drastic measures such as a leucotomy were frequently carried out. The technique that Meyer developed, called 'modification of expectations' (now usually referred to as 'exposure and response prevention'), heralded a vastly more optimistic future for people with this kind of problem. The important point to note about this development was the variety of evidential sources that Meyer drew upon in building up an argument for his selected intervention. Meyer cited academic literature, his own previous therapeutic successes, self-report from clients, informal clinical observations during the therapy process and behavioural monitoring. His use of academic knowledge was sometimes based on an argument by analogy with, or speculative extension of, previous research findings. He attempted to account for inconsistencies in the evidence and alternative hypotheses were considered, sometimes only to be discounted. The conceptual model that Meyer eventually developed allows a therapist to generate testable predictions about any particular client who complains of compulsive rituals.

To summarize the abductive reasoning process in Meyer's case, the evidence was appraised as a whole and fitted together using different types of argument. This is what makes it an idiographic process when applied to the individual case. Meyer reported the results of his technique on only two cases, and he sought to find parallels between them on the assumption that the mechanism of ritual development and maintenance would be similar in both. This reasoning has subsequently proved to be sound because general models of obsessions have been developed that seem to identify processes that are shared between people with different obsessions; therapy based on these models can be shown to be effective. However, each new client who presents with an obsession has to be considered afresh.

ICF does not set itself up in opposition to nomothetic knowledge but insists that the latter can provide only a subset of the arguments for solving a problem in one way rather than another. The abductive reasoning process cannot be put to one side in any single-case conceptualization in the hope that prescriptive rules will suffice. Even airline pilots need to know how to fly a plane when the instruments fail.

References

Barlow, D. H., Nock, M. K., & Hersen, M. (2008). *Single case experimental designs: Strategies for studying behavior change* (3rd ed.). Boston: Allyn & Bacon.

Bennett-Levy, J., Butler, G., Fennell, M., Hackmann, A., Mueller, M., & Westbrook, D. (Eds.) (2004). *Oxford guide to behavioural experiments in cognitive therapy*. Oxford, UK: Oxford University Press.

Bernard, C. (1957). *An introduction to the study of experimental medicine [1865]*. (Translated by H. C. Greene, introduced by L. J. Henderson, with a foreword by I. B. Cohen). New York: Dover Publications.

Evers, C. W., & Wu, E. H. (2006). On generalising from single case studies: Epistemological reflections. *Journal of Philosophy of Education, 40*, 511–526.

Godoy, A., & Gavino, A. (2003). Information-gathering strategies in behavioral assessment. *European Journal of Psychological Assessment, 19*, 204–209.

Hackmann, A., Bennett-Levy, J., & Holmes, E. A. (2011). *Oxford guide to imagery in cognitive therapy.* Oxford, UK: Oxford University Press.

Hallam, R. S. (2013). *Individual case formulation.* Oxford, UK: Academic Press.

Haynes, S. N., & O'Brien, W. H. (2000). *Principles and practice of behavioral assessment.* New York: Kluwer Academic.

Jose, A., & Goldfried, M. R. (2008). A transtheoretical approach to case formulation. *Cognitive and Behavioral Practice, 15*, 212–222.

Kahneman, D., & Tversky, A. (1973). On the psychology of prediction. *Psychological Review, 80*, 237–251.

Kuyken, W., Padesky, C. A., & Dudley, R. (2009). *Collaborative case conceptualization: Working effectively with clients in cognitive-behavioral therapy.* New York: Guilford Press.

Lindsley, O. R. (1959). Reduction in rate of vocal psychotic symptoms by differential positive reinforcement. *Journal of the Experimental Analysis of Behavior, 2*, 269.

Meehl, P. E. (1954). *Clinical vs statistical prediction.* Minneapolis, MN: University of Minnesota Press.

Meyer, V. (1966). Modification of expectations in cases with obsessional rituals. *Behaviour Research and Therapy, 4*, 273–280.

Muller, J. M. (2011). Evaluation of a therapeutic concept diagram. *European Journal of Psychological Assessment, 27*, 17–28.

Nezu, A. M., Nezu, C. M., & Lombardo, E. (2004). *Cognitive-behavioral case formulation: A problem-solving approach.* New York: Springer.

Raimy, V. (Ed.). (1950). *Training in clinical psychology.* New York: Prentice Hall.

Ross, L. (1977). The intuitive psychologist and his shortcomings: Distortions in the attribution process. In L. Berkowitz (Ed.), Advances *in experimental social psychology* (Vol. 10, pp. 173–240). Orlando, FL: Academic Press.

Shapiro, M. B. (1961). The single case in fundamental clinical psychological research. *British Journal of Medical Psychology, 34*, 255-262.

Turk, D. C., & Salovey, P. (Eds.). (1988). *Reasoning, inference, and judgments in clinical psychology.* New York: Free Press.

Wolpe, J., & Turkat, I. D. (1985). Behavioral formulation of clinical cases. In I. D. Turkat (Ed.), *Behavioral case formulation* (pp. 5–36). New York: Plenum Press.

4

Case Formulation and the Therapeutic Relationship

Peter G. AuBuchon

Listen to your patients, and they'll tell you what they need.
Henry Adams (1978)

The value of the therapeutic relationship in psychotherapy has been studied by seasoned and expert therapists of every therapeutic orientation. Whether the clinicians have been psychodynamic, client-centred, interpersonal or behavioural, a similar conclusion has been reached: A 'good therapeutic relationship' is a necessary ingredient in any type of psychotherapy[1] (e.g. Beck, Rush, Shaw, & Emery, 1979; Benjamin & Critchfield, 2010; Goldfried, 1983; Greenson, 1965; Meyer & Gelder, 1963; Rogers, 1957).

Consistent with this, the American Psychological Association (APA) Task Force on Empirically Supported Therapy Relationships recently reviewed the empirical literature on the therapeutic relationship and presented their findings (Norcross, 2001). They concluded, among other things, that "(a) the cumulative research convincingly shows that the therapy relationship is crucial to outcome; (b) the therapy relationship makes substantial … contributions to psychotherapy outcome independent of the specific type of treatment; (c) treatment guidelines should explicitly address therapist behaviors … that promote a facilitative therapy relationship; (d) the therapy relationship acts in concert with discrete interventions … in determining treatment effectiveness and (e) adapting or tailoring the therapy relationship to specific patient needs and characteristics (in addition to diagnosis) enhances the effectiveness of treatment" (Norcross, 2001: pp. 495–497).

Beyond Diagnosis: Case Formulation in Cognitive Behavioural Therapy, Second Edition.
Edited by Michael Bruch.
© 2015 John Wiley & Sons, Ltd. Published 2015 by John Wiley & Sons, Ltd.

The third, fourth and fifth points mentioned above were components of one approach to the therapeutic relationship in cognitive–behavioural therapy (CBT), namely, the case formulation approach to the therapeutic relationship (AuBuchon & Malatesta, 1998). This chapter will provide an update on that approach, as well as what is hoped to be a more sophisticated and evolved view on the therapeutic relationship. It is also hoped that this chapter will offer some suggestions on how to manage the therapeutic relationship according to the case formulation and illustrate ways in which the therapeutic relationship, in and of itself, can be a potent treatment intervention. To start, however, the current chapter will review the literature on the therapeutic relationship in behaviour therapy, highlighting two of the more impressive approaches to this relationship, and briefly review the case formulation approach to behaviour therapy.

Review of the Literature

The importance of the therapeutic relationship has been emphasized by prominent clinicians throughout the history of behaviour therapy (e.g. Beck et al., 1979; Brady, 1980; Goldfried & Davison, 1976; Kohlenberg & Tsai, 1991; Linehan, 1988; Meichenbaum, 2006; Meyer & Gelder, 1963; Wolpe & Lazarus, 1966). In addition, the therapeutic relationship in behaviour therapy has been studied in a variety of ways. First, there have been studies that have compared behaviour therapists with those of different orientations on a variety of characteristics. Behaviour therapists were found to be at least as warm, empathic, genuine and caring as therapists from other orientations (e.g. Brunink & Schroeder, 1979; Fischer, Paveza, Kickertz, Hubbard, & Grayson, 1975; Sloan, Staples, Cristol, Yorkston, & Whipple, 1975). Behaviour therapists were also found to be more active and to demonstrate more initiative, support and direction than therapists from other orientations (e.g. Greenwald, Kornblith, Hersen, Bellack, & Himmelhoch, 1981; Sloan et al., 1975).

A second group of studies have examined how the therapeutic relationship may improve the efficacy of behaviour therapy. For example, the role of the therapist as a nonfearful model, reassuring stimulus, safety signal or 'reciprocal inhibitor', has been addressed (e.g. AuBuchon & Calhoun, 1990; Bandura & Menlove, 1968; Meyer, 1957; Rachman, 1983; Wolpe, 1980). In addition, Wright and Davis (1994) have offered strategies for modifying therapist behaviours based upon assessment of the patient's expectations of the therapy and/or therapist. Taking the concept one step further, Linehan (1988) and Rosenfarb (1992) have written clinically useful analyses of the therapeutic relationship within the practice of behaviour therapy. These authors discuss the therapeutic relationship both as a vehicle for therapy and as a therapeutic agent in itself (e.g. through modelling and social reinforcement). Linehan (1988) also discusses the beneficial effects of being in a therapeutic relationship, for *both* the patient and the therapist (e.g. 'The relationship as life enhancing': p. 286). All in all, it is an insightful and sophisticated article and one recommended for all cognitive–behavioural therapists.

Third, studies have demonstrated that certain types of therapist behaviours are more effective with various clinical populations. These behaviours include acceptance, limit setting and validation with borderline personality-disordered patients (e.g. Linehan, 1993; Shearin & Linehan, 1992); focusing, challenge, encouragement and praise with anxiety-disordered patients (e.g. Grayson, Foa, & Steketee, 1982; Gustavson, Jansson, Jerremalm, & Ost, 1985; Rabavilas, Boulougouris, & Perissaki, 1979; Williams & Chambless, 1990); lenient and flexible behaviours with anorexic patients (Touyz, Beumont, & Dunn, 1987); and initiative, support and direction with depressed patients (Greenwald et al., 1981).

In addition to the studies mentioned above, two recent approaches to the therapeutic relationship in CBT merit a more elaborate discussion. The first of these is Meichenbaum's 'Core tasks of Psychotherapy: What "Expert" Therapists Do' (Meichenbaum, 2001). In this approach, seven behavioural tasks are identified, which Meichenbaum proposes are done by expert psychotherapists regardless of therapeutic orientation. These are as follows: (a) developing a collaborative therapeutic alliance with the patient via compassionate listening and helping the patient identify strengths of theirs that can be built upon in treatment; (b) educating the patient about their problem and possible solutions; (c) reconceptualizing the patient's problems in a more hopeful way; (d) ensuring that the patient has the necessary intrapersonal and interpersonal coping skills; (e) encouraging the patient to perform personal experiments; (f) ensuring that the patient takes credit for positive changes and (g) conducting relapse prevention strategies. Subsequently, Meichenbaum has identified five additional tasks for patients who have been victimized and/or are suffering from post-traumatic stress disorder (PTSD) (Meichenbaum, 2006).

The other notable approach to the therapeutic relationship is Kohlenberg and colleagues' *Functional Analytic Psychotherapy* (e.g. Tsai, Kohlenberg, & Kanter, 2010).In this approach, patient difficulties are conceptualized in accordance with behavioural principles and operant learning history. The authors further propose that the patient demonstrates behaviours with the therapist that are reflective of their problems outside of the therapeutic relationship and in their daily lives (i.e. 'clinically relevant behaviours [CRBs]'). In this way, the approach bears some similarities to psychoanalytic approaches and to the case formulation approach written about by AuBuchon and Malatesta (1998). Kohlenberg and colleagues then outline in behavioural and interpersonally sensitive terms five guidelines that specify therapist behaviours ('tasks'), which use operant and interpersonal techniques to modify the patient's behaviour in accordance with their goals. It is notable that when describing these tasks, the authors also address issues such as how to increase therapist awareness of CRBs and how to address *problematic behaviours and issues of the therapist*, which may have a negative effect on the therapy. Also commendable is that Kohlenberg and colleagues have demonstrated empirical support for their approach through a series of studies (e.g. Kanter, Schildcrout, & Kohlenberg, 2005; Kohlenberg, Kanter, Bolling, Parker, & Tsai, 2002).

The Case Formulation Approach

The preceding section reviewed and described various approaches to the therapeutic relationship in CBT. In a previous edition of this book, AuBuchon and Malatesta (1998) outlined an approach to the therapeutic relationship that was guided by the case formulation. In this approach, various therapist behaviours are ideographically and systematically demonstrated with each patient, as determined by the therapist's formulation of the patient and their difficulties. The integral role of the case formulation in guiding and influencing the therapeutic relationship will be again described in the following section and in the following chapter. Before those topics are discussed, however, a brief review of the case formulation approach in CBT is offered.

Case formulation approaches to behaviour therapy can be traced to the pioneering work of Victor Meyer (1957). Emphases on (a) an individualized approach to understanding each patient's problems via sensitive listening and hypothesis testing and (b) tailoring scientifically backed treatment interventions for each patient were hallmarks of Meyer's approach. I had the pleasure and honour of working with, and observing, Dr. Meyer during the 1980s and 1990s and will never forget his half-serious complaint that he 'wished [he] had never invented exposure and response prevention (for treatment of obsessive-compulsive disorder), because nobody thinks about their patients anymore' (V. Meyer, personal communication, London, 1985). Dr. Meyer worked alongside Dr. Edward Chesser, one of the few behaviourally oriented psychiatrists, for several decades. They co-directed an innovative inpatient psychiatric unit, delivering intensive treatment according to behavioural principles. Furthermore, they worked with complex and treatment-refractory cases, all the while displaying a great deal of sensitivity and dignity towards their patients. In addition, they wrote about behaviour therapy in clinical psychiatry (Meyer & Chesser, 1970). As for the case formulation approach in CBT, it has been elaborated upon by Meyer (1975), Turkat (1985), Persons (1989a) and Bruch and Bond (1998). In addition, interesting and thorough accounts of the development of case formulation approaches to CBT can be found in a previous edition of this book (e.g. Bruch, 1998a, 1998b).

In 1979, Meyer and Turkat defined formulation as 'an hypothesis which (a) relates all the client's complaints to one another, (b) explains why the individual developed these difficulties, and (c) provides predictions concerning the client's behavior given any stimulus conditions' (pp. 261–262). This definition still serves us well, not only in specifying what a case formulation *is* but also in guiding and challenging us as clinicians. That is, having to meet the criteria specified in the definition given by Meyer and Turkat helps to ensure that we as clinicians really understand our patient and their difficulties. This case formulation approach has also been demonstrated empirically to be effective with a range of disorders including schizophrenia (Adams, Malatesta, Brantley, & Turkat, 1981), chronic pain (AuBuchon, Haber, & Adams, 1985), complex phobia (AuBuchon, 1993), complex obsessive–compulsive disorder (OCD), personality disorders (AuBuchon & Malatesta, 1994; Malatesta, 1995; Turkat & Carlson, 1984) and tic disorders (Malatesta, 1990). It also has utility for guiding and managing the therapeutic relationship as demonstrated by Turkat and Brantley (1981), Persons (1989b) and AuBuchon and Malatesta (1998).

Beyond Therapist Style: Current Thinking on the Therapeutic Relationship

In the first edition of this book, AuBuchon and Malatesta (1998) described an approach for managing the therapeutic relationship that was based upon and guided by the case formulation. First, they proposed that the behaviour the patient demonstrated towards the therapist could be understood in terms of the case formulation. For example, a patient who experienced severe criticism growing up in her family of origin might misinterpret the therapist's behaviour as being critical of her and/or might become severely upset or defensive when feeling criticized by her therapist. Second, AuBuchon and Malatesta maintained that the case formulation was valuable in guiding the therapist's interactions with the patient. For instance, if based upon the case formulation, the therapist hypothesized that the patient would have strong negative reactions to feeling controlled, the therapist would make sure that he did not unnecessarily trigger these feelings in the patient. He would do this by sharing control with the patient during the course of the therapy (e.g. by letting the patient choose the frequency of therapy sessions or other treatment activities).

AuBuchon and Malatesta (1998) also presented two sets of therapist behaviours. The first of these was derived from seminal research on the therapeutic alliance (e.g. Frank, 1984; Strupp, 1984) and would be demonstrated with nearly all patients. The other set of behaviours would be systematically varied, and differentially emphasized, on the basis of the therapist's formulation of the patient and on their experiences with the patient during the course of therapy. They went on to state that this second set of therapist behaviours were 'hypothesized to be valuable in (a) strengthening the therapeutic alliance, (b) improving the likelihood that the patient will benefit from implementation of specific therapeutic techniques, and (c) helping patients modify interpersonal anxieties and skill deficits likely to be demonstrated in interactions with the therapist' (AuBuchon & Malatesta, 1998: p. 145). They also introduced and operationally defined a relationship intervention, the 'therapist style'. Therapist style was defined as 'a collection of purposeful interpersonal behaviors exhibited by the therapist when in contact with the patient' (p. 144). It was emphasized that these behaviours were not only genuine for the therapist but also primarily determined by the therapist's formulation of the patient's difficulties. For example, with a patient with fears of revealing difficulties, the therapist may elect to disclose something that the therapist struggled with in his life. Again, this appears consistent with the APA Task Force's recommendations cited earlier in this chapter. That is, treatment guidelines need to explicitly address therapist behaviours that promote a facilitative therapy relationship, and that tailoring the therapy relationship to specific patient needs and characteristics, *in addition to diagnosis*, enhances treatment effectiveness (Table 4.1).

The formulation-guided approach to the therapeutic relationship described by AuBuchon and Malatesta represented a step forward within CBT. It *remains* a highly effective way to manage the therapeutic relationship, and one with many benefits. First, it emphasizes the value of a thoughtful and systematic approach to the therapeutic relationship (i.e. one guided by the case formulation). This means a very individualized relationship with each patient, based on their learning history and interpersonal presentation. In effect, no two therapeutic relationships are the same. This differs from traditional psychoanalytic approaches with a heavy reliance on technical neutrality and from client-centred approaches relying primarily on unconditional positive regard. The formulation-guided approach also differs from cognitive–behavioural approaches, which often focused too much on treatment techniques for specific disorders, thereby ignoring the interpersonal context in which these disorders developed, or were maintained (e.g. interpersonal dependency with an agoraphobic patient). In addition, this individualized approach appears to be a more natural approach to the therapeutic relationship. One could argue, for instance, that **no two interpersonal relationships in nature are the same**: that is, no two parent–child relationships, no two husband–wife relationships, no two friendships or no two relationships between colleagues.

Table 4.1   Two sets of therapist Behaviours.

I. Constant	II. Systematically varied	
Will be demonstrated with nearly all patients	Will be varied according to the therapist's formulation of the patient and clinical experimentation. These will vary in amount and type.	
A. Respect	A. Nurturing provided	M. Frequency of sessions
B. Trustworthiness	B. Structure in session	N. Modelling/admitting shortcomings
C. Interest	C. Self-disclosure	O. Sharing notes and/or formulation
D. Caring	D. Directiveness	P. Limit setting
E. Understanding	E. Criticism	Q. Confronting maladaptive behaviours
F. Acceptance	F. Praise/social reinforcement	R. Validating the patient's feelings and experiences
G. Accurate empathy	G. Encouragement	
H. Appears competent	H. Play	
I. Instills the expectation for change	I. Humour	
J. Genuineness	J. Control	
	K. Therapist availability	
	L. Length of sessions	

Reproduced from AuBuchon and Malatesta (1998).

Second, the strengthened therapeutic alliance that results from the formulation-guided approach yields several additional benefits for patients. One such benefit is the increased effectiveness of specific ('non-relationship') treatment techniques (e.g. exposure and response prevention; assertiveness training). This increased effectiveness seems to occur for various reasons. First, patients seemed to like or trust their therapist more. Second, patients report feeling well understood by their therapists. Third, in the context of a strong therapeutic alliance, patients have expressed feeling strongly affirmed and supported by their therapists. It is easy to see that if a patient is experiencing these positive emotional states they would be more willing to experiment with therapeutic suggestions, expose themselves to challenging situations or emotions or comply with therapeutic homework. Additionally, the strong therapeutic alliance that can result from the formulation-guided relationship helps clinicians avoid therapeutic ruptures and roadblocks. Finally, the formulation-guided approach helps therapists conceptualize, understand and treat various maladaptive cognitive, autonomic and behavioural responses demonstrated within the therapeutic relationship (e.g. automatic thoughts about the therapist's motives, overwhelming emotional reactions like fear or anger and behaviours such as withdrawal or criticism).

Since the publication of the 'Therapist Style' chapter, my primary concern with it has been that the *'therapist-style intervention'* would be implemented in a 'cookbook' fashion (i.e. akin to matching treatment techniques to diagnoses). This would not be consistent with a formulation-based approach. I was also concerned that therapists would choose behaviours from 'column A' or 'column B' and apply them in a contrived manner instead of relating to their patients in a genuine, sensitive and caring fashion. In addition, the therapeutic relationship skills of listening intently to the patient and trusting one's intuition and then responding sensitively and accurately to 'where the patient is', in a moment-by-moment fashion, need to demonstrated as well.[2] **The goal, therefore, is to do both: Demonstrate sensitive and attentive clinical skills while having the therapist's way of interacting with the patient be informed and guided by the case formulation.**

In the 14 years since the 'Therapist Style' chapter was written, clinical experience with hundreds of patients has deepened my appreciation of the richness of therapeutic relationships. These experiences have also demonstrated to me the power and potential of this component of therapy to bring about meaningful and lasting changes for the individuals we treat. **'Good' therapeutic relationships enhance the effectiveness of treatment techniques, are an intervention in and of themselves, provide for corrective emotional experiences for patients (e.g. patients can feel valued, likable, worthy and even lovable), can turn therapeutic ruptures into unique learning experiences that result in lasting changes in core problems (e.g. feelings of being unwanted and expectations of abandonment) and can minimize treatment dropout rates.**

Therapeutic relationships improving specific treatment interventions

Examples of how formulation-guided therapeutic relationships improve the effectiveness of specific treatment techniques include the following. In the chapter of this book focusing on the role of the therapeutic relationship in the treatment of complex PTSD and OCD, a case is presented of a 40-year-old Roman Catholic Sister. This woman grew up having a mother who suffered from paranoid schizophrenia and a father with OCD and obsessive–compulsive personality disorder. In addition, and severely traumatizing for the patient, was the father's extremely invalidating style in response to the patient as she experienced multiple extreme stressors. These stressors included repeatedly watching a mother deteriorate into psychosis, having inadequate food and heat in the home and having to function as a *de facto* parent: that is, caring for siblings while the father was at work and/or when her mother was either psychotic or hospitalized. It became very clear in the first session that one of the most traumatic and enraging experiences for the patient *was not* the mother's schizophrenia but rather the father's invalidating responses to the overwhelming stressors (e.g. 'Oh, Mom is fine'; physically or verbally abusing the patient if she expressed fear for her mother's condition). Understanding the traumatizing effects of this invalidation was a key part of the case formulation. As such, no intervention for treatment of this woman's PTSD (e.g. psychoeducation, writing about and processing traumatic events, coping skills training and assertive self-care) could be undertaken without first validating how awful certain experiences and emotions were for the patient. If accurate validation was given, treatment gains were achieved. If it was not, for instance when well-intentioned attempts at psychoeducation were experienced as critical lectures by the patient, PTSD-related flashbacks were triggered and therapeutic setbacks occurred.

Other examples of how formulation-guided therapeutic relationships improved the efficacy of specific treatment techniques include exposure and response prevention with patients with OCD (AuBuchon & Malatesta, 1998; Bond, 1998; Malatesta, 1995) and contingency management with an adolescent with conduct disorder (AuBuchon & Malatesta, 1998).

Therapeutic relationship as an intervention in and of itself

The power and importance of the therapeutic relationship as an intervention in and of itself cannot be understated. There are several ways in which this happens. First, as succinctly described and empirically supported by Kohlenberg and colleagues (e.g. Kohlenberg & Tsai, 1991), interpersonal and intrapersonal issues of the patient *do* show up in therapy sessions and in the therapeutic relationship. Through the use of therapist awareness of CRBs, therapist awareness of their own reactions to the patient's behaviour and sensitive and well-timed feedback to the patient about their behaviour (e.g. how the patient's behaviour is experienced by the therapist), patients can have immediate, and deeply meaningful, new learning experiences. An example from my own practice illustrates these points. The patient is an attractive, intelligent and extremely likable 46-year-old single man who presented with a complex anxiety disorder, self-image problems and depression. His anxiety disorder featured intense fears of engaging in activities away from his small town neighbourhood and of getting in serious trouble for acting in spontaneous or fun ways. These fears generalized to the point that he feared that he would be imprisoned for having a friendship with an influential authority figure, who once demonstrated caring for the patient. Additional problems included avoidance of dating and intense distress characterized by endless obsessing about his perceived inadequacies. The patient also experienced anger, rage, depression and severe self-criticism when certain women did not want to date him or when he viewed himself as not being aggressive enough ('not man enough'). Treatment included discussion of the case formulation: That is, the patient had learned fears that others would do harmful things to him if he strayed too far from home or if he pursued his ambitions and desires. He had also acquired a learned self-image of being an inadequate and inferior man ('the little sissy boy in the corner'). Learning to recognize and conceptualize automatic thoughts of inferiority in terms of this case formulation, learning new responses to these thoughts and *in vivo* exposure to avoided situations were key formulation-based interventions. In addition, treatment also included psychoeducation and treatment of obsessive thoughts and mental rituals (e.g. Freeston & Ladouceur, 1998; Rachman, 2006). Equally important, however, was the positive regard, caring and interest I demonstrated towards the patient. This was done by taking an interest in his suffering and redirecting the patient back to the case formulation and treatment strategies designed to reduce the importance of his automatic thoughts (rather than 'siding' with attitudes that he was a defective or an inferior person in some way). This care and interest was also demonstrated via therapeutic self-disclosure (e.g. letting the patient know that I actually looked forward to our sessions, that I enjoyed our discussions of 'non-treatment topics' such as film or art and that if we did not have a professional relationship, that he would be the type of man I would be friends with). These self-disclosures on my part were calculated risks (i.e. boundary crossings) but ones that were consistent with the case formulation and the length and nature of the therapeutic relationship (i.e. I knew the patient well, and there was no personality disorder symptomatology). In addition, awareness of my own behaviour and feelings (i.e. that it was easy to lapse into conversations about movies and actors) enabled me to use disclosure of these feelings as real and positive interpersonal experiences for the patient. What Kohlenberg would classify as immediate and natural reinforcement.

The phrase 'Use oneself as an instrument of change' also has a certain appeal to it (Tsai et al., 2010: p. 181). In the example above, demonstrating interest and caring for the patient and using formulation-guided self-disclosure were examples of natural and immediate interpersonal responses that became therapeutic for the patient. Therapeutic self-disclosure was also used to provide the patient with feedback about how I experienced him. For this patient, experiencing my genuine enjoyment of spending time with him was a corrective emotional experience. One that was possible because of my willingness to share my feelings with the patient. Of course, with any self-disclosure by the therapist, the therapist should ask themselves whether the self-disclosure advances the patient's therapeutic goals or whether the self-disclosure simply gratifies the therapist's needs. Other examples of the therapeutic relationship being an agent for change include the following:

- The 42-year-old married white woman with a long history of subjugating her emotional, social and professional needs to those of significant others being asked by the therapist what would be a good time **for her** to have the next session. Another opportunity was pointing out how concerned the patient was about the spelling of the therapist's name on her check, rather than finishing a discussion about one of **her** concerns.

- My being willing to share a few details of what I would be doing on vacation with the aforementioned Roman Catholic Sister. This was done in order to counteract severe PTSD symptomatology related to experiences of abandonment and isolation caused by her mother's multiple psychiatric hospitalizations. Because the patient was so young at the time and because of a lack of explanation and validation from the patient's father, the patient's experience was that her mother completely disappeared (e.g. 'I didn't know what my mother was doing or even seeing'). Knowing just a few things that I would be doing (like working on this manuscript) calmed the patient tremendously. Of course, the meaning of the patient's requests was discussed, and the emotional processing of these traumatic memories and feelings was done, but these interventions could not have been undertaken until after her requests were granted, and the overwhelming autonomic reactions quieted. It was also essential to discuss the meanings of these requests when the patient was not in the middle of a PTSD reaction, so as to not trigger other PTSD reactions related to having been told there was something wrong with her.

As can be seen above, my behaviour within the various therapeutic relationships was determined by each patient's case formulation. It also appears that 'using oneself [and the therapeutic relationship] as an agent of change' can produce treatment results that may not be achievable in other ways. The immediate and genuine experience the patient has with the therapist leads to new learning, as only actually experiencing an event can. Also, as pointed out by Ferster (1967), Skinner (1982) and Tsai et al. (2010), natural and immediate reinforcement is more effective in the learning of new behaviour than delayed or contrived reinforcement.

A quick word on self-disclosure and boundaries: As can be seen in the examples above, therapeutic self-disclosure can be a powerful intervention. It is, however, also a boundary crossing. With any boundary crossing on the therapist's part, the therapist needs to ask themselves several questions:

- Is this boundary crossing/self-disclosure in the patient's best interest or mine?
- Does this boundary crossing/self-disclosure help the patient achieve their goals?

- Does this self-disclosure/boundary crossing increase the patient's focus on their problems and issues or does it shift the focus to my issues?
- Does this boundary crossing/self-disclosure reinforce harmful or excessive dependence on the therapist?
- Is this a boundary crossing or a boundary violation?

Boundary crossings are essentially any deviation from the traditional frame and parameters of psychoanalytic therapy. They happen all the time in therapy and are not harmful to either the patient or the therapist (e.g. sharing with a patient of Italian descent that my wife is Italian, in order to build some rapport). Boundary violations are boundary crossings that do harm to either the patient or the therapist. The most severe example of a boundary violation would be a therapist having sexual relations with a patient. Knapp and Van de Creek (2012) provide an excellent discussion of boundaries as well as other ethical matters in their book on 'positive ethics' in psychology. Likewise, Bloomgarden and Menutti (2009) have edited an excellent book on therapist self-disclosure.

In addition to the aforementioned benefits of using the therapeutic relationship as an agent of change, one could argue that the modification of interpersonal problems and maladaptive cognitions about relationships (e.g. expectations and interpretations) is best and most effectively accomplished via the therapeutic relationship. As discussed above, the immediate and natural reinforcement that occurs within the therapeutic relationship will have more powerful effects on patients' behaviour, and lead to stronger treatment effects, than delayed or contrived reinforcements. For example, if feelings of rejection occur in the therapeutic relationship and are responded to immediately by the therapist, this will have stronger treatment effects than simply talking about feelings of rejection that arose outside of therapy sessions. Furthermore, as can be seen from the examples above, many of these experiences with the therapist become corrective emotional experiences for the patient (e.g. 'feeling as though people do want to spend time with me'; 'others think about me when I am not with them' and 'someone cares about my feelings and needs').

Therapeutic ruptures as opportunities for meaningful change

Another powerful opportunity that can occur in the therapeutic relationship is that of a 'rupture in the therapeutic alliance'. These are defined by Safran and Muran (1996) as 'deterioration in the quality of the relationship between patient and therapist', are considered reflective of important interpersonal issues for the patient and '[indicate] critical points in therapy for exploring and understanding ... maladaptive interpersonal schema' (p. 447). Therapeutic ruptures are bound to happen with any complex case.

They, however, can be understood in terms of the case formulation and do indeed provide special opportunities in therapy. They provide the chance for the therapist and patient to understand and make lasting and meaningful changes in core problems (e.g. feeling not cared about and feelings of mistrust). Typical examples of core issues that trigger therapeutic ruptures include when patients feel criticized by the therapist; when therapists make well-intentioned suggestions that end up traumatizing the patient in a session; therapeutic impasses concerning fees; seemingly innocuous comments about the health benefits of exercise with a patient with body image, weight or eating disorder issues or patients with a history of neglect, abandonment or abuse feeling as though the therapist is not taking their side in an interpersonal conflict. Therapist behaviours that appear crucial in resolving and learning from these ruptures include genuine and nonjudgemental validation of the patient's feelings, nondefensiveness on the therapist's part as the rupture is discussed and the therapist owning their contribution to the interpersonal event that caused the therapeutic rupture (e.g. not being clear about the fees for an extended *in vivo* exposure session). Other essential interventions during therapeutic ruptures include discussing the patient's feelings and reactions in terms of their life experiences and/or conceptualizing the patient's reactions as learned self-protective coping responses. **That is, these feelings and responses are discussed in terms of the case formulation.** If these essential relationship-based interventions are done well enough, the patient ends up feeling validated and listened to, can look at their contributions in a less defensive manner and can gain new insights about their interpersonal difficulties. Therapeutic ruptures can then be healed, progress is made and patients stay in treatment versus prematurely dropping out of it.

Preventing premature termination

This brings us to the final benefit of 'good therapeutic relationships': They reduce the risk of patients prematurely terminating their therapy (aka 'psychotherapy dropout'). Dropout rates in psychotherapy remain generally high. Stanley and Turner (1995) reported that 30% of patients with OCD either refused behavioural treatment or dropped out of therapy prematurely. In addition, a recent meta-analysis of psychotherapy dropout concluded that the mean dropout rate was 46.86% (Wierzbicki & Pekarik, 1993). It is my experience, and that of colleagues who use a formulation-based treatment approach, that if the therapist has an accurate understanding of the patient's difficulties and uses this formulation to guide his treatment with the patient – including both the tailoring of specific interventions and management of the therapeutic relationship – individuals are more likely to stay in treatment and benefit from it. An example of this, with empirical support, is found in Victor Malatesta's treatment of a 47-year-old woman with complex OCD (AuBuchon & Malatesta, 1998). Dr. Malatesta's formulation of this woman's difficulties indicated the need to share control with the patient in all phases of treatment. It also indicated that it would be essential to provide the patient with full explanations and information about assessment and treatment procedures. Without these formulation-guided relationship strategies, it is doubtful that a good therapeutic alliance would have been established, and it was likely that the patient would have terminated treatment prematurely (V. J. Malatesta, personal communication, Narberth, PA, 2012). Other examples of the value of a good therapeutic relationship in guarding against treatment dropout include the finding that perhaps the most important factor in the treatment of alcohol abuse is whether the patient likes his therapist/treatment programme. If he does, he tends to go to treatment sessions, groups or meetings more often; and if he attends treatment activities more often, he tends to drink less (Meichenbaum, 2001). A second example of how **critical** it is to have a strong therapeutic alliance is in the treatment of suicidal patients. Linehan (1993), e.g. has stated that it is essential to have a strong therapeutic relationship with patients who are suicidal and/or who suffer from borderline personality disorder – it keeps them alive or in treatment.

A final point regarding patients' abilities to stay in therapy: The corrective emotional experiences that patients have in good therapeutic relationships (e.g. feeling lovable and feeling that people want to spend time with them) yield additional benefits. To begin, they usually enhance the patient's general emotional state and self-esteem. This in turn gives patients more energy to tackle difficult problems and stay the course in therapy. These emotional benefits, in addition to identifying and targeting self-critical cognitive patterns, also help patients develop more loving, compassionate and accepting attitudes *towards themselves*. These attitudes, in addition to all the aforementioned benefits of a good therapeutic relationship, allow therapy to progress at a faster rate, as opposed to an inadequate rate of therapeutic progress, which can also lead to treatment dropout.

Summary and Conclusions

In this chapter, the point was made that a cornerstone of effective psychotherapy, including cognitive–behavioural psychotherapy, is that of a good therapeutic relationship. It was argued that managing the therapeutic relationship according to the case formulation provided the clinician a means of maximizing the usefulness and power of the therapeutic relationship, both as a treatment intervention and as a component of psychological treatments. The chapter began with a review of the scientific literature on the therapeutic relationship in CBT. This literature reflected the evolution of our study of the therapeutic relationship in CBT, starting with studies that examined traits of behaviour therapists as compared with therapists of other psychotherapeutic orientations. These findings demonstrated that cognitive–behavioural therapists were as empathetic and warm and cared for their patients as much as psychotherapists from other orientations. They also showed that behaviour therapists demonstrated more initiative, support and direction than therapists of other orientations.

Other early studies indicated that therapist presence often had beneficial (i.e. anxiolytic) effects while the patient was encountering fearful or difficult situations. In addition, they suggested that the presence of the therapeutic relationship in patients' lives had facilitative effects for patients as they pursued their treatment goals. Based on my experience with hundreds of patients, I would agree with this hypothesis. For many patients, especially those who experienced abusive and/or negligent relationships with significant others, their relationship with an affirming, supportive, validating and nurturing therapist may have been their first experience with such a healthy relationship. And, as discussed in this chapter, these new learning experiences with their therapist often result in better self-esteem, greater energy to address difficult problems and less self-defeating self-critical attitudes.

Finally, the initial studies on the therapeutic relationship in CBT demonstrated that certain therapist behaviours needed to be demonstrated at a higher rate with individuals presenting with certain types of problems (e.g. validation and limit setting with patients with borderline personality disorder; focusing, challenge, encouragement and praise with patients with anxiety disorders and initiative and support with patients suffering from depression). These studies pointed cognitive–behavioural therapists toward the approach of tailoring their relationship with each patient on the basis of their understanding of that individual. Ideally, this understanding would go beyond their patient's diagnosis and more towards the therapist's formulation of that individual's difficulties, strengths, personality traits and unique learning history – in a sense who they were as a person.

The present chapter also acknowledged two notable approaches to the therapeutic relationship in CBT: Meichenbaum's 'Core tasks of Psychotherapy – What Expert Therapists Do' and Kohlenberg's Functional Analytic Psychotherapy (FAP). These two approaches were highlighted because I believe that they offer effective and powerful interventions to cognitive–behavioural psychotherapists. Meichenbaum has studied the behaviours of highly effective psychotherapists from various therapeutic orientations and identified those behaviours that are associated with the best clinical outcomes. This empirical approach, as opposed to a theoretical or orientation-bound approach, is consistent with Gottman's (1997) highly effective approach to marital therapy. It is also reminiscent of Adams'

(1984) imploration that psychologists be scientific and empirical in their therapies and research, rather than 'religious' or 'cultish' in their adherence to their theoretical orientation.

Kohlenberg's FAP is notable for several reasons. First, there is a parsimony and consistency evident throughout the approach. From the basic experimental psychology findings that underlie the approach to the conceptualization of the patient's behaviour, to the therapeutic rationale and treatment interventions and to the empirical studies that have demonstrated the approach's effectiveness, Kohlenberg and colleagues rely on operant learning principles. Second, they argue that because of the greater effectiveness of immediate and natural reinforcement, over that of delayed and contrived reinforcement, the therapeutic relationship offers a powerful venue in which to modify the patient's intra- and interpersonal problems. Third, the approach emphasizes the use of the functional analysis in understanding and modifying problematic behaviour. It is refreshing to see the use of this technique in CBT and reminds me of earlier publications by Meyer and colleagues (Meyer & Turkat, 1979; Meyer, AuBuchon, & Olasov, 1988). Unfortunately, it is a term that seems to have disappeared from the CBT literature. Finally, FAP ought to be commended for recommending that therapists themselves need to be aware of their own intra- and interpersonal issues that may interfere with treatment effectiveness and to continually engage in their own 'personal work' (e.g. peer supervision and personal psychotherapy) in order to optimize their effectiveness with their patients. Cognitive–behavioural therapists would benefit from familiarizing themselves with both Meichenbaum's and Kohlenberg's approach to clinical work and the therapeutic relationship. In addition, Linehan's insights and expertise with the therapeutic relationship are extremely valuable and clinically useful (e.g. Linehan, 1988, 1993). I would also recommend that cognitive–behavioural therapists read her treatises on the subject.

The present chapter also briefly reviewed the development of the case formulation approach to behaviour therapy and the invaluable contributions of Victor Meyer. It again presented the definition of formulation given by Meyer and Turkat and cited empirically supported case studies that utilized the case formulation approach. The present chapter then reviewed the formulation-based approach to the therapeutic relationship by AuBuchon and Malatesta (1998). In this approach, two sets of therapist behaviours were identified. The first set of behaviours included respect, trustworthiness, acceptance, expectation for change and empathy. These behaviours were considered essential for the development of a productive therapeutic alliance with any patient. The second set of behaviours included nurturing, self-disclosure, humour, control, validation and limit setting, among many others. These behaviours were to be systematically varied and demonstrated based on the therapist's formulation of each individual patient. This case formulation–based approach was seen as a step forward in managing the therapeutic relationship in behaviour therapy. It represented a thoughtful and systematic approach to the therapeutic relationship, based on the case formulation rather than a standard approach to the relationship as in psychoanalytic or client-centred therapies or on the patient's diagnosis (e.g. borderline personality disorder and anxiety disorder).

In the years since Victor Malatesta and I wrote our chapter on managing the therapeutic relationship according to the case formulation (AuBuchon & Malatesta, 1998), I have had the privilege of working with hundreds of individuals in psychotherapy. These gratifying experiences have deepened my understanding of clinical work and of the importance of the therapeutic relationship. Hopefully, my growth as a clinician has contributed to a more sophisticated and effective yet still formulation-based approach to the therapeutic relationship. In the remainder of this chapter, examples have been discussed on how formulation-guided relationships enhanced the effectiveness of specific treatment techniques; how the therapeutic relationship in itself was used as a treatment intervention for modifying intra- and interpersonal problems (e.g. 'using oneself as an instrument of change'); how care must be taken with regards to therapeutic boundaries; how relationship-based interventions and the case formulation can be used to turn therapeutic ruptures into opportunities for therapeutic progress and how good therapeutic alliances can minimize dropout rates in psychotherapy.

Perhaps, the most important contributions of this chapter come from the case examples and accompanying insights discussed above. The example of the formulation-guided relationship with the Catholic Sister details how sophisticated an analysis of an individual's experiences needs to be. This analysis, which pointed to the role of invalidation in this woman's trauma, was critical in guiding therapist behaviour. Without validation of the patient's emotional experiences, *those that occurred in the therapy sessions and those that occurred in her past*, no treatment of her OCD or PTSD would have been possible.

The examples of 'using oneself as an agent of change' come from accurate formulations of those individuals' difficulties and openness on my part. An openness I believe that comes from years of experience with therapeutic relationships and the willingness to take risks in these relationships – not blind risks, however, but risks informed by hypotheses generated by the case formulation.

In conclusion, I wish to thank not only the patients who gave their permission to be included in this chapter but also all of the patients I have worked with over the course of my career. It has been a privilege to be let into these people's lives, and it has been a profound and gratifying education. Our work together has deepened my understanding of clinical work and of the importance of the therapeutic relationship. Hopefully, this new knowledge has contributed in some way to an evolution of formulation-based approaches to the therapeutic relationship in CBT.

Notes

1. Interestingly, this finding seems to hold not only for mental health treatments but also for medical treatments as well. Meichenbaum (2006) has pointed out, for instance, that when controlling for the type of surgical procedure, better results are realized when patients like their surgeons than when they do not.
2. I would also endorse therapeutic relationship guideline of Tsai and Kohlenberg "fostering an exquisite sensitivity and benevolent concern for the needs and feelings of clients, and caring deeply" (Tsai et al., 2010: p. 182).

References

Adams, H.E. (1978). Personal communication as told to Victor Malatesta, Athens, GA.

Adams, H. E. (1984). The pernicious effects of theoretical orientations in clinical psychology. *The Clinical Psychologist, 37,* 90–94.

Adams, H. E., Malatesta, V. J., Brantley, P. J., & Turkat, I. D. (1981). Modification of cognitive processes: A case study of schizophrenia. *Journal of Consulting and Clinical Psychology, 49,* 460–464.

AuBuchon, P. G. (1993). Formulation-based treatment of a complex phobia. *Journal of Behavior Therapy and Experimental Psychiatry, 24,* 63–71.

AuBuchon, P. G., & Calhoun, K. S. (1990). The effects of therapist presence and relaxation training on the efficacy and generalizability of *in vivo* exposure. *Behavioural Psychotherapy, 18,* 169–185.

AuBuchon, P. G., & Malatesta, V. J. (1994). Obsessive compulsive patients with comorbid personality disorder: Associated problems and response to a comprehensive behavior therapy. *Journal of Clinical Psychiatry, 55,* 448–453.

AuBuchon, P. G., & Malatesta, V. J. (1998). Managing the therapeutic relationship in behavior therapy: The need for a case formulation. In M. Bruch & F. W. Bond (Eds.), *Beyond diagnosis: Case formulation approaches in CBT* (pp. 141–165). Chichester, UK: John Wiley & Sons.

AuBuchon, P. G., Haber, J. D., & Adams, H. E. (1985). Can migraine headaches be modified by operant pain techniques? *Journal of Behavior Therapy and Experimental Psychiatry, 16,* 261–263.

Bandura, A., & Menlove, F. L. (1968). Factors determining vicarious extinction of avoidance behavior through symbolic modeling. *Journal of Personality and Social Psychology, 8,* 99–108.

Beck, A. T., Rush, A. J., Shaw, B. F., & Emery, G. (1979). *Cognitive therapy of depression.* New York: The Guilford Press.

Benjamin, L. S., & Critchfield, K. L. (2010). An interpersonal perspective on therapy alliances and techniques. In J. C. Muran & J. P. Barber (Eds.), *The therapeutic alliance: An evidence-based guide to practice* (pp. 123–149). New York: The Guilford Press.

Bloomgarden, A., & Mennuti, R. B. (Eds.). (2009). *Psychotherapist revealed: Therapists speak about self-disclosure in psychotherapy*. New York: Routledge; Taylor & Francis Group.

Bond, F. W. (1998). Utilising case formulations in manual-based treatments. In M. Bruch & F. W. Bond (Eds.), *Beyond diagnosis: Case formulation approaches in CBT* (pp. 185–206). Chichester, UK: John Wiley & Sons.

Brady, J. P. (1980). Some views on effective principles of psychotherapy [special issue]. *Cognitive Therapy and Research, 4*, 271–306.

Bruch, M. (1998a). The development of case formulation approaches. In M. Bruch & F. W. Bond (Eds.), *Beyond diagnosis: Case formulation approaches in CBT* (pp. 1–17). Chichester, UK: John Wiley & Sons.

Bruch, M. (1998b). The UCL case formulation model: Clinical applications and procedures. In M. Bruch & F. W. Bond (Eds.), *Beyond diagnosis: Case formulation approaches in CBT* (pp. 19–41). Chichester, UK: John Wiley & Sons.

Bruch, M., & Bond, F. W. (Eds.). (1998). *Beyond diagnosis: Case formulation approaches in CBT*. Chichester, UK: John Wiley & Sons.

Brunink, S. A., & Schroeder, H. E. (1979). Verbal therapeutic behavior of expert psychoanalytically oriented, gestalt, and behavior therapists. *Journal of Consulting and Clinical Psychology, 47*, 567–574.

Ferster, C. B. (1967). Arbitrary and natural reinforcement. The *Psychological Record, 22*, 1–16.

Fischer, J., Paveza, G. J., Kickertz, N. S., Hubbard, L. J., & Grayson, S. B. (1975). The relationship between theoretical orientation and therapists' empathy, warmth, and genuineness. *Journal of Consulting Psychology, 22*, 399–403.

Frank, J. D. (1984). Therapeutic components shared by all psychotherapies. In J. H. Harvey & M. M. Parks (Eds.), *The master lecture series: Volume 1, psychotherapy research and behavior change* (pp. 9–37). Washington, DC: American Psychological Association.

Freeston, M. H., & Ladouceur, R. (1998). *Treating obsessions without overt compulsions*. ADAA Reporter, 9, 1–19. Rockville, MD: Anxiety Disorders Association of America.

Goldfried, M. R. (1983). The behavior therapist in clinical practice. *The Behavior Therapist, 6*, 45–46.

Goldfried, M. R., & Davison, G. C. (1976). *Clinical behavior therapy*. New York: Holt, Rinehart, & Winston.

Gottman, J. M. (1997). *Clinical manual for marital therapy: A scientifically-based marital therapy* (304 p.). Seattle, WA: The Seattle Marital and Family Institute, Inc.

Grayson, J. B., Foa, E. B., & Steketee, G. (1982). Habituation during exposure treatment: Distraction versus attention-focusing. *Behaviour Rewsearch and Therapy, 20*, 323–328.

Greenson, R. R. (1965). The working alliance and the transference neurosis. *Psychoanalytic Quarterly, 34*, 155–179.

Greenwald, D. P., Kornblith, S. J., Hersen, M., Bellack, A. S., & Himmelhoch, J. M. (1981). Differences between social skills therapists and psychotherapists in treating depression. *Journal of Consulting and Clinical Psychology*, *49*, 757–759.

Gustavson, B., Jansson, L., Jerremalm, A., & Ost, L. G. (1985). Therapist behavior during exposure treatment of agoraphobia. *Behavior Modification*, *9*, 491–504.

Kanter, J. W., Schildcrout, J. S., & Kohlenberg, R. J. (2005). In vivo processes in cognitive therapy for depression: Frequency and benefits. *Psychotherapy Research*, *15*, 366–373.

Knapp, S., & Van de Creek, L. (2012). *Practical ethics for psychologists: A positive approach* (2nd ed.). Washington, DC: American Psychological Association.

Kohlenberg, R. J., & Tsai, M. (1991). *Functional analytic psychotherapy: Creating intense and curative therapeutic relationships*. New York: Plenum Press.

Kohlenberg, R. J., Kanter, J. W., Bolling, M. Y., Parker, C., & Tsai, M. (2002). Enhancing cognitive therapy for depression with functional analytic psychotherapy: Treatment guidelines and empirical findings. *Cognitive and Behavioral Practice*, *9*, 213–229.

Linehan, M. M. (1988). Perspectives on the interpersonal relationship in behavior therapy. *Journal of Integrative and Eclectic Psychotherapy*, *7*, 278–290.

Linehan, M. M. (1993). *Cognitive-behavioral treatment of borderline personality disorder*. New York: Guilford Press.

Malatesta, V. J. (1990). Behavioral case formulation: An experimental assessment study of transient tic disorder. *Journal of Psychopathology and Behavioral Assessment*, *12*, 219–232.

Malatesta, V. J. (1995). "Technological" behavior therapy for obsessive-compulsive disorder: The need for adequate case formulation. *The Behavior Therapist*, *18*, 88–89.

Meichenbaum, D. (2001). *Core tasks of psychotherapy: What "expert" therapists do.* Continuing education workshop presented at Philadelphia, PA.

Meichenbaum, D. (2006). *Treating traumatized adults and children: A life span approach.* A two day continuing education workshop presented at Lancaster, PA.

Meyer, V. (1957). The treatment of two phobic patients on the basis of learning principles. *Journal of Abnormal and Social Psychology*, *55*, 261–266.

Meyer, V. (1975). The impact of research on the clinical application of behavior therapy. In R. I. Thompson & W. S. Dockens (Eds.), *Applications of behavior modification*. New York: Academic Press.

Meyer, V., & Chesser, E. S. (1970). *Behaviour therapy in clinical psychiatry*. London: Penguin Books.

Meyer, V., & Gelder, M. G. (1963). Behaviour therapy and phobic disorders. *British Journal of Psychiatry*, *109*, 19–28.

Meyer, V., & Turkat, I. D. (1979). Behavioral analysis of clinical cases. *Journal of Behavioral Assessment*, *1*, 259–270.

Meyer, V., AuBuchon, P. G., & Olasov, B. (1988). Multilevel approaches to behavioural analysis and treatment. In J. Gemplar & B. V. Barrientos (Eds.), *Psicologia clinica compotamontal analisis de casos (Clinical behavioral psychology: Case analysis)*. Bogata, TX: Pontificia Universidad Javeriana.

Norcross J. C. (Chair). (2001). Empirically supported therapy relationships: Conclusions and recommendations of the Division 29 task force. *Psychotherapy, 38,* 495–497.

Persons, J. (1989a). *Cognitive therapy in practice: A case formulation approach.* New York: W.W. Norton.

Persons, J. (1989b). The therapeutic relationship. In J. Persons (Ed.), *Cognitive therapy in practice: A case formulation approach* (pp. 158–222). New York: W.W. Norton.

Rabavilas, A. D., Boulougouris, J. C., & Perissaki, C. (1979). Therapist qualities related to outcome with exposure *in vivo* with neurotic patients. *Journal of Behavior Therapy and Experimental Psychiatry, 10,* 293–294.

Rachman, S. (1983). The modification of agoraphobic avoidance behavior: Some fresh possibilities. *Behaviour Research and Therapy, 21,* 567–574.

Rachman, S. (2006). *The treatment of obsessions.* Oxford, UK: Oxford University Press.

Rogers, C. R. (1957). The necessary and sufficient conditions of therapeutic personality change. *Journal of Consulting Psychology, 21,* 95–103.

Rosenfarb, I. S. (1992). A behavior analytic interpretation of the therapeutic relationship. *The Psychological Record, 42,* 341–354.

Safran, J. D., & Muran, J. C. (1996). The resolution of ruptures in the therapeutic alliance. *Journal of Consulting and Clinical Psychology, 64,* 447–458.

Shearin, E. W., & Linehan, M. M. (1992). Patient-therapist ratings and relationship to progress in dialectical behavior therapy for borderline personality disorder. *Behavior Therapy, 23,* 730–741.

Skinner, B. F. (1982). Contrived reinforcement. *Behavior Analyst, 5,* 3–8.

Sloan, R. B., Staples, F. R., Cristol, A. H., Yorkston, N. H., & Whipple, K. (1975). *Psychotherapy versus behavior therapy.* Cambridge, MA: Harvard University Press.

Stanley, M. A., & Turner, S. M. (1995). Current status of pharmacological and behavioral treatment of obsessive-compulsive disorder. *Behavior Therapy, 26,* 163–186.

Strupp, H. H. (1984). The outcome problem in psychotherapy: Contemporary perspectives. In J. H. Harvey & M. M. Parks (Eds.), *The master lecture series: Volume 1, psychotherapy research and behavior change* (pp. 43–71). Washington, DC: American Psychological Press.

Touyz, S. W., Beumont, P. J., & Dunn, S. M. (1987). Behavior therapy in the management of patients with anorexia nervosa: A lenient flexible approach. *Psychotherapy and Psychosomatics, 48,* 151–156.

Tsai, M., Kohlenberg, R. J., & Kanter, J. W. (2010). A functional analytic psychotherapy (FAP) approach to the therapeutic alliance. In J. C. Muran & J. P. Barber (Eds.), *The therapeutic alliance: An evidence-based guide to practice.* New York: The Guilford Press.

Turkat, I. D. (Ed.). (1985). *Behavioral case formulation.* New York: Plenum.

Turkat, I. D., & Brantley, P. (1981). On the therapeutic relationship in behavior therapy. *The Behavior Therapist, 4,* 16–17.

Turkat, I. D., & Carlson, C. R. (1984). Data-based versus symptomatic formulation of treatment: The case of a dependent personality. *Journal of Behavior Therapy and Experimental Psychiatry, 15,* 153–160.

Wierzbicki, M., & Pekarik, G. (1993). A meta-analysis of psychotherapy dropout. *Professional Psychology: Research and Practice, 24*, 190–195.

Williams, K. E., & Chambless, D. L. (1990). The relationship between therapist characteristics and outcome of *in vivo* exposure treatment for agoraphobia. *Behavior Therapy, 21*, 111–116.

Wolpe, J. (1980). *The practice of behavior therapy* (3rd ed.). New York: Pergamon Press.

Wolpe, J., & Lazarus, A. (1966). *Behavior therapy techniques*. New York: Pergamon Press.

Wright, J. H., & Davis, D. (1994). The therapeutic relationships in cognitive-behavioral therapy: Patient perceptions and therapist responses. *Cognitive and Behavioral Practice, 1*, 25–45.

5

The Therapeutic Relationship as a Critical Intervention in a Case of Complex PTSD and OCD

Peter G. AuBuchon

Accounts of long-term, intensive treatment of individuals with severe and complex problems arising from a history of chronic multiple traumas are relatively few in the cognitive–behavioural therapy (CBT) literature. An exception would be Linehan (1993). Even more rare are publications describing a formulation-driven CBT for individuals presenting with these difficulties. What follows is a detailed account of an intensive cognitive–behavioural psychotherapy with a female patient who presented with a history of severe trauma and abuse. As a consequence of these horrific experiences, the patient developed severe and complex post-traumatic stress disorder (PTSD), had a severe obsessive–compulsive disorder (OCD) triggered and also had to endure several other difficult problems. The critical roles of the case formulation, the therapeutic relationship and specific relationship interventions based on the case formulation are emphasized in the following case study.

Identifying Information and Presenting Problem

The patient is an intelligent, energetic and very likable 40-year-old Roman Catholic Sister. We shall call her 'D.'. At the time of the first session, D. lived in a convent with 12 other sisters in a suburb of Philadelphia, Pennsylvania.

Beyond Diagnosis: Case Formulation in Cognitive Behavioural Therapy, Second Edition.
Edited by Michael Bruch.
© 2015 John Wiley & Sons, Ltd. Published 2015 by John Wiley & Sons, Ltd.

The patient was employed as a fifth and sixth grade teacher at a Catholic elementary school and had been a Sister for approximately 16 years. D. completed bachelor degrees in economics and philosophy/religion at a mid-sized university, where she was president of her sorority, and also excelled athletically on the field hockey and lacrosse teams. She had also earned her master's degree in multicultural education from a second university. The patient was the third of four children born to an intelligent, fun-loving, caring and 'very gentle' woman with paranoid schizophrenia. The patient's father worked as a chemist whom D. described in the second session as 'bright, well read, very calm and even-tempered; with a great sense of humour, and who was also very religious'. In addition, *in the beginning of this second session*, D. reported that she 'felt close to her father and had no bad memories of [him]'.

The patient also told me in the first session that her mother had died of cardiac arrest '2 years ago and was still very sad about it' but stated that what brought her to therapy was that she was 'in a difficult convent situation'. D. explained that she had been through several big changes recently in her life: Changing the order of sisters to which she belonged, losing two supportive principals at the school where she taught, having to take a teaching job at a new school and having to move into a new convent. Consequences of these moves included losing contact with several friends from her previous congregation whom she found very supportive and moving in with 12 new sisters who reportedly were 'all mean and very abusive'. D. further reported that these women 'were all very set in their ways, and very nasty about it'. The patient reported that she found three of these new 'housemates' particularly stressful: two would 'huff and puff and yell at you if things were not put back exactly where they wanted things to be'; and the third was very frightening for the patient because she would stalk the patient at various locations, would barge into the patient's room and would call the patient names in a hostile and paranoid fashion (e.g. 'backstabber'). D. reported that living in this new convent was so stressful for her that she only slept a few hours per night and had lost 30 lbs in the 2 months she had been living with these new sisters. The first session ended with a discussion of informed consent to treatment, session fees, assessment procedures and involvement of the referral source.

Commentary
Because D. seemed to be experiencing significant levels of frustration and anxiety and because it seemed that she had a need to express these feelings and talk about her current stressful living situation, I decided to let her express these feelings and 'tell her story' over the first few sessions. This is what seemed clinically indicated at the time. Therefore, clinical activities

such as developing a comprehensive list of D.'s problems, having her articu-
late her treatment goals, etc. unfolded in a natural and flexible manner over
the course of the first several sessions.

After D.'s first session, I had a conversation with the referring doctoral-
level psychologist, who was also a Roman Catholic Sister. The referral
source stated that she had seen the patient when her mother had died and
that D. had really taken care of her mother when she was growing up. The
referring psychologist also reported that the patient has had OCD since she
was 14 years old and that she stopped therapy with her previous therapist
(not the referral source) because this therapist wanted D. to take medication
for her OCD.[1] The referring psychologist went on to state that D. was 'very
intense' and frequently complained that 'no one listens to me or understands
me'. The referring psychologist also reported that the Sister who stalked the
patient suffered from paranoid schizophrenia and had at times publically
criticized the patient, causing her to become very upset. Finally, the referral
source reported that D. was excessively exercising, was restricting food, had
a suspected eating disorder and would sit at school for hours and then com-
plain that the principal would not make her leave.

Commentary
One thing that I have learned from working with many sisters is that the
environments in which they live are very intense. They not only live with
several other women in the convents but also must share bathrooms, cars,
cooking duties, meals, etc. There is very little personal property and also
very little private space. The sisters pray together, often more than once a
day, and often work together as well. From my conversation with the
referral source and my first session with D., my first impressions of the
patient were that she too was 'very intense' (i.e. seemed to experience,
demonstrate and communicate her feelings intensely). In addition, D. also
was quite distressed emotionally and had recently experienced multiple
significant stressors (e.g. changing orders, losing two supportive supervi-
sors and moving into a new living situation with critical and threatening
housemates). Furthermore, while there was something I really liked about
D., I wrote in my initial assessment note that she seemed 'unassertive,
sensitive to perceived criticisms and slights and very sensitive in general.'
I hypothesized that given these interpersonal sensitivities and dissatisfac-
tion with her previous therapist and others in her order (e.g. 'nobody
understands me, or listens to me'), our therapeutic relationship was going
to be of critical importance in D.'s treatment. My initial impressions of
D. were about to change significantly over the course of the next two
sessions, however; and while my hypothesis of how important our
therapeutic relationship was going to be in D.'s treatment was accurate, I
*had no idea **how important** it was going to be.*

Session 2

In addition to the aforementioned descriptions of her parents, in the second session, D. began describing what things were like growing up in her home when her mother would have her psychotic episodes. D. reported in *this second session* that when she was 8 or 9 years old she would notice that her mother's psychotic episodes would start with her not taking care of the house. They would then progress to her mother 'being afraid of everything' and then to a state in which she suffered from paranoid delusions and auditory and visual hallucinations. D. reported that when she 'was younger', her mother 'would have to be hospitalized one to two times a year, and by the time she was 8 or 9 years old, her mother could be hospitalized five or six times per year'. The patient reported that she felt sad but relieved when her mother was hospitalized. When I reflected how difficult it must have been to have a mentally ill mother, D. became angry and told me that what was most stressful about her mother's schizophrenia was her father's response when her mother started demonstrating symptoms. The patient went on to state that it was extremely stressful, frustrating and infuriating to have her father not get the severity of her mother's mental state and suffering. He would often criticize the patient for being concerned about her mother, say that 'she was not that bad' and fail to take D.'s mother to her psychiatrist or the hospital when she needed treatment. When I reflected how **invalidating** this must have been for D., she became intensely upset stating that her father was so invalidating that she could not even stand to hear the word '**invalidation**'. We talked further about D.'s anxiety that her mother would get hurt while in one of her psychotic episodes (e.g. by walking out into the street and getting hit by a car or by jumping out of a moving car – something that D.'s mother actually did while in a paranoid state). It seemed, however, that the patient demonstrated the most intense affect when speaking of her attempts to get her father to take her mother's condition seriously, recalling that she would often state 'Come on Dad, aren't you seeing this?'

Finally, towards the end of this second session, the patient presented me with a writing of hers. It was as follows:

> 'D.
> Who needs to be loved
> Wonders about heaven and eternal life
> Believes in feminine images of God
> Often feels misunderstood
> Wishes her Mom didn't have a mental illness
> Is afraid of flying
> Likes to learn about history and philosophy
> Never ate a peanut butter and jelly sandwich

Still can't be by herself all the time
Is a germ freak
Doesn't understand why she's so determined
Gets annoyed when people brag
Makes time for friends
Is trying to be more patient
Regrets trying to live up to other people's expectations
Is thankful for her optimism
Laughs often
Devotes time to the contemplative life
Rarely gets lonely
Hates to be criticized
Can't accept all of the teachings of the Catholic Church
Has a bad habit of skipping ahead to the end of a book
Always tries to do her best
Appreciates nature
Feels guilty about saying things out of frustration
Refuses to believe that there is no cure for OCD
SOMEDAY HOPES TO MAKE SENSE OF HER LIFE'

Commentary
*The first thing that struck me about D.'s poem was how sad it was. Never having eaten a peanut butter and jelly sandwich, such a normal part of an American child's life. The lack of this experience led me to hypothesize that there must have been so many **losses** for D. because of her mother's schizophrenia and her father's inabilities to help the children cope with their mother's mental illness. It also suggests that there were many everyday normal experiences the patient did not get to know (generating the hypothesis that **deprivation** experiences would be a factor in D.'s trauma). In addition, D. would tell me in subsequent sessions of how many holidays and special occasions would also 'be ruined' because her mother typically would have to be hospitalized before such events and how painfully sad and traumatic this was for her (e.g. 'My last memories of my mother before she would be hospitalized was that of a completely disheveled, fearful, frightening woman...that image would be stuck in my mind throughout the holidays'). I further hypothesized that her mother's absence, as well as her father's neglect and lack of sensitivity to what his children needed, contributed to perhaps the most severe type of PTSD for D.: **That of feeling abandoned.** As it turned out, abandonment-themed PTSD flashbacks were one of the most difficult and frequent treatment targets in D.'s therapy, thereby confirming this hypothesis.*

In addition to D.'s losses, sadness, anxiety and suffering, however, my experiences with D. in our first two interviews, showed me her many strengths.[2] *Here was a person who was incredibly resilient and determined given all the traumatic experiences she endured (e.g. 'does not understand why she is so determined...refuses to believe there is no cure for OCD'). Her ability to persevere in the face of so much terror, abandonment, neglect, disappointment and heartbreak enabled D. to survive this traumatic childhood and to accomplish so much. In addition, she was also an original thinker and problem-solver (e.g. 'female images of God...can't accept all of the teachings of the Catholic Church'). Looking back, I am sure that this creativity was one of D.'s strengths that helped her survive and cope with immeasurable trauma from her childhood. Other strengths so apparent also included good interpersonal skills (e.g. 'making time for friends'), optimism, a good sense of humour, intelligence, hard work and ability to enjoy and appreciate learning new things and nature. Without these strengths, it is easy to imagine D. having succumbed to substance abuse or suicide.*

Another primary hypothesis was generated in these first two interviews. This hypothesis was that **invalidation of D.'s experiences, emotions and concerns**, *and the traumatizing and exacerbating effects of this invalidation, was a significant precipitating and maintaining factor in D.'s psychological problems (i.e. D. had experienced damaging invalidation repeatedly growing up in her home and in the convent to which she had just moved). In addition, in the very next session, and many times over the course of our therapy together, D. would have severely upsetting reactions to me, and others, who, at times, inadvertently, invalidated her experiences. These events repeatedly confirmed my hypothesis. As a result, I learned that* **validation of D.'s experience was going to be a critical and essential therapeutic relationship intervention.** *One that not only had both immediate therapeutic benefits by itself (e.g. repaired therapeutic ruptures allowed for the processing of painful emotions and soothed the patient) but also allowed for the implementation of other therapeutic interventions (e.g. exposure, coping skills training and self-care).*

Sessions 3–7

D.'s third session began with her describing traumatic and embarrassing events related to her mother's schizophrenia and her father's invalidation of how mentally ill the mother was. D. reported that her father would often bring her mother out with them, even though it was obvious that her mother was experiencing severe symptoms of schizophrenia ('Dad never seemed to see what the big deal was'). The patient elaborated that she was very fearful that her Mom would scream out, act paranoid or behave in an odd fashion out in public. In addition, D. stated that she was also quite apprehensive of the reactions of those who 'were not used to' psychotic behaviour, fearing that they would be critical of her mother. This was something that the patient's paternal grandmother did quite often (i.e. she would criticize D.'s mother when she demonstrated severely psychotic symptoms, saying the mother was 'just doing it for attention'). The patient further reported that her grandmother was also very critical of how D. did many things around the house (e.g. ironing and cooking). These chores and daily activities were things that the patient had to do at a prematurely young age because of her mother's incapacitating mental disorder and were also tasks D. had to do without ever being shown how to do them. In later sessions, D. reported that her father was also very critical of how she did these chores and that he would invalidate, criticize or beat the patient when she expressed concerns for her mother's mental state or about the lack of food in the house.

Other fears reported by the patient in the third session included those of the family running out of money because of her mother's treatment expenses and of her mother becoming seriously ill because of her heavy cigarette smoking. Finally in this session, D. reported how infuriating it was to have others invalidate her present-day stressors (e.g. being harassed by sisters D. lived with), by attributing the patient's distress to growing up in a difficult situation. 'For some people', D. would state, 'my mother being sick was the magic carpet explanation'.

In sessions 4–7, we assessed the patient's OCD, compiled an initial problem list and identified D.'s goals for treatment. D.'s OCD included four different 'sets' of obsessive–compulsive (OC) symptoms. The first of these featured fears of contamination by germs, rituals (i.e. excessive hand washing – 'till my hands were raw' and washing dishes with 'burning hot water and scrubbing until everything was spotless and germ free') and avoidances (i.e. not eating meat if D. suspected it was undercooked and throwing out food if D. 'even suspected' it was contaminated). These appeared to be the first OC symptoms D. experienced, and therefore the onset of her OCD seems to have occurred when the patient was in third grade (i.e. 8 years old). This was a severely stressful year for the patient. To begin, the patient's maternal grandmother, 'Nanny', died suddenly during this year. This woman had provided much positive attention and nurturing for the patient and had been incredibly supportive and helpful to the patient's mother and the rest of the family. She served the role of a much-needed 'buffer' for the children against the terrifying and traumatic effects of their mother's schizophrenia and their father's invalidation and abuse. The patient stated in this fourth session that when her Nanny died, 'Nobody there to help me, I had to [go through the rest of my childhood] myself'. A second series of stressors were a consequence of the maternal grandmother's passing: The patient's mother started requiring frequent and lengthy hospitalizations. This **exposed the patient to traumas of many kinds: deprivations, abuse, abandonment, criticisms, severe disappointments,** etc. Also in third grade, the patient reported that she suffered a 'huge beating' at the hands of her father. She explained that her father 'beat everybody for something that [her] brother had done'. The patient further stated that she confronted her father that what he had done was illegal – an example of D. already being parentified – and that after this confrontation the subsequent beatings decreased in severity. Other factors in the development of these OCD symptoms appear to have been paternal modelling of ritualistic dish washing and cooking and the patient's father telling D. while she was in a terrified and hyperaroused state (and thereby more vulnerable to traumatic conditioning) that dishes needed to be washed with scalding hot water and that meat had to be cooked excessively. These contamination fears/cleaning rituals waxed and waned but essentially continued into D.'s adulthood.

A second set of OC symptoms involved ordering and straightening out things. Rituals included putting things away in a certain way or in a certain place or doing things in a specific order, a certain number of times, or in a certain way (e.g. the morning routine and packing her school bag). They also included repeating rituals. For instance, while reading or praying, the patient reported that it 'felt like it did not count' if she was not concentrating hard enough or focusing on every single word, so she would 'do it all over again'. These rituals were attempts to neutralize the feeling that things 'were not right/out of control/chaotic/disorganized'. The patient stated that she had to do these rituals 'until it felt right'. Stressors that existed during the onset of these OC symptoms (ages 9–11) included the patient's mother not being home, physical abuse by the father, the absence of the patient's Nanny and the patient's sister and younger brother developing 'emotional troubles'. It was during this time that the patient was pushed into the role of taking care of these siblings, and it was during this time the patient recalled feeling 'that things were out of control in the family, and that [she] felt totally overwhelmed'.

Obsessive fears of somebody dying comprised the third set of OC symptoms and seemed to have their onset around age 14. D. attempted to neutralize these obsessions by performing certain actions in an exact way (e.g. having her foot land in the exact centre of a step while descending a staircase) or by repeating an action to prevent a disaster from occurring. D. reported that she was very ashamed of these obsessive fears and in fact had never told anyone of these fears for the past 26 years; that is, until she told me in this session. Consistent with this, the patient reported that she had also not revealed much of the traumatic events in her life until the start of this therapy. D. further reported that she traced the onset of these feelings of shame to 'around age 12', in response to her *paternal* grandmother saying disparaging things about the patient's mother and 'constantly belittling and criticizing' the patient for how she did various household chores, chores, in fact, that were often developmentally inappropriate for the patient to be doing in the first place (e.g. ironing clothes).

Around this time, D. developed her fourth set of OCD symptoms. Primarily, these symptoms involved D. repeatedly checking to make sure she had done something (e.g. having her keys, putting homework in her school bag, setting her alarm clock, having her money and locking the car door). The patient explained that these checking rituals neutralized the feeling that she had not done something (i.e. 'that it didn't "register" that I had done it'). It also appears that these rituals served the function of ensuring that D. had not made a mistake that she would then be belittled or criticized for.

The severity of D.'s OCD symptoms fluctuated throughout her life, depending on the amount of stress she was under (e.g. 'at times, the OCD was so severe, it took over my life'). The patient described a major exacerbation of these symptoms when she moved into the new convent described above. At this time, D. reported that she 'would be trapped at school doing OCD rituals for hours, not getting home till 9 pm and missing dinner completely'. The aforementioned stressors, 'people yelling at me, blaming me for things I didn't do, giving me way too many jobs to do' and experiencing *invalidation* (i.e. 'no one seemed to understand how stressful this was for me....everyone kept telling me I'd be fine') appeared to fuel the exacerbation of the patient's OCD (and PTSD). It is certainly easy to see how the experiences of being verbally abused, blamed and invalidated would be especially stressful for the patient given her traumatic history of these experiences from her father and father's mother. **In fact, as confirmed by many experiences in her therapy with me, instances where D. felt abandoned, blamed, criticized or invalidated by me were not only stressful for the patient but also triggered PTSD flashbacks for her**. Indeed, these experiences also triggered these flashbacks for the patient during her time at the new convent. The exacerbations of her OCD and PTSD in combination with being cut off from her friends culminated in an inability to sleep, loss of appetite, loneliness, 'crying all the time', headaches, oversensitivity, generalized anxiety/worry and – in an attempt to cope – over exercising. In addition, D. seemed very distressed by the fact that when she was so consumed by various symptoms, 'nobody said anything' – reminiscent of her father's response to her mother.

Commentary
At this point in time, D. seemed to be suffering from severe and complex PTSD manifested by high levels of chronic anxiety; fears of abandonment, invalidation and criticism; flashbacks; dissociation; sleep disturbance; cognitive difficulties; etc. She also obviously was suffering from severe OCD. I hypothesized that D.'s PTSD was her primary and most 'central' problem, with her OCD 'a close second'. I conceptualized D.'s problems in this way because the PTSD-related problems were so pervasive, easily triggered, earlier learned and often incapacitating. In addition, onset of D.'s OCD occurred in

a highly stressful and traumatic environment, and aside from the usual main-
taining factors of anxiety reduction/neutralization of obsessions, D.'s compul-
sive rituals served various functions in her life. For instance, washing and
checking rituals helped her avoid verbal and physical abuse; rituals designed
to reduce the fear of a loved one dying and increase a sense of safety in her life
occurred in an environment where there was an actual risk of her mother or
one of the children dying (e.g. the patient's mother was having command hal-
lucinations to kill her children and the mother threw herself out of a moving
car) and ordering rituals provided a sense of control in a home environment
where things felt dangerous and chaotic, and in which D. felt abandoned.

Comprehensive Problem List

Through the course of the first seven sessions with D. and the completion of
several self-report inventories[3] [e.g. Beck Depression Inventory (Beck, Ward,
Mendelsohn, Mock, & Erbaugh, 1961); Personal Problems Checklist for
Adults (Schinka, 1985)], the following problem list was generated:

1. PTSD – D. had experienced multiple, perhaps countless, traumatic
    events in her life that involved the threat of death, serious injury or loss
    of physical integrity to herself or others (e.g. her mother holding a
    butcher knife over D. as a child and telling D. that 'the voices were tell-
    ing [the mother] to kill D.'; not having food in the house during times
    when D.'s mother was hospitalized; being left alone in the house as a
    child with inadequate food or heat; being beaten by her father and
    witnessing her mother throw herself out of a moving automobile).
    D. responded to these events with intense fear, helplessness and, as
    child, disorganized behaviour. She also demonstrated flashbacks, disso-
    ciation, nightmares, intense psychological distress ('crying fits') and
    physiological reactivity when exposed to PTSD triggers; efforts to avoid
    conversations associated with the traumas; feelings of detachment or
    estrangement from others; sleep disturbance; difficulty concentrating
    and hypervigilance. *Beyond these diagnostic criteria* (Diagnostic
    and Statistical Manual of Mental Disorders; DSM-IV; APA, 1994),
    and clinically more useful, we organized D.'s PTSD into *types of trau-*
    matic experiences. The clinically most important types of trauma for
    D. seemed to revolve around the experiences of **invalidation, abandon-**
    ment and **being criticized.** When D. was triggered by these types of
    experiences, she could dissociate or become completely incapacitated
    for days (e.g. being curled up in the foetal position on the floor). Other
    important types of traumatic experiences that caused intense sadness or
    agitation for D. included experiences that triggered memories and feelings

of **being trapped, neglected or deprived** and **disappointment** ('having special occasions ruined').

2. OCD – D.'s OC symptoms are described in detail above and clearly reflect the themes of trying to prevent disastrous things from happening to her or loved ones and of trying to avoid making mistakes that would lead to physical and/or verbal abuse. In addition, one could hypothesize that another function of D.'s OCD symptoms was to provide a sense of control, predictability or certainty in a world where there was none, on account of her mother's schizophrenia and her father and grandmother's physical and emotional abuse.

3. Severe and chronic anxiety – In addition to the fears and anxieties associated with traumatic memories and triggers and with her OCD, D. suffered a great deal from what she would describe as 'nearly constant high levels of anxiety'. This anxiety appeared to have resulted from the additive and cumulative effects of repeated trauma, constant fears of being criticized, obsessive fears, psychosocial stressors and the experience that D. had to cope with all these threats **completely on her own.**

4. Stressors and the traumatic effects of D.'s recent move and current living situation – As D. wrote in an early therapeutic homework assignment, at the time of her referral to me she had recently 'moved into a new – and hostile – convent and had no supports. [She] repeatedly asked for help, but everyone kept saying not to worry about it and it would be fine.' Specifics of this highly critical and stressful living arrangement are described above, but to me what it most striking is that these experiences mirror D.'s experiences growing up: High levels of **criticism**, the presence of a woman with paranoid schizophrenia and massive **invalidation** of D.'s experience.

5. Moderate to severe levels of depression – D. complained of many depressive symptoms including depressed mood, lowered energy, suicidal ideation, sleep disturbance, tearfulness, feelings of failure and feelings of worthlessness.

6. Post-traumatic symptomatology secondary to being attacked – D. reported that 7 years prior to the start of her therapy with me, another sister, who 'was mentally ill', had tried to kill the patient by strangulation. D. obviously had managed to get away, but she stated that she still experienced flashbacks reminiscent of when D.'s mother had threatened to kill the patient when she was psychotic. D. also reported that she often feared for her safety. Again, the patient complained of a 'lack of response from [her] superiors', when she complained about her safety.

7. Sadness in response to the loss of D.'s previous community – These losses included not only the loss of 'really good friends' but also the loss of opportunities for career advancement (e.g. 'getting to work at the college level').

8. Job dissatisfaction – D. reported that even though she really liked the children that she taught, she was feeling very bored as a sixth grade teacher. She further complained that she 'did not feel challenged at all and had to make an effort not to be bored'.

9. Extreme sensitivity to criticism – Even though this problem area can be easily understood given all the traumatic criticism, verbal abuse and physical beatings D. experienced growing up, D. complained that this was a particularly difficult problem for her. And, as I witnessed multiple times over the course of D.'s therapy with me, perceived criticism by me often set off severe PTSD reactions for the patient (e.g. flashbacks, severe anxiety, dissociation and migraine headaches).

10. 'Emotional eating' – Again, clearly traceable to traumatic experiences growing up, the patient coped with feelings of abandonment and deprivation by bingeing on large amounts of candy and other sweets.

11. 'Misophonia' – D. reported that she experienced an unbearable agitation and anxiety in response to others gulping their drinks or the sounds of others chewing their food. This reaction was so severe for the patient that she either dissociated at the dinner table or had to leave the room where others were eating.

12. Fear of flying – This was especially significant for D. because it prevented her from experiencing many special vacation opportunities that her younger brother could provide for D. because of a perk of his job. The feelings of loss secondary to this flying phobia were compounded by all of the traumatic loss associated with special occasions for D. when she was growing up (e.g. holidays and birthdays when her mother was hospitalized).

D.'s Goals for Therapy

At the beginning of her fourth session, D. provided a written account of her goals for therapy. They were as follows:

- 'Look at my past experiences and identify where healing/integration is still needed and work on accomplishing that.
- Establish alternative and healthier ways to handle my anxiety.
- Grieve the loss of my mother and the loss that comes from leaving my former congregation'.

In addition to the previously stated goals, D. spoke of how frustrated she was with all of the protocols of religious life and how she'd like to work better within that system. She also wished to pursue a more stimulating profession and to 'understand the whole OCD thing better'.

Commentary and Case Formulation

*In these first several sessions, D. described a childhood filled with nearly constant emotional trauma. There were **terrifying and dangerous** events such as her psychotic mother holding a knife over the patient and threatening to kill her. There were repeated **abandonment** experiences secondary to her mother's hospitalizations and her father's inability to provide emotional support, adequate food and heat or explanations for what was happening with the children's mother. There was infuriating **invalidation** of the patient's mother's mental state; of how overwhelming the family situation was and of the needs for adequate food, heat or emotional support. The patient also lived with intense **fears of being beaten, criticized or blamed** if she were to express concerns about her mother's or siblings' emotional states or if she complained about lack of food or other necessities.*

*In addition, D. also experienced 'soul-crushing disappointments' when the patient's mother was not home on holidays, birthdays or special events. Finally, there were high levels of **neglect and deprivation** due to D.'s mother's frequent hospitalizations and her father's inability to compensate for his wife's absences (e.g. by providing adequate physical or emotional support for the children).*

*Given the above, the following **formulation**[4] of D.'s problems was generated:*

The primary psychological mechanisms that appear to determine D.'s problems are intense and severe fears of, and extreme sensitivity to, situations in which she feels abandoned, invalidated or criticized.

Predisposing factors for the development of D.'s difficulties include her mother having paranoid schizophrenia and her father's psychological limitations (e.g. extreme insensitivity to his children's needs, strong tendencies to invalidate D.'s concerns and emotional states and being highly critical and verbally and physically abusive). The combination of these factors exposed D. to a highly stressful home environment characterized by high levels of fear, anxiety, sadness, loss, deprivation, etc. Exposure to these stressors put D.'s nervous system and 'psyche' into an overtaxed and vulnerable state making traumatic conditioning and the onset of mental problems inevitable.

It is not as easy, however, to classify the previously described exposure to multiple chronic traumas as either predisposing or precipitating factors for D.'s problems. Growing up in this traumatic environment appears to have predisposed D. to her traumatic reaction to her recent move, her job dissatisfaction (i.e. from the effects of years of criticism and invalidation) and her misophonia (i.e. an overloaded nervous system making her highly sensitive to the sounds of someone chewing). In addition, exposure to all these traumatic events certainly precipitated D.'s PTSD-related problems (e.g. high levels of chronic anxiety and fears, flashbacks and dissociation when feelings of abandonment, invalidation or criticism were triggered). For some of D.'s problems, however, exposure to these multiple and chronic traumas served as both predisposing and precipitating factors. The overwhelmed emotional state she was in made her more vulnerable to the onset of her OCD. It also necessitated self-soothing via emotional eating. Exposure to these traumas conditioned severe fears and sensitivity to criticism and also resulted in the loss of reinforcers and loss of control over her problems leading to a state of clinical depression.

Maintaining factors for her problems included attempts to cope 'all by herself' with any negative emotion or problem that should arise. This 'hyper-independence' was due to conditioned fears of being retraumatized by being exposed to abandonment, invalidation, or criticism should she seek help or express a concern. Other maintaining factors include dissociation (i.e. a severe form of avoidance of overwhelming emotional distress), being unable to express her traumatic feelings and memories, and OC rituals and avoidances.

*Because **the most important determinants of D.'s problems seemed to be these fears and sensitivities to feeling abandoned, invalidated or criticized;** because these fears were of an interpersonal nature and learned via her experiences with her parents and because **D. was incredibly alone in her efforts to manage her distress, I hypothesized that the most important factor in D.'s treatment was going to be our therapeutic relationship.** I also hypothesized that various relationship interventions (e.g. validation, 'being there for D.' [i.e. the opposite of abandoning her]) were going to be critical components of treatment as well.*

As such, the formulation-guided treatment plan, of which a formulation-guided therapeutic relationship was the most important intervention, was as follows:

*D. would need a validating, noncritical and constant therapeutic relationship due to the many traumas and losses she experienced in her relationships with her mother and father.[5] This relationship would need to psychologically 'hold' the patient as she got treatment for her OCD, worked through her PTSD, learned how to cope with flashbacks, grieved her many losses, learned how to cope with negative emotions rather than engaging in emotional eating and pursued a higher academic degree and more stimulating career. What followed these initial sessions was a 6-year behaviourally oriented psychotherapy that did exactly that. In addition, as D.'s therapy progressed, it became apparent that the therapeutic relationship not only helped the patient benefit from nonrelationship interventions but also various **relationship interventions were actually the most important interventions in D.'s treatment.***

Response to Formulation-Guided Relationship and Initial Nonrelationship Interventions

As consistent with the case formulation, but genuinely and naturally, I took care to listen closely to D. and validate whenever I could what it must have been like for her as she described various traumatic events from her childhood or recent past. I also made sure to validate how awful her present-day OCD and/or PTSD symptoms were. In addition, I took care to convey an affirming attitude towards D. rather than a critical or blaming one. As will be described later in this case study, however, there were many times in which I inadvertently triggered intense and prolonged PTSD reactions in D. by saying or doing something she perceived as invalidating and/or critical or blaming of her. These 'clinical mistakes' served to be important learning experiences for both of us and nearly always therapeutic growth experiences for the patient.

In D.'s fourth session, she expressed satisfaction with our therapeutic relationship and positive feelings about me (e.g. 'Really liked [PGA]'; '... exactly what she looked for in a therapist.... pleasantly surprised actually... smart but understands what [she] is saying' (i.e. **validation**). Also in this session, we worked on D.'s frustration with her supervisors for not helping her out with her convent situation. Again, care was taken to express validation of D.'s feelings of frustration. Also, feedback was given to the patient that it made '**perfect sense**' that she would have such an intense reaction to her supervisors' responses to her situation given her childhood experiences with her father and paternal grandmother (e.g. D.'s father often seemed 'oblivious' to the emotional needs of the family and in denial of the severity of D.'s mother's psychosis; her grandmother often came up with solutions that made things emotionally stressful and worse for D's mother [i.e. **invalidating** and **unsupportive**]). Labelling these reactions as 'PTSD reactions', a form of conditioned emotional responses (CERs), was also helpful to the patient.

As reported above, in sessions 4–7, assessment of D.'s OCD was conducted. In addition, initial treatment interventions for the patient's OCD were also implemented (e.g. psychoeducation about the disorder as per Freeston & Ladouceur, 1997; Meyer & Levy, 1973). D. reported in her seventh session that it was very helpful to have the mechanisms of OCD explained to her (e.g. negative reinforcement of ritualistic behaviour via the reduction of anxiety, that OCD sufferers can learn that their anxiety will come down on 'it's' own if they can resist performing rituals). She also stated that she was 'very grateful' to be able to tell me about her OCD. It also seemed that it was extremely important to D. that I understood the severity of her OCD symptoms (e.g. 'At times, they took over my life'). I conceptualized this need for me to 'understand how bad things could be' as consistent with the case formulation: That is, it was traumatic for D. to have her father **invalidate** how bad things were for D.'s mother and the children.

Commentary and D.'s Response to Treatment of Her OCD
Approximately 2 months after the start of therapy, D. reported that her OCD was significantly improved; this being so without any formal exposure or response prevention sessions having been conducted. D. reported that understanding the determinants of the disorder and its maintaining factors (e.g. negative reinforcement of ritualistic behaviour) were very useful interventions for her. In addition, interventions such as accepting the presence of obsessive thoughts without trying to neutralize them (i.e. response prevention) were reported to be useful by D. What appeared to be especially important in the treatment of D.'s OCD were actually **relationship interventions**. *D. stated that 'just hearing that [PGA] knew what OCD was, and how to treat it, was a 'Huge Miracle' for (her)' (i.e. she was* **not alone** *with her problem). The patient also reported that for her, PGA telling her that she 'did not have to do her rituals' was 'extremely helpful'. To me, these interventions worked so well because they followed the case formulation. In fact, the way D. stated that I told her she did not have to do her rituals seemed very much like what a child would say (i.e. 'My Dad told me I didn't have to do them anymore'). This advice also occurred in the context of a safe and secure therapeutic relationship.*

Natural follow-ups on D.'s progress with her OCD indicated that the disorder improved steadily over the course of the next year of D.'s therapy. At times, the patient reported that she was conducting what amounted to self-directed exposure and response prevention 'all day long' (e.g. packing her gym bag without checking). The bulk of the in-session activities during this year focused on treatment of PTSD (e.g. writing about and processing painful emotions and memories) and on relationship interventions – especially ones made necessary by in-session events triggering PTSD reactions. Both the patient's PTSD symptoms and our relationship improved over the course of this year. I believe that decreasing the patient's PTSD symptoms and increasing her sense of having a good therapeutic relationship in which she felt validated, secure and 'backed-up' gave her the security to more confidently attack her OCD. D.'s report confirmed this hypothesis.

Treatment of D.'s PTSD

As per Meichenbaum (2006), between the eleventh and twelfth sessions, D. constructed a time line of the various traumas in her life. This time line reflected D's energy and creativity – it was made of poster board and was 10 feet long and 18 inches wide! On this time line were the many significant traumatic 'events' that D. had experienced in her life. 'Events' is in quotation marks because many of these traumatic experiences were not single events but rather variable and chronic traumatic events that D. repeatedly experienced in her childhood (e.g. coughing up blood for 2 years between the ages of 8 and 10 without her father ever taking D. to a physician [**neglect**]; repeated exposure to a mother deteriorating into psychosis and not being home for holidays [**abandonment, terror** and **disappointment**]; repeatedly being told everything was OK when her mother was exhibiting mentally ill or dangerous behaviours, when siblings were exhibiting emotionally disturbed behaviours or when there was inadequate food or heat in the house [**invalidation** and **abandonment**]).

Meichenbaum (2006) has stated after decades of research with PTSD that 'the single most important factor for humans in overcoming a traumatic event is to have a sympathetic listener to "tell the story" to'. This 'telling of the story' is present in most empirically supported treatments for PTSD (e.g. exposure therapies [Boudewyns & Hyer, 1990; Foa, Hembree, & Rothbaum, 2007] and cognitive processing therapy [Resick & Schnicke, 1992]). The time line provides an excellent vehicle for which the patient's story can be told, listened to and validated. In addition to the time line, D. and I made great use of therapeutic writing and journaling throughout the course of her therapy.[6] The writing served several purposes: First, it enabled the patient to write about various traumatic events in her life, have me read what she had written and then discuss and process these painful memories in session. Often, part of this process is to have the patient read aloud an account of a traumatic event in order to facilitate exposure to previously avoided memories and feelings. A modification of this technique seemed to work better for D.'s therapy. This modification was for me to read what she had written and have us discuss the material. **Consistent with the case formulation**, I think this worked well because of the need for D. **to be able to tell another person** of her horrors and to have that person listen to and **validate** her experience. It was also an essential part of D.'s healing (i.e. 'new learning') **to not have to go through all of these terrible experiences 'on her own'** (i.e. not be abandoned with all of the horror). An interesting bit of clinical data from these writings that supports this hypothesis and that **underscores this writing as a therapeutic relationship intervention** was that every single one of these therapeutic writings was written to me [PGA]. That is, the writings were addressed to me or had my name in them, as though the patient was *telling me* what she had experienced.[7] In addition, I had no concerns about avoidance of traumatic memories as D. did yeoman's work getting exposed to the painful feelings and memories when she wrote about them between sessions. Finally, at one point in her therapy, D. constructed her 'PTSD book'. This book had pages and illustrations for nine different types of PTSD experiences (i.e. 'themes'; for instance, abandonment, shame, deprivation, danger and 'lost my mind'). This book was not only useful for talking about and processing various traumatic memories in session but also provided D. with a coping tool between sessions (e.g. by helping the patient correctly identify and label various reactions and flashbacks as PTSD-related CERs rather than threatening events in her present-day life).

Other key interventions that were implemented throughout D.'s therapy included psychoeducation about PTSD in general and the patient's personal PTSD reactions specifically (e.g. triggering events, dissociative or terrified reactions and flashbacks); skills training for coping with flashbacks (e.g. grounding techniques and 'inner child' imagery); judicious and supportive pharmacotherapy[8] and maintaining a 'safe' therapeutic relationship. That is, a relationship in which D. did not feel **invalidated, criticized** or **abandoned.** Unfortunately, these PTSD reactions *were* triggered multiple times in the course of D.'s therapy by innocuous or (very) well-intentioned statements or behaviours on my part. At times, these reactions were so painful, intense or prolonged (i.e. 'retraumatizing') for D. that it was difficult for her to continue her treatment.[9]

Thankfully, D. persevered in her therapy. And fortuitously, these 'retraumatizing' events turned out to be extremely important new learning experiences for D. (and myself). **In fact, it seemed that these events and their processing were perhaps the most important, powerful and therapeutic components of D.'s treatment.** While these events probably happened dozens of times over the course of D.'s therapy, examples of some of the most important ones are presented below.

Examples of Invalidation

As discussed above, it seemed that the experience of invalidation, particularly from D.'s father, was an especially toxic phenomenon for the patient. It created much frustration, aggravation and anger for the patient when she was an adolescent and young adult. Her father's invalidation of D.'s concerns about her mother's psychotic state also led to terrifying and traumatizing experiences for D. (e.g. D.'s mother speaking of people coming to kill the family; her standing over D. with a butcher knife telling the patient that the voices were telling the mother to kill D. and D.'s mother trying to throw herself out of a moving car when the family was driving the patient to college). Another terrifying period in D.'s life that was a consequence of her father's invalidation occurred during the patient's childhood after she was diagnosed with asthma and allergies. D. reported that her father stated that 'D. doesn't have asthma and everyone has allergies'. The patient wrote of how traumatizing this was for her, 'Sometimes at night when I couldn't breathe, I used to stay awake because I thought if I fell asleep I wouldn't be able to make sure I was breathing, and I could die'.

A striking example of D.'s experiences having been invalidated and the powerful effects of corrective validation by me occurred about 3 months into the patient's treatment. D. reported that until age five or six she had done everything with her left hand. Once she began writing in school, her father 'made [her] become right-handed because he said, "You're not left-handed. You can't be because no one in our family is left-handed"'. D.'s father's insistence that D. was right-handed led to high levels of frustration, confusion and humiliation for the patient in academic and athletic endeavours and made doing her chores around the house a traumatic experience (e.g. getting verbally and/or physically abused for being clumsy and burning herself while ironing clothes). For approximately 35 years, D. lived her life as a right-handed person. After a few sessions of discussing the effects of her father's invalidation of her left-handedness, I suggested that D. gradually start doing things with her left hand. After some initial anxiety about 'dropping all of the right-handed behaviours', D. experienced an incredible easing of doing many things in her life. Writing, cooking, working and daily activities felt much more natural and less tension-filled. The patient also reported that she experienced some sort of 'neuropsychological shift' after returning to do things with her left hand, 'It was as though the whole world was reorganized, and I could see things more naturally – everything [perceptually] seemed to make sense'. In addition, D. also reported that once she 'acknowledged [her] left-handedness, [she] immediately knew for the *first time in [her] life, [her] left from [her] right'*.

Because it seemed clear to me that D. became very upset when she felt invalidated[10] and because of her history of traumatic invalidation, I made sure to demonstrate validating behaviours consistently with D. I borrowed, and used liberally, Linehan's (1993) phrase 'that makes perfect sense' (i.e. D.'s feelings, behaviours and thoughts made perfect sense in the context of her history and current life situation). I listened and demonstrated empathy for the patient's experience. I also made sure I demonstrated that I understood, accepted and did not judge D.'s feelings and perceptions. As such, there were not as many severely frustrating or retraumatizing 'invalidation events' in our therapy. Two types that did occur, however, were (1) when I overemphasized a scientific or psychological explanation for one of D.'s reactions without returning to her feelings and (2) when early on in D.'s treatment, she would be telling me of negative experiences in her life and she felt that I was not seeing the severity of these situations. In the first of these scenarios, D. felt that I was minimizing her distress, even though she knew 'this bothered [her] because [her father] intellectualized absolutely everything, and that always felt like he was minimizing my thoughts, feelings, and needs'. A second type of event occurred primarily because of the patient's learned fears of showing that she was upset about something (i.e. she was invalidated and/or verbally or physically abused if she showed she was upset about something important). After many instances of D. feeling that I 'did not get' the severity her complaints, the patient and I had an interesting discussion. D. reported that she often felt that she was 'screaming out' her distress. My perception of the patient at these very same times, however, was that she actually appeared euthymic. As with other types of PTSD reactions, D.'s writing proved very useful in pointing out to me what I was inadvertently doing to trigger her invalidation reactions.

Examples of Abandonment

D. had experienced so much abandonment in her life. Often, this was triggered by her mother disappearing into a psychiatric hospitalization or her father being unreachable at work when D. had to cope with a psychotic mother or having inadequate food in the house. It made perfect sense, therefore, that events during the course of our therapy such as vacations; missed sessions because of holidays, conferences (PGA) or retreats (D.) or even the time between sessions when D. did not see me would often trigger 'abandonment PTSD' reactions for the patient. These reactions were extremely painful for D. and were characterized by an intense dissociative state/flashback she poignantly described as follows:

'*I'm in a gray, rectangular square that stretches on to infinity...I'm in the middle of it, no one can hear me. No one can see me, because no one knows I'm there. No one can help me. I think my Mom is far away...she is looking my way. And I'm outside...and there is no strong feeling, and there's no talking; nobody has anything to say, and I'm probably only 4. I'm going to be there a long time in that state – in that gray void – for a long time. Sometimes if I scream, sometimes nobody can hear me, and my Mom doesn't say anything*'.

This was obviously one of the saddest, despairing PTSD reactions the patient experienced and one that still registers today as I write this. We worked assiduously on this reaction in D.'s therapy using emotional processing and therapeutic relationship interventions (see below). Other experiences often present in D.'s abandonment reactions included anger and rage at PGA in response to feeling that I knew she was suffering but would not reach out to help her; depressing flashbacks of not knowing where her mother was and an intense feeling of disconnection from PGA or feeling as though PGA 'did not exist'. These reactions seemed clearly to be CERs related to D.'s experiences when her mother was hospitalized. The patient reported that when her mother was in the hospital she missed her terribly and often did not know where her mother was hospitalized. In addition, the patient's father often did not allow the children to telephone or visit their mother. The patient also knew that her mother was often so psychotic that she may have forgotten about her children or had little psychological resources available to her to think of them very much. D. often coped with these intensely painful feelings by disconnecting emotionally.

Given the interpersonal nature of abandonment, it is easy to see that therapeutic relationship strategies would prove to be very valuable. With regards to missed sessions due to vacations, etc., two relationship strategies seemed especially effective. The first of these was called 'The Reconnection List'. Because two painful aspects about D.'s mother's hospitalizations were that D. did not get to share life experiences with her Mom *and* did not get to know what her mother was experiencing while she was hospitalized. The following two items were included on 'The List'. The first was for D. to tell me some of the 'highlights and lowlights' from her life during the time which we did not meet. The second was that I would tell D. one highlight from my time away. Other items on the list included D. writing down daily activities and progress reports on therapeutic or personal goals and sharing these with me upon resumption of our sessions. And of course, the first item on the list was always to greet D. with a hug after a prolonged absence.[11]

A few months after the implementation of The Reconnection List, D. asked me if I could tell her where I went on vacation in order to counteract feeling abandoned, adrift in the grey unknown and PTSD flashbacks of not knowing where her mother was when she was hospitalized.[12] Because I did not answer immediately, feelings of shame, humiliation and hurt feelings were triggered in D. These feelings were processed over several sessions. In addition, many of our therapy experiences were reviewed in which I always worked very hard to help D. and demonstrated my caring for her. During these discussions, D. realized, and then stated, that '[PGA] had never let her down'. After the next break in therapy (the Christmas holidays), D. reported that her abandonment reactions had improved 85–90%. This improvement seemed clearly related to our hard work together, and, *especially to the relationship interventions* described above.

Another extremely distressing, and at times incapacitating, reaction that D. experienced in her life were those of multiple PTSD reactions occurring 'on top of each other' (see 'in crisis' reactions below). At times, these reactions were also triggered in our therapy. To explain, a 'Criticism PTSD' reaction could be triggered by a meant-to-be-helpful, innocuous comment or facial expression on my part. Then, despite my best efforts to relieve the reaction, D. would leave the session still triggered and have to go home and cope with the reaction 'on [her] own'. This would set off a cascade of other PTSD reactions, one piling on top of the other: feeling that her suffering was being ignored, on top of abandonment, on top of being told there was something wrong with her.

A few sessions before D. was able to render that poignant description of 'Lost in the Grey', she spoke of how extremely sad, depressing and disappointing it was to not have her mother home for the Christmas holidays. She also started having the emergence of memories of being abandoned 'in the grey' but could not yet articulate them. Around this time, the patient reported experiencing intense fear and a feeling of being out of control. Despite my best efforts to help her, D.'s experience of a key session was that I did not recognize how hard she was trying to cope and instead felt criticized by me. This set off the cascade described above. Through a series of phone messages and sessions, D. described how much she hated leaving a session upset,[13] '...the worst part about it is that I feel completely **abandoned**. That's what sets off the PTSD hell'. Also through these sessions, we identified many interventions, most of them relationship interventions, that helped with these reactions. These interventions included the following:

- Labelling intense reactions as PTSD (e.g. 'if it's really intense, it's PTSD')
- Reminding herself that she is 'not in this alone, that [PGA] is in this with me, and we'll figure it out together'
- Reminding herself that she 'does not have to do this on her own'
- Using her PTSD book
- PGA saying to D., 'I know you're upset, if you don't feel better in a little while, I want you to call me so we can finish talking about this. Remember you are not alone'
- Validating for the patient, 'that must be horrible; but I'm in it with you, and we'll figure it out'
- Reminding herself that whenever there are extreme reactions, 'it's PTSD, but we are fine' (i.e. the therapeutic relationship).
- PGA calling D. after an upsetting session to see how she was doing[14]

The patient reported that the above interventions were extremely helpful to her and specifically stated that it was 'especially helpful to hear that [PGA] wanted to help [her] with this... that [she] did not have to cope with it all on [her] own(**not abandoned**)... that [she] did not have to know how to cope, was never taught how to cope, but now was learning it from [PGA]... that we'd figure it out, even if we did not know what would help at this moment(**not abandoned**)... and that [she] felt better because [PGA] really understood her situation'(**validated**).

Examples of Feeling Judged, Criticized or Blamed

Approximately 1 year after the start of D.'s therapy, she requested that I sit next to her on the couch in my office to discuss what she had written about traumatic memories. Up until this point in her treatment, D. had sat in a chair across from me. Given the patient's extreme sensitivity to rejection and perceived criticism, I sat next to her on the couch. D. sat significantly closer to me than I had expected. Later in the session, the patient stated that she had often leaned up against her mother as she slept on the couch, 'drugged up' from her antipsychotic medication. D. also revealed that there was a complete lack of physical affection from her father. For several weeks prior to this session, D. had done courageous work processing traumatic memories from the 'hardest time in [her] life' (ages 7–13). D. reported that her mother was often psychotic during this time and was often hospitalized, triggering intense feelings of **fear, abandonment** and **sadness** in the patient. She also stated that she was not allowed to tell anyone that her mother was mentally ill or in the hospital (**shame**). D. also reported that during this time her father constantly criticized the patient's appearance and would hit D. if she complained about being hungry or for the way she performed household chores (**criticism** and **abuse**). D. also reported that she was told during this time that she was not left-handed and was forced to do everything with her right hand and she was also told whenever she told her father that her mother needed to go to the hospital that she 'did not know what she was talking about' (**invalidation** and **frustration**). *I understood her request to sit next to me on the couch as needing a sense of safety as she continued to do this work and as also a function of unmet needs for physical comfort and affection during her childhood. I was not exactly correct.*

In the next session, D. again requested that I sit next to her on the couch in order to help her talk specifically about traumatic memories associated with her mother. And again D. sat quite close to me on the couch (about 15 inches from me). I offered an interpretation that perhaps D. felt like she needed to sit that close to me because of unmet needs in her relationship with her mother. D. bristled in response to my interpretation and seemed to shut down emotionally. Obviously, she felt **criticized and judged to have behaved inappropriately.**[15] I apologized for any perceived criticism and the poor timing of my interpretation, and this seemed to help D. reconnect a bit. It was her writing about these issues and our processing of these traumatic memories over the next several sessions, however, that proved to be much more therapeutic for the patient.

Through in-session discussions and poignant and impressive therapeutic writing done between sessions, D. explained that she 'just needed to be closer to [PGA] when she was trying to relay an extremely painful and traumatizing memory about [her] Mom.' She would subsequently reveal, and we would process, horrific memories of D. being 4–6 years old and believing what her mother said about people coming to kill D.'s mother, D. and the rest of her family. *The patient explained that one reason she sat so close to me when processing these horrific memories was that as a child she was unable to share her fears and worries with her mother for fear that it would overwhelm her mother, become part of her psychosis and trigger a full-blown psychotic episode.* To cope with her own terror and stress, D. would lean up against her mother for comfort and try to think of a solution to her problems. D. elaborated that this provided her with the only sense of **safety** she had her 'whole life until [she] started therapy with [PGA]'. Another reason why D. wanted to sit so close to me while processing these memories was related to the prohibition against talking to others about the mother's mental illness. There was so much conditioned shame for D. about her mother's schizophrenia. D. wrote that sitting in close proximity made talking about all these traumas easier because 'it's too much too reveal all the shame and secrecy I've carried my whole life by blabbing it across the room!! When I sit closer to you, I don't talk as loudly and it makes me feel like only you can hear it, not anyone else'. Sitting closer also provided sort of a *graduated exposure* to the traumatic material in that when D. whispered about the traumatic events they seemed less real at first and therefore less overwhelming.

Commentary
*As can be seen above, the therapeutic relationship intervention of honouring D.'s request to sit close to her on the couch as we processed the most horrific of her PTSD memories proved to be extremely therapeutic for D. Most importantly, it provided the patient with a **sense of safety** when discussing dangerous and terrifying events. It also provided a sense that it was normal and healthy to discuss her mother's mental illness without feeling ashamed of it. These discussions, with me seated next to D. on the couch, went on for several months, until she no longer needed that proximity to help her process traumatic memories. I doubt if we could have done this processing without this relationship intervention.*

A second example of feeling judged and criticized occurred approximately 4 years after the start of D.'s therapy. At that time, the patient began pursuing her doctorate in education (Ed.D.). While D. was working on her Methods Section for her dissertation, she left me a voicemail asking me if I could work on the section with her (i.e. be interviewed as an expert in the area). Naturally, this triggered a conflict within me as it represented a boundary crossing (i.e. me being in the role of D.'s therapist and in the role of informal advisor on her dissertation). I answered D.'s voicemail in the most gentle and sensitive way that I could. I told her that I did not want her to feel that she had done anything wrong by making her request and that 'most likely this would be OK'. I also stated, however, that since my helping her on her dissertation represented a boundary crossing (see Knapp & Van de Creek, 2012), I thought we should think about her request and talk about it in our next session. This triggered an intense, overwhelming PTSD reaction for the patient, the theme of which seemed to be **feeling criticized and told there was something deeply wrong with her**. D. explained in session that my comments about a possible boundary crossing triggered thoughts that she 'needs too much, expects too much, wants too much, is too much of a problem and is annoying PGA too much'. Reframing her reaction as PTSD and a CER from her being emotionally abused, providing corrective feedback and appropriate self-disclosure of how much I cared for D. and **asking D. to bring to session what she wanted me to see in her Methods Section** seemed to be very helpful to the patient. After this session, D. left me another voicemail stating 'How helpful the session had been', and that she had some 'new insights' about [the severity] of this PTSD reaction – a level of severity D. described as being 'in crisis'.

In our next session, D. presented another example of her good use of therapeutic writing. It described what the patient experienced when she was 'in crisis'. Her words are as follows:

'A typical PTSD episode for me has the regular stuff, like overwhelming anxiety/depression, flashbacks, just sitting and staring for long periods of time, inability to sleep, crying, lack of concentration and/or dissociation, headaches or migraines, etc. When I use the phrase 'in crisis' ....my whole body goes into **convulsions** or something....I begin to feel really cold... I start shaking uncontrollably...my body feels so stiff that's it's almost impossible to move...the feelings that infuse and permeate these convulsions are twofold – I LITERALLY FEEL SHOCKED AND PETRIFIED COMBINED....the only thing that seems to help is when I pile a bunch of blankets and pillows on top of me...the weight...makes me feel safer, and after a while the convulsions do subside....I'm thinking it has something to do with childhood experiences where I felt shocked and petrified, and God knows there are a million of those in my past, right?!?!...Thanks again for listening ...I know it's your interest in me and your desire to hear what I have to say that enabled me to write this paper....I'm beginning to realize that many things I thought were just 'D.' are really PTSD, and that makes me feel relieved'.

Once again, **relationship factors proved vital in D.'s therapy** – 'it's your interest in me and your desire to hear what I have to say that enabled me to write this paper'. We discussed these extreme reactions that included curling up in a foetal position and shaking, and D. reported that she was convinced that they were a response to a real-life traumatic childhood event. I hypothesized that her reactions reflected an experience in which she felt attacked, perhaps emotionally or physically, and in which she seemed to fear for her safety. And as simple as it sounded, we agreed that one of the most useful coping skills for D. to implement when she was 'in crisis' was to call me and say 'I'm in crisis'. Again, a **relationship intervention** in that this provided new learning that someone would be there for her and **validate** the emotional distress she was experiencing. In addition, over the next several sessions, I agreed to have D. 'interview me' for her dissertation. This seemed therapeutic for the patient as it provided a new learning experience in the context of an important relationship and also seemed to be, for lack of a better word, *healing* for the patient.

Commentary
The power of the therapeutic relationship and relationship-based interventions can be seen in the above examples. As emphasized by Kohlenberg and Tsai (1991) in their Functional Analytic Psychotherapy, the therapeutic relationship provides a powerful opportunity for clinical change, therapeutic growth and new learning for the patient (and therapist). This is because of the immediate and natural interpersonal reinforcement that can occur between the patient and the therapist (i.e. the 'within-session contingencies'). In addition, Meyer and Liddell (1975) advocated for an individualized therapeutic relationship based on the clinician's formulation of the patient, as did AuBuchon and Malatesta (1998) in their 'therapist-style' publication.

The terrifying and incapacitating 'in crisis' reactions that D. experienced did not stop occurring, however, until about 5 months later. A series of events over the span of 6 weeks proved to be some of the most important in D.'s therapy and captured several of the most important themes to D.'s PTSD (e.g. criticism/being told there was something wrong with her; abandonment and neglect and disappointment). These events also provided valuable opportunities to make extremely meaningful progress on these traumas and severe symptoms. (They also demanded extremely hard work from me.)

Examples of Combined Abandonment, Being Criticized and Disappointment

Things started with D. asking me if I could again help her with another aspect of her dissertation (i.e. the Institutional Review Board [IRB] questionnaire regarding interview questions and informed consent). I actually helped the patient in that session by answering some of these questions in a general way, but I apparently had a thoughtful look on my face as I heard her request. D. experienced a 'being criticized or being told there was something wrong with her PTSD reaction' in response to my facial expression and angrily stated 'Forget it! I'll never bring it up again in session, and just talk to other psychologists!' In addition, the patient left me a voicemail after the session letting me know she was "in crisis"' and was enraged that 'another special day had been ruined' and also that I 'did not call her after the session to see how she was doing'. A series of voicemails were exchanged with validation and an apology from me about triggering her PTSD. In addition, a phone session was agreed upon, as D. reportedly was too afraid to be retraumatized again if she showed up for our next face-to-face session. **Perhaps, the most important thing I did, however, was to communicate to D. that I 'hated it when she felt so bad'.**

In the phone session and in several face-to-face sessions that followed, it became clear that D. had experienced a sequence of several types of PTSD reactions. The first, a **'being told there was something wrong with me'**, was triggered by the thoughtful look on my face. Then because the session ended, D. had to leave with that PTSD reaction, which in turn triggered the experience of having to **'deal with feeling traumatized all by myself (abandonment, invalidation and neglect)'**. This was an experience D. knew all too well. The patient reported that many times in her life, she had approached her father about a serious, stressful or terrifying problem only to be ignored, invalidated and **'left to cope with the problem completely on [her] own'**. D. further explained that when she was in one of these reactions she often thought that I knew that she was suffering and yet *would not* help her (e.g. 'This is killing me and you're not helping me'). A third type of PTSD reaction, **'another special day was ruined' (disappointment and loss)**, was also triggered. These reactions as well as relevant traumatic childhood events, coping skills and therapeutic relationship interventions were all discussed and implemented. During one of these sessions, D. explained that it 'seemed impossible' for her to call for support when she was experiencing these reactions, due to the nearly incapacitating symptomatology described above and high levels of shame associated with asking for help. As such, D. requested that if I thought she was upset after a session that I would call her and see how she was doing. Even though in some cases this type of behaviour on the part of a therapist might reinforce excessive dependency and confusion with a patient, I decided to honour D.'s request. This decision was based on clinical need, the case formulation and because when I had honoured these types of requests in the past (e.g. sitting next to D. on the couch, providing a few minor details about my vacation and the dissertation interview), things worked out well. That is, D. usually made therapeutic progress, only needed the request granted once or for a short period of time and never demonstrated 'needy' behaviour in these situations.[16]

The honouring of D.'s request and actually calling her after a session in which I believed she was very upset was one of several important interventions that occurred over the course of these several weeks. I believe it **demonstrated** to D. that I indeed did care about her emotional state, wanted to help her with her problems and would not abandon her. In addition, as with other requests in the past, D. made progress in this area also. Soon she was able to call for support when she was distressed and eventually progressed to the point where she did not even need a call back from me – just letting me know what was going on, and trusting that I cared about her, was enough.

While I did consult with colleagues about the appropriateness of my helping D. with the IRB questionnaire,[17] **I also did help the patient in session with her questions.** This seemed to be the third of several powerful relationship interventions that proved to be extremely therapeutic for the patient. The first was **communicating to D. that I 'hated it when she felt bad'**. The second was **calling her when I suspected that she was having a PTSD reaction.**[18]

The **power of these relationship interventions** became clear several months after these events and intense sessions. At that time, D. reported that she 'did not dissociate anymore and actually sort of missed it'. The patient also reported that this was incredible progress as she had 'spent most of her waking hours' since childhood in a dissociated state. D. also reported that '[she] had not had a major PTSD reaction, nor been "in crisis", [since these sessions]'. **It seemed that D.'s PTSD reactions to being judged, abandoned and left to cope on her own had all greatly improved.** Of course, I interviewed the patient about this remarkable progress, in hopes of identifying the critical factors that led to such improvement. D. answers demonstrated that these gains were **directly attributable to relationship interventions.** The patient stated that she 'knew that [PGA] does not want her to feel bad, would not let her down and would not abandon her'. The patient also reported that '[PGA] was much more relaxed with and in our relationship... was way calmer... that there was no anxiety in [his] reactions to [D.], and was more accepting of what [the patient] said [and requested]'. It appeared that my genuine communications to D. that I hated it when she felt bad, my willingness to endure some therapeutic boundary crossings and my willingness to reach out to the patient when she had difficulty reaching out to me provided D. with new learning experiences that helped significantly decrease her severe PTSD.

Commentary
*While there were many different types of traumas that D. experienced in her life, **the combined traumas of being criticized/judged, with that of being abandoned, proved to be the most traumatic and damaging for the patient.** D. experienced this '1–2 punch' of trauma multiple times in her life and had had this type of combined PTSD reaction (including flashbacks) triggered many times as an adult. Not long after D. and I worked through the combined reaction described above, the patient reported a very interesting insight about why being criticized had become so traumatizing for her. D. explained that her father and paternal grandmother had been the ones who criticized her the most. The occurrence of these criticisms, because they were often about how D. would perform chores and/or for her expressions of concern for her mother, meant that D.'s mother 'was not there'. That is, 'she was either very impaired or hospitalized'. The patient further stated that the **traumas of being criticized and abandoned 'became fused together'.** The patient explained that 'Their criticism made it real that my mother was not there'. Based on classical conditioning therefore, it's easy to see how the experience of being criticized became traumatic via association with the*

*trauma of abandonment. In addition, the experience of being criticized could also trigger the conditioned response of feeling abandoned and/or PTSD abandonment flashbacks, thereby setting off the combined reaction described above. Given the severity of D.'s reactions (e.g. curled up in a foetal position and shaking uncontrollably for hours) and given her response to our work together (e.g. stopped having severe PTSD reactions; stopped dissociating and marked decreases in hypervigilance), **it appeared to me that the most central and important component of D.'s PTSD treatment was the use of relationship interventions when PTSD reactions were triggered within the therapeutic relationship.** This seems to be where the most important work was done – within the therapeutic relationship. The relationship interventions described above (e.g. validation, nurturing and reaching out to the patient when she was unable to reach out to me) were critical in this psychotherapy. They were also generated and guided by the case formulation. That is, D. would need a therapeutic relationship in which she felt cared for, nurtured and validated, and one in which she did not feel criticized, shamed or abandoned while she processed traumatic memories and feelings as well as worked on her other problems (e.g. OCD, emotional eating and fear of flying). The patient's self-report confirmed this hypothesis:*

'When I came to see you, and a big part of my therapy, was learning to put words on my traumatic memories and painful feelings. Because I could trust you within our therapeutic relationship, I could take major risks in my therapy, without knowing what the ramifications might be, and say things or ask for things, that I didn't understand – only because I knew you wouldn't abandon me and you'd help me figure it out and make sense of it all. I guess what I'm saying is my lack of words for my trauma and my conditioned sense of shame and secrecy were overcome by the security of our relationship.'

Progress to Date

D. has made remarkable progress over the past 6 years. Looking back at her initial problem list helps us organize and review all of her clinically significant gains. Starting with the patient's PTSD, D.'s treatment gains in this area are many and are extremely meaningful. The patient's severe PTSD reactions and flashbacks no longer occur. The remaining PTSD reactions the patient does experience are 'far less severe', and when they do occur, the patient reports that she 'knows that [she is] seeing things through historical eyes' (i.e. that she can separate the PTSD reaction from what is happening in her present-day life and in the therapeutic relationship). D. estimates that her abandonment PTSD reactions are '95% improved'. The patient further reports that currently when PTSD reactions are triggered, she knows that these feelings will pass and that she uses her coping skills and tools effectively (e.g. the PTSD book, reaching out for help, using internalized things that [PGA] has said). D. also reports that she no longer dissociates.

In terms of being able to utilize a helping relationship, the patient reports many other meaningful changes. To begin, D. stated that she has 'learned that [she] can talk to somebody about a painful feeling or problem and feel like [she'll] be heard and helped'. This has meant that the patient does not have to function in an excessively independent fashion anymore. It has also meant that D. 'does not have to cope by using OC rituals anymore and that there is 'no need to cope' via emotional eating (i.e. bingeing on sugary foods). Of course, these gains started within our therapeutic relationship and not only generalized to other helping relationships[19] but were also **essential if D. was going to stay in a difficult treatment and benefit from nonrelationship interventions** (i.e. without them D. would have dropped out of treatment). The patient reported that she felt safe and secure in our relationship and no longer feared being abandoned, criticized, neglected or shamed by me. She also reported that she no longer feared having sessions trigger PTSD reactions, that she could now 'ask for help instead of feeling like [she] had to do everything [herself]' and that she 'could tell [PGA] anything and that he would validate [her] experience'.

Other significant improvements in D.'s PTSD include the following. The patient describes decreased hypervigilance ('after 40 years of living 24/7 in survival mode... [D.] no longer feels that the world is a dangerous place'). She also reports that she can 'sleep at night and get a full uninterrupted night's sleep every single night'. In addition, D. reports that she is less sensitive to criticism in general and that her father's criticism 'does not throw [her] anymore'. Finally, the patient reports that she believes in herself and trusts her own experiences (self-validation), can do public speaking with ease and can plan on things now 'because [she] does not assume they will be ruined'. Furthermore, the patient states that she 'knows that when [she] gets sick that [she will] get better', takes far less psychotropic medication, does not think she is a 'bad person' anymore and is no longer afraid that 'others will hit [her]'.

Regarding the patient's OCD, D. reported clinically significant decreases in obsessional fears and compulsive rituals. Specifically, the patient reports that she does not 'live with the fear of loved ones dying any more'. She also reports a 98% reduction in ritualistic hand washing, a 98% reduction in scrubbing things with boiling hot water, a 90% reduction in ordering rituals, a 99% reduction in rituals designed to prevent disasters from happening and a 99% reduction in checking rituals. These are highly significant improvements, as D. reported prior to treatment these fears and associated rituals often 'consumed her'. The patient also stated that she does not 'feel overly responsible to do everything and help everyone all the time' and that 'most of her OCD is gone'.

D. also demonstrated marked improvements in several other problem areas. The patient reported that she no longer suffered from depression or suicidal ideation. She also demonstrated terrific improvements in her fear of flying. D. reported that she can 'get on an airplane with little distress' and actually has flown to London, Paris, Madrid and Rome for vacations with her brother over the past few years. For someone who could not take these type of vacations due to her flying phobia and who has had countless special occasions in her life 'ruined' by traumatic experiences, these vacations were especially meaningful for D. Similarly, being able to perform all sorts of tasks naturally and with much greater ease with her left hand is a great improvement in D.'s life. The patient can also engage in public speaking without freezing up or stuttering. Her sensitivity to the sounds of others eating ('misophonia') is also greatly improved. D. attributes this to various relationship interventions (e.g. being able to discuss the problem with [PGA], knowing that [PGA] did not want her to feel bad and knowing that she could leave me a voicemail after a dinner party letting me know how it went). Other interventions reported to be helpful with this sensitivity included grounding techniques (i.e. orienting self to the present), labelling this reaction as 'a PTSD reaction', D. herself eating crunchy foods in a vigorous way and the patient reminding herself that she could leave the situation if it became too painful (i.e. she was not trapped there and did not have to endure a situation 'masochistically').

D. has also demonstrated clinically significant improvements with regard to food in her life. She is much freer and more likely to prepare nutritious meals. She no longer hoards food and is much less likely to cope with intense emotions via emotional eating.

Finally, D. recently defended her dissertation and earned her doctorate. Not only does this represent progress in terms of realizing her professional potential but it also represents an incredible victory over her PTSD, OCD, trauma and neglect. The importance of our therapeutic relationship and the relationship-based interventions in our work together was highlighted by D.'s response to my pointing out this major victory for the patient. She stated, 'Peter, it's like you have 3 daughters'. That is, D. was expressing her gratitude for all the nurturing, support, validation and 'parenting' I gave her over the course of the past 6 years.

Concluding Comments

A 6-year psychotherapy in which the therapeutic relationship is such an essential and powerful component can raise questions regarding the duration of the treatment, the possibility of maladaptive dependency on the part of the patient and of termination issues. I will draw upon two sources of data – D.'s behavioural responses to relevant relationship interventions during the course of her treatment and the patient's self-report – in addressing those issues. I will also point out why these issues are not problematic *for this patient* in light of the case formulation.

To begin, treatment duration simply reflected clinical need. That is, D. presented with multiple problems that were extremely complex and severe. Second, D. had experienced years of chronic trauma and abuse. Consequently, there were many traumatic memories and feelings to process, reflecting several types of trauma (e.g. **abandonment, criticism and deprivation**), and much new learning to occur (e.g. learning that one can express their concerns without being invalidated or ask for help without being criticized). In addition, much of D.'s trauma occurred in the context of key interpersonal relationships (e.g. **abandonment, criticism, invalidation and neglect**), and she also had limited experiences of security and safety within these relationships. As a consequence, one would predict that these types of PTSD reactions would be easily triggered in the therapeutic relationship (in which they were) and that D. would need time to develop security in our relationship, which she did, and that many sessions would be required to process the PTSD reactions that were triggered in her therapy (which were). Furthermore, the patient stated that she 'has no worries about the duration of her treatment [because her] life is so much better now'. Given her outstanding progress to date, I would concur.

Regarding the dependency concern, the most powerful data that indicate that this is not a problem for this patient come from her responses to the formulation-based relationship interventions conducted in D.'s therapy (e.g. granting her requests to sit next to her on the couch when processing especially traumatic memories, telling D. about one thing I did on vacation and being willing to answer questions about her dissertation). The patient explained why she was not concerned about excessive dependency in our relationship, and her words put it best: 'Based on everything else that has happened… that is, everything that I asked for in the therapy has always been a temporary need… once these needs were met, I was the one that initiated saying that 'I don't need that anymore', like sitting on the couch, knowing about [PGA] on vacation…. I just sort of grew past it… also I knew there was never any pressure to stop doing these interventions because [PGA] said 'we'd do it as long as we needed to'…this enabled me to move through [these issues] more quickly; if I would have been rushed, it would have made me feel trapped and triggered lots of PTSD reactions [i.e. feeling criticized and/or abandoned]….also just knowing it was OK, reduced the need for it…because I had so much anxiety asking for it….besides my big problem has been that I've been too independent, I've always had to solve things on my own'. D.'s comments of 'just knowing it was OK and reduced the need for it' are consistent with the case formulation and the formulation-guided treatment in that the traumatic effects of **deprivation and criticism** were reversed by the relationship interventions of **demonstrating** that these requests were appropriate given her learning history.

D.'s self-report matched her behaviour in therapy (i.e. she was indeed the one who initiated discontinuation of the aforementioned relationship interventions). Other data that allay concerns of maladaptive dependency include the following: D. has for most of her life prior to therapy functioned in an excessively independent way; she has always had, and continues to have, several close friends; she lives in a religious community and she has never acted in a needy way between sessions. In addition, I believe that the therapeutic relationship provided D. with the validation, acceptance, security and opportunity to talk about and process traumatic memories and feelings and helped D. build skills that enabled her to be less reliant on me to cope with traumatic memories and feelings (e.g. therapeutic writing, the PTSD book and distancing skills ['seeing PTSD through historical eyes']), manage her OCD and get her interpersonal needs met. Again, the patient's words are consistent with these data: '[PGA] has taught me to help myself in a healthy manner, and that's very, very important...I use that a lot...before I wouldn't ask anybody for help and would be overwhelmed and anxious, but now I've learned ways to help myself. Also [PGA] never pressured me by saying, 'Oh, you should ask somebody else to help you with that' ... [PGA] trusted the process and knew that I had other people in my life and would eventually transfer that to them; that is, being able to ask for things and find the words and courage to ask for help...If [PGA] hadn't done that, I would have never have been able to ask [PGA] or anybody else for help... [PGA] always trusted that the process would evolve and expand to my getting help from others'.

Regarding decreasing the frequency of sessions and termination, again the case formulation and D.'s response to treatment interventions thus far provide us with hypotheses and guidance. As the patient stated above, when an accepting, nurturing and validating relationship is demonstrated for her and she does not feel pressured to discontinue an intervention (including meeting twice a week), she makes progress on that issue faster, stops needing that particular intervention and initiates discontinuation on her own. I would hypothesize that the same process will happen with regards to decreasing the frequency of sessions and termination. Over time, D. will simply need to see me less often. I say this because she will have recovered from her traumatic memories and feelings; she will have unmet needs for constancy and security, validation and nurturing met via the therapeutic relationship and she will have acquired the skills to mange her problems and get her interpersonal needs met. This can be seen as analogous to a healthy parent–child relationship: The child acquires the security and skills to function independently from their parents and naturally decreases their contact with their parents.

Treatment of individuals with histories of severe and chronic multiple traumas, abuse and abandonment do, however, raise an important question about termination of therapy: Is a formal and permanent termination of therapy clinically indicated? Put another way, are there cases where the most therapeutic approach to 'termination' is one in which there is an explicit understanding with the patient that there will be an 'open-ended' arrangement? That is, the patient may request a session from time to time (e.g. every few to several months) **indefinitely**. Aside from Linehan, I know of no other cognitive–behavioural therapist who has addressed this question (i.e. 'With [other patients], ongoing if intermittent contact with their former therapists may be very important; Linehan 1993: p. 461). Based on D.'s history and case formulation, I believe this is the best approach. She seems to concur: 'My insight regarding termination starts with being aware that just getting that word out of my mouth is tremendous progress, because before that [idea] would send me into total PTSD trauma. I see this termination happening very gradually and very naturally. Due to the chronic nature of my horrific trauma and abuse that began long before I could remember, I feel that in a certain way [PGA] has re-raised me, which is why I said I feel like your third daughter. Even after our sessions have been completed, I'm sure there will occasionally be times when I'll need a little help from you because you know my complicated life story. But even more than that, after all we've worked on together I can see myself wanting to let you know when something good or significant happens, because of the relationship that we've established. Also anything wonderful that happens to me in the future will be a direct result of what [PGA] has helped me overcome. Because the place I was in when I started therapy would have never allowed that to happen'.

The preceding case study provided a detailed account of an intensive behavioural psychotherapy with a resilient, intelligent and spirited woman, 'D.'. D. had experienced countless severe traumas and heartbreaking losses throughout her life. As a consequence of these horrific experiences, D. developed severe and complex PTSD, had a severe OCD triggered and also had to endure several other extremely difficult problems. While empirically supported treatment interventions were implemented in the patient's therapy, the most important components of her treatment were the therapeutic relationship and the relationship interventions employed. This relationship and these interventions were guided and determined by the case formulation and were critical in D.'s recovery. They enabled the patient to vanquish her many traumas and recover from the devastatingly sad losses associated with growing up with a mother who suffered from paranoid schizophrenia and a father who was psychologically overmatched by this tragic situation. D.'s victory over these traumas and losses makes this a joyous case study, as well as one filled with sadness and hard work.

Notes

1. According to D., this was this therapist's 'only solution' for OCD.
2. In his discussion of case conceptualization, Meichenbaum (2006) repeatedly admonishes and encourages therapists to identify not only the patient's problems but also their strengths and to use these strengths in treatment. Utilizing these strengths was an essential component of D.'s therapy.
3. These self-report inventories were given because they often yield useful clinical data (e.g. a problem the patient has not revealed yet; severity level of depression) or help to ensure that I have a comprehensive list of a patient's difficulties.
4. For an operational definition of 'formulation' and a discussion of case formulation approaches to CBT, the reader is referred to Meyer and Turkat (1979) and Bruch and Bond (1998).
5. In fact, during a conversation with the psychiatrist involved in D.'s treatment, I commented that I often felt like I was both D's mother and father.
6. All told, D. has produced over 120 therapeutic writings over the course of her treatment, all of which were read and discussed in session.
7. After reviewing a draught of this chapter, D. confirmed this hypothesis stating that these writings were addressed to me because she needed to tell another person about what happened to her, so she would not have to continue being alone with all these traumatic feelings and memories.
8. During the time when D. began processing traumatic memories from 'the hardest time in her life' (see below), the patient requested that she receive some pharmacological help. She took a relatively low dose of a selective serotonin reuptake inhibitor (first citalopram, 20 mg/day; then escitalopram, 10 mg/day) for approximately 4 years. During this time, D. was also prescribed a low dose of clonazepam, 1.0 mg/day. At the time of this writing, D. has progressed so well in her therapy that the only medication she currently takes is clonazepam, 0.25 mg once a day, and reports that soon she will probably no longer feel the need for that medication.
9. Indeed, dropout from treatment of PTSD is a common occurrence, one that is probably due to these types of 'retraumatizing' experiences in the therapy itself (Meichenbaum, 2006).
10. Remember at the start of D.'s therapy, she could not even stand hearing the word, 'invalidate', and stated once 'if [she] could have shoved a sock in my mouth to keep me from saying that word, [she] would have done it'.
11. Of course, physical contact with a patient is a boundary crossing, but these hugs seemed to feel 'parental' in nature, and even I, who is probably an overly conscientious psychologist, never felt uncomfortable with these hugs. Most importantly, they (another relationship intervention) clearly had a therapeutic effect on D.
12. D.'s father did not tell the children where their mother was hospitalized, nor would he let the children talk to the mother over the telephone or visit her in the hospital.
13. It was not always leaving a session feeling criticized that would trigger the cascade of PTSD reactions. At times, it was being left alone with something

important or upsetting that D., usually out of a sense of shame or fear that she would be criticized, could not tell me. These experiences were incredibly disappointing and frustrating for the patient.

14. This intervention would be revisited several months later (sometimes it takes a while for us to learn).

15. D. later explained that my reaction to her sitting so closely to me triggered shameful memories of her father always telling D. that she sat too close to him, implying that she was doing something inappropriate.

16. Indeed honouring these requests could be seen as examples of courageous clinical experimentation on my part (e.g. Bruch, 1998).

17. The consensus was that helping the patient with her dissertation was clinically indicated as she had benefited from these interventions in the past and from discussing these events *after* the PTSD reaction had subsided. In fact, one of my colleagues usefully commented that these boundary crossings were 'messy, but that there's nothing wrong with messy'.

18. Coping cards were also developed for D. to use between sessions. As consistent with the rest of her therapy, two of the three most useful coping statements were relationship focused (e.g. '[PGA] hates it when I feel this bad, he really cares about how I feel' and 'I don't have to do it all by myself'). The third coping statement reminded D. that these intense reactions 'were all PTSD'.

19. D. reported that she 'can now, without any discomfort, ask others who are more seasoned than [she] in a given area for help or advice' (e.g. advisors, principals and co-workers).

Acknowledgement

The author would like to thank 'D.' for her willingness 'to have her story told' in this case study.

References

American Psychiatric Association. (1994). *Diagnostic and statistical manual of mental disorders* (4th ed.). Washington, DC: APA.

AuBuchon, P. G., & Malatesta, V. J. (1998). Managing the therapeutic relationship in behavior therapy: The need for a case formulation. In M. Bruch & F.W. Bond (Eds.), *Beyond diagnosis: Case formulation approaches in CBT* (pp. 141–165). Chichester, UK: John Wiley & Sons.

Beck, A. T., Ward, C. H., Mendelsohn, M., Mock, J. E., & Erbaugh, J. K. (1961). An inventory for measuring depression. *Archives of General Psychiatry, 4,* 561–571.

Boudewyns, P. A., & Hyer, L. A. (1990). Physiological response to combat memories and preliminary treatment outcome in Vietnam veteran PTSD patients treated with direct therapeutic exposure. *Behavior Therapy, 21,* 63–87.

Bruch, M. (1998). The UCL case formulation model: Clinical applications and procedures. In M. Bruch & F. W. Bond (Eds.), *Beyond diagnosis: Case formulation approaches in CBT* (pp. 19–41). Chichester, UK: John Wiley & Sons.

Bruch, M., & Bond, F. W. (Eds.). (1998). *Beyond diagnosis: Case formulation approaches in CBT*. Chichester, UK: John Wiley & Sons.

Foa, E. B., Hembree, E. A., & Rothbaum, B. O. (2007). *Prolonged exposure therapy for PTSD: Emotional processing of traumatic experiences*. New York: Oxford University Press.

Freeston, M. H., & Ladouceur, R. (1997). *The cognitive behavioral treatment of obsessions: A treatment manual* (75 pp). Unpublished research report, Universite Laval, Quebec, Canada.

Kohlenberg, R. J., & Tsai, M. (1991). *Functional analytic psychotherapy: Creating intense and curative therapeutic relationships*. New York: Plenum Press.

Knapp, S., & Van de Creek, L. (2012). *Practical ethics for psychologists: A positive approach* (2nd ed.). Washington, DC: American Psychological Association.

Linehan, M. M. (1993). *Cognitive-behavioral treatment of borderline personality disorder*. New York: The Guilford Press.

Meichenbaum, D. (2006). *Treating traumatized adults and children: A life span approach*. A two day continuing education workshop presented at Lancaster, PA.

Meyer, V., & Levy, R. (1973). Modification of behavior in obsessive-compulsive disorders. In H. E. Adams & I. P. Unikel (Eds.), *Issues and trends in behavior therapy* (pp. 77–137). Springfield, IL: Thomas.

Meyer, V., & Liddell, A. (1975). Behaviour therapy. In D. Bannister (Ed.), *Issues and trends in psychological therapies*. London: Wiley.

Meyer, V., & Turkat, I.D. (1979). Behavioral analysis of clinical cases. *Journal of Behavioral Assessment, 1*, 259–270.

Resick, P. A., & Schnicke, M. K. (1992). Cognitive processing therapy for sexual assault victims. *Journal of Consulting and Clinical Psychology, 60*, 748–756.

Schinka, J. A. (1985). *Personal problems checklist for adults*. Odessa, FL: Psychological Assessment Resources, Inc.

6

Generalized Anxiety Disorder
Personalized Case Formulation and Treatment

Kieron O'Connor, Amélie Drolet-Marcoux,
Geneviève Larocque and Karolan Gervais

Introduction

Generalized anxiety disorder (GAD) is traditionally considered a residual disorder diagnosed in the absence of criteria for other disorders. In DSM-III-R, GAD became its own category characterized by apprehensive expectation in a limited number of specific worry domains (Watson & Friend, 1969). Core symptoms of GAD include a disarming array of somatic, behavioural and cognitive signs, including both autonomic hyperarousal and hypoarousal, and most reliably muscle tension and worry (Barlow, 2002).

Despite strong somatic signs, GAD is considered mainly a cognitive disorder. Research in GAD has therefore focused predominantly on clarifying the nature and function of worry: worry and meta-worry. In worry, the person dwells endlessly and aversively on the future aspects of a problem or event, anticipating negative outcome and an ensuing inability to cope. In meta-worry, people worry about the fact that they worry (Cartwright-Hatton & Wells, 1997). Both meta-worry and worry thought sequences can interact in handicapping real problem solving and increasing anxiety (Mathews, 1990).

Worry reduces somatic activation and attempts to control worry may be forms of experiential avoidance that are self-perpetuating and that distract from what would be more effective behavioural forms of responding to the environment (Hayes, Strosahl, & Wilson, 1999).

Clinically, treating GAD can lead to a tortuous process where anticipation produces worry, which produces somatic symptoms, which produce

---

Beyond Diagnosis: Case Formulation in Cognitive Behavioural Therapy, Second Edition.
Edited by Michael Bruch.
© 2015 John Wiley & Sons, Ltd. Published 2015 by John Wiley & Sons, Ltd.

further worry and meta-worry about the worry and further anxiety and performance difficulties.

In keeping with the diverse nature of the disorder, there are a number of evidence-based standardized treatment packages, mostly cognitive–behavioural therapy, available. These include protocols highlighting imaginal exposure, problem solving (Craske, 1999), programme relaxation (Ost, 1987), cognitive and meta-cognitive restructuring (Wells, 1999), intolerance of uncertainty (Ladouceur et al., 2000), interpersonal processes (Borkovec, Alcaine, & Behar, 2004) and narrative approaches (O'Connor, Gareau, Gaudette, & Robillard, 1999).

In this chapter, we illustrate how the vagueness and seeming contradictions of GAD can be overcome by a case formulation approach that centres evaluation and treatment around the person and contextualizes worries within personal and interpersonal domains.

We discuss three cases, all of which received an 'official' diagnosis of GAD (by structured clinical interview) but required separate and independent case formulations. The GAD symptoms in each case were linked together with an interactive case formulation using individual schemas in collaboration with the person. The schemas allowed progressive targeting of the contents of the worry in a way that was meaningful to the person and allowed them to understand how worry functioned in their life domains. So, the individual case formulations were idiosyncratic and not comparable, despite all three cases sharing a common diagnosis. The three cases also received different treatment modalities, so illustrating how case formulation can lead to tailored treatments.

In particular, we moved beyond a matching symptom to technique approach towards a matching person to treatment approach, in order to uncover the individual variation regarding development, presentation and maintenance of the disorder. The complexity of the model is brought together through a personalized rather than standard focus on interlocking behaviours. The principle of this case formulation approach is that though there may be several symptoms, there is only one person and understanding the underlying mechanism in personal terms allows the clinician to pinpoint how problems interact in daily life and so to provide a singular solution.

Case 1 – John

Definition of presenting problem

The first client, John, was in his early 30s and living with his common-law spouse and their newborn baby. He was a university-educated civil servant. His presenting complaint was periods of anxiety that he could not link to any particular stressor in his life. John reported that his first such period of intense anxiety had happened 7 years earlier and that he had had regular episodes since then. His objective was to experience less of the thoughts and have more 'control of my thoughts'.

The therapist detected a conflict in John's non-verbal and verbal discomfort of expressing his problem. He was torn between admitting his thoughts and seeking help and protecting himself. The therapist noted that the client was clearly uncomfortable talking about his anxiety, and discussion seemed to make him more anxious. This discomfort had led to abandoning previous therapy.

The therapeutic alliance with the therapist was initially tense, largely because John also had some narcissistic traits that led him believe he ought to be able to control his thoughts on his own and that prevented John from accepting therapist suggestions. So he was constantly critical of the therapist, convinced she did not understand his anxiety and would make it worse. As noted, John was very anxious about discussing his anxiety, and his tone was monotone, indicating a desire to avoid emotion, which he felt not only showed control but also presented him as someone correct and superior. Sometimes, the therapist's suggestions were met by an attacking attitude where John would deny having said or agreed to a plan previously. One hypothesis to account for this behaviour was a dislike for or resistance to the therapist. This hypothesis was dismissed by John's own account, who reported independently how he liked the therapist.

Finally, the therapist realized that John was only half-listening to her due often to absorption in his thoughts and so had not fully understood the formulation. But due to his narcissistic traits and high standards, he could not admit to not understanding. The pace of conversation was slowed to allow time for feedback and understanding. The therapist was also aware of her own reaction to these episodes and consequent dislike of the patient interaction, which she set off by focusing on the behaviour in the context of the patient's suffering.

So the therapist summed up John's problems as anxiety caused by thoughts John felt he should not have or should be able to control. This anxiety was fuelled further by his narcissistic traits and a perfectionism that heightened his judgement about the admissibility of his thoughts. There was also a lack of understanding of the nature of thought control and of how thoughts work and finally the use of self-sabotaging strategies such as thought suppression that paradoxically increased the intensity of the thoughts.

Exploration

According to John's description of his principal problem, a negative thought would come to his mind (e.g. 'I could stop loving my spouse') and set off a series of further negative thoughts (e.g. 'I could hurt my spouse or my baby'; 'I could become so anxious I would be unable to be a good father' and 'I would be a failure and go crazy'). John said that these thoughts and the anxiety symptoms that accompanied them (nausea, loss of appetite and sleeping problems) could last several days to a few weeks.

The therapist decided to explore exactly what anxiety meant for this client. This deconstruction of anxiety is important in a clinical setting since anxiety is an umbrella term with a different sense to everybody. The therapist established with the client that John's principal fear was losing control. By identifying a list of possible consequences (death, illness, loss of relationship, becoming non-functional, losing control and going crazy) of his anxiety, the therapist established that for John, losing control meant loss of self and potential mayhem and becoming crazy and non-functional. The therapist began to collaboratively explore with John a general model of his anxiety. In particular, the sequence of thoughts leading to John's anxiety was unclear.

In John's own words, he would anticipate a negative thought, then anticipate feeling guilty about the thought and consider he was not strong, then wonder if the thought would make him crazy. He was torn between considering he should not have the thought and feeling he should attend to it, so ending up with mental neutralization and avoidance. Since there was no external trigger, the hypothesis was that anticipation of this conflict was the principal trigger.

The therapist also evaluated the coping strategies used by John and his attitudes about the usefulness of worrying in general. John answered that he put a moderate amount of effort into controlling his worries. The main strategies he used were trying to distract himself, rationalizing the worry by trying to argue against it and trying not to think of the things that worry him. The main beliefs about worrying endorsed by the client were that worrying creates stress for the body, worrying could do him harm and worrying too much could cause him to lose control.

John had developed a series of cognitive avoidance strategies that he used to cope with anxiety. He described how he would avoid things that could trigger negative thoughts (e.g. images of people apparently out of control, as in wild enjoyment, and places (e.g. billboards) where he might see these images). He would seek reassurance from his spouse and friends. The reassurance seeking involved asking questions such as the following: Did I say or do anything wrong? He also practised meditation and took baths to calm himself during periods of extreme anxiety. He also used relaxation techniques regularly in order to reduce, as he put it, his general 'susceptibility to anxiety'. Most often, John would repeat to himself that his negative thought was 'unrealistic', as a form of self-reassurance until he was able to mentally neutralize the thought.

So the question in the therapist's mind was how aware was John of the link between his anxiety and avoidance. In order to make John more aware of the succession of his thoughts, the therapist found it useful to map out in a diagram triggers and how the thought triggers led to more thought triggers and more anxious thoughts and more triggers.

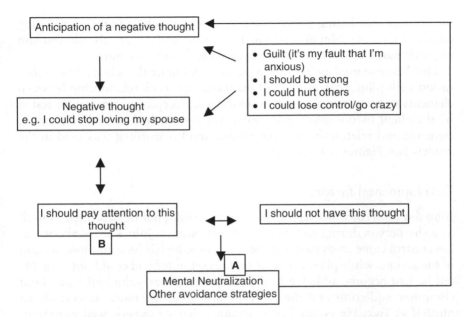

Figure 6.1 General model. This schema shows how John's anticipation of a negative thought elicited a negative reaction leading to the conflict between feeling he should attend to the thought and that he should not have the thought leading to avoidance.

A general diagram or schema was elaborated with John (see Figure 6.1) and seemed to show that John maintained his anxiety by anticipating having anxiety-provoking thoughts. He used certain cognitive strategies (mental neutralization and self-monitoring) and behaviours (avoidance, reassurance seeking and relaxation) in order to reduce his anxiety symptoms, but these strategies worked only on a short-term basis. In the long run, they increased his susceptibility to anxiety by augmenting his anticipation through rendering the negative thoughts more salient. (These were treated as if they really were dangerous and must be avoided.) The model also contained personal themes that determined the content of the negative thoughts (his guilt and excessive sense of responsibility) and gave some insight into why these thoughts were salient for John (why he attributed importance to them). So the next task for the therapist was to explore why the content of the thoughts was so important to John.

Clearly, an additional factor affecting John's anxiety was his perfectionism, which interacted with his fear of losing control. In dialogue with John, what appeared at first to be a rigid moral value that he should not have thoughts about not loving his wife turned out not to be morally inspired but rather an expression of his perfectionism that there must always be a 'correct' way of acting and he must always be 'correct' and never lose control. As the therapist noted to John, and he agreed, the fear of loss of control led onto the further fear that letting a therapist help would also be a sign of him losing control. Involving John in designing the schema collaboratively allowed him to participate in the therapy and in part to feel more 'in control'.

The therapist used an iterative process to elaborate the schema in collaboration with John. Each element of the model and each relationship between elements were proposed as a hypothesis to be accepted or rejected or tested by the client before moving on. John was also invited to add or propose elements and relationships to the model, and his wording was used in the models (see Figures 6.1 and 6.2).

Developmental factors

John did not remember having anxiety as a child, but he described himself as a shy person during childhood and adolescence. John's story about losing control came from past experiences where he felt he could lose control of his actions while playing games on the computer and could not stop. He felt he had become addicted to the computer games. John had read about computer addiction and the more he reflected, the more he considered himself at risk. He pointed to sensations that he experienced automatically, like excitement, as proof of his impulsivity. He could not let himself

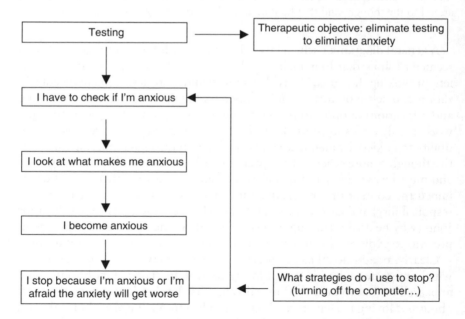

Figure 6.2   This schema illustrated how John's testing behaviour to check he was anxious far from keeping him anxious increased his anxiety, which made him abort his exposure and incubate the anxiety further.

go and have pleasure because of his fear of losing control, and so he monitored his thoughts anxiously. John reported frequently experiences of anxiety when he had pleasure as a child. John recalled one or two examples of family outings where he had enjoyed himself. He had run too quickly for an ice cream and fell and grazed his knees. Later, he had turned over the day increasingly, regretting his lack of discipline. To him, his very childish immaturity seemed a sign of being out of control, compared with his parents' composure. Although his parents were strict, they were not moralistic, but there seemed religious overtones, where religious examples were often invoked to install sense of worth (e.g. What would Jesus say about that idea?). Actually, John told the therapist he believed in God and had quit smoking as a promise to God, and he now could not let God down.

Formulation

The formulation was elaborated in a series of schema connecting distinct elements contributing to his anxiety. Part of developing the schema was educational wherein connecting up interacting problems John realized how the problems built on one another and what transition points he could address to change the course. Each schema was associated with a therapeutic goal negotiated with John (see below), and John was asked if he recognized his way of functioning in these schemas and if so did he wish to work towards these goals. All three schemas, with their respective goals, are shown (see Figures 6.2, 6.3 and 6.4).

The schemas were developed with the client by firstly listing all elements of the problem. The therapist worked with John to put these elements into a sequence. So, for example, John would anticipate thinking a thought, feel guilty about the thought and consider he was not strong that he would not be able to stop going crazy and that he would lose control. This sequence allowed both the therapist and John to reflect on the anxiety built up largely through anticipation of feeling anxious and John realized he was torn between wanting to not have the thought and feeling he should however attend to it. It seemed to the therapist that there was also an inner struggle between what John thought and what he thought he should think, which had led to the guilt and avoidant strategies and the constant reassurance seeking. Through the schema, John was able to see how the push and pull dynamic 'wanting to attend – not wanting to' also maintained the anxiety. The therapist reflected on whether the anticipation, the conflict or the avoidances was the principal root of the problem. There were several elements to target since his avoidance strategies and his evaluation of his thoughts were both factors maintaining anxiety. The therapist's plan of action was to break the vicious circle by either dealing with avoidance first or addressing John's thoughts. But the therapist was unsure which to target.

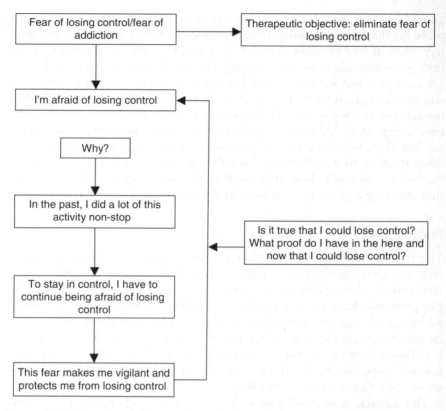

Figure 6.3   This schema illustrated to John how his attempts to monitor his loss of control produced a fear of losing control and hence more anxiety.

Intervention

The initial goal was to break the vicious cycle of – anxiety – avoidance – short-term relief – more anxiety – progressively. So it was important to identify the right point of entry to break the cycle. Was it through changing his thoughts or his behaviour? After looking at the sequence with John, it seemed avoidance was the more doable option. The therapist first targeted the elimination of John's avoidance strategies, and he agreed to gradually stop using them.

This target was intended to break the cycle by helping John let go of the notion that he should keep control through avoidance (see Figure 6.1, entrance into the cycle marked by the letter A). John was successful in this first step, in which he gained knowledge of his idiosyncratic ways of avoiding negative thoughts, such as mental neutralization and behavioural avoidance of images and situations where he would anticipate getting anxious. His remark was 'Yes I see how this works'. John also came to understand that

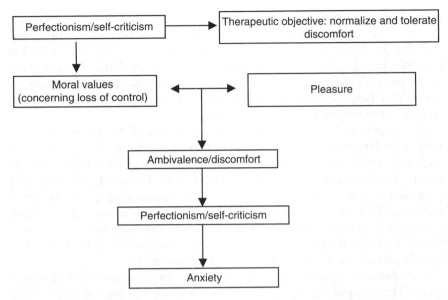

Figure 6.4 This schema illustrates how John's perfectionist and self-critical tendencies lead to a conflict between enjoying an activity and feeling bad. This activity might lead to enjoyment, losing control and hence transgress his values. This ambivalence in turn led to more self-criticism and anxiety.

avoiding anxiety-provoking thoughts was in a way, in his words, 'training his brain to believe that these thoughts are actually dangerous'.

The second step of the exercise consisted in identifying the positive significance the client attributed to his negative thoughts (e.g. 'these thoughts will help me to plan for the worst') in order to completely dismantle the cognitive mechanism by which John was attributing so much importance to his negative thoughts (see Figure 6.1, section of the cycle marked B). John started this second step of the exercise, but he found it difficult to find occasions to put it into practice as his anxiety had greatly diminished over the first period of treatment as had the frequency of his anxiety-provoking thoughts. Partly as a result of avoiding avoidance and exposing himself to anticipation and the fear of becoming anxious, his anticipation had decreased. John indicated that he feared anxiety itself much less than he did at the beginning of therapy. So the therapist reasoned that the hypothesis about anticipation as the trigger for more anxiety seemed supported.

Addressing avoidance strategies by avoiding avoidance was sufficient to eliminate a number of meta-cognitive elements that were maintaining John's cycle of anxiety since the worst did not occur ('Anticipating the worst' was not helpful.) As the client came to understand more fully the rationale behind the intervention ('anxiety fuels itself by the use of strategies that make anxiety more likely'), he also felt a decrease in his fear of anxiety itself. It became obvious to him that to a certain extent he could simply stop maintaining his own anxiety by modifying his meta-cognitive style. For example, he was sure he had to monitor his anxiety level and even test it out in the presence of anxiety by thinking thoughts to make himself anxious. So a series of behavioural experiments were devised to decide whether not testing out made John feel better or worse.

The schema in Figure 6.2 represents how John had developed a habit of testing his level of anxiety by engaging in an anxiety-provoking behaviour and then withdrawing from the activity before his anxiety level could go down (as it would do if he maintained exposure). The therapeutic objective proposed was to avoid increasing anxiety by eliminating this withdrawal. John was able to carry through the task with some anxiogenic thoughts about his future and some pleasant activities like reading adventure stories where he became stimulated. He realized when carrying on instead of withdrawing, he felt better and he did not lose control.

The schema in Figure 6.3 represents John's fear of losing control, as discussed above. The therapist was partly able to work on this fear, using cognitive restructuring techniques to reduce fear of losing control. John would frequently monitor his thoughts and behaviour for any sign of losing control. Unfortunately, this very monitoring made him anxious. He would often go further and test himself by thinking certain thoughts and gauging his reactions. If his reaction was at all ambivalent, he would be anxious. So, for example, he would think, 'Do I love my wife?' and then would ruminate if his reaction was correct.

In a similar fashion, as soon as he undertook an enjoyable activity, for example, playing games on the computer, he began to fear losing control. Losing control for the client was synonymous with becoming addicted and hence implied inability to inhibit a behaviour. The theme of exerting tight control was explored in several life domains with John. How could one control every aspect of a behaviour? Was it feasible or desirable to control every component of an act? By exerting too much inhibition, could one not impede the flow of an automated act? John agreed to observe how he functioned in everyday life and test the effects of losing control. Was action aided or compromised by his testing and monitoring behaviour? But although John admitted he felt more confident and in control with less testing, he still feared losing control. The therapist was initially puzzled. The irony was that his testing and questioning increased his anxiety and worry, which augmented his belief that he could lose control. Intellectually, John had understood how testing (Figure 6.2) can favour anxiety and was making efforts to abstain from engaging in this habit. The therapist decided to re-emphasize the connection between his beliefs and anxiety.

The therapist's aim in constructing these schemas was to plan treatment specifically to address different elements underpinning John's anxiety problems that had been uncovered during work on the general model (Figure 6.1). These elements were his habit of anxiety testing (Figure 6.2), his self-monitoring, his fear of losing control (Figure 6.3) and his perfectionism/self-criticism (Figure 6.4). The therapist's aim was that revealing how the elements contributed jointly to the anxiety would facilitate John's readiness to work on each one. However, John saw the element addressed in Figure 6.3 (fear of losing control) not so much as a problem but as a protective mechanism helping to avoid having behaviour that he did not want to have. The therapist explained to John that he would be freer, not less free, to choose his behaviours if he got rid of his anxiety (his fear of losing control). But regardless of the outcome of the behavioural experiments, John held on to the belief that his behaviour could become out of control if not monitored. This quandary suggested to the therapist that a deeper strongly held belief was controlling the monitoring.

The schema in Figure 6.4 illustrates how John's perfectionism turned what might have been an acceptable discomfort into full-blown anxiety. Here, the therapist's aim was to use cognitive restructuring to normalize the fact that John could sometimes be unsure if his way of behaving was absolutely correct (moral or otherwise) and that this kind of discomfort is a common experience. Initially, John considered his problem with the computer and other pastimes was a fear of losing control. But a behavioural experiment with playing a game on his computer for a limited time showed that in the here and now he could not lose control even if he wanted. However, this vigilance about losing control had become a conflict between what he termed values and pleasure.

The experimental work on the schema in Figure 6.4 reached an impasse when John changed his mind and no longer accepted that his discomfort came from ambivalence between the conflict between moral values about being correct and having pleasure, which was then magnified into anxiety by a perfectionist attitude. Instead, John insisted that his ambivalence was between the risk of engaging in an activity that on the one hand was pleasurable but on the other hand could provoke anxiety. This new formulation represented a new contradiction for the therapist. John considered that any pleasurable activity, one that was enjoyed too much, could by itself become anxiogenic. Although the fear of losing control was evident here, it was also supplemented by an implicit moral censure about enjoyment. The therapist explored this moral dimension using downward arrow technique. If he enjoyed himself, what did this mean? That he was lazy, irresponsible and sinful even? John realized in his mind there was a fusion between enjoying himself too much and becoming out of control. A fear that enjoying himself too much signalled addiction, which signalled loss of control. The therapist and John devised a behavioural experiment where John would carry on with a very pleasant activity such as playing on the computer until tired and show how any activity tires in the end without loss of control.

However, John terminated therapy before his paralyzing reasoning about enjoying and losing control could be put to the test and be fully understood. The therapist tried to clarify with a new model this implicit contradiction fuelling distress in his personal functioning. John managed partial exposure to a number of situations where he was able to immerse himself in activity naturally, but other activities, especially related to more sensual pleasure, where he felt stimulated, even erotic, he felt were forbidden, not for moral reasons but because enjoyment implied implicitly that he might lose control.

Outcomes and Evaluation of Therapy

Although therapist and John agreed that there was more work to be done on his beliefs concerning enjoyment in order to eliminate more fused anxiety-provoking/-maintaining mechanisms, John reported that he was satisfied with the understanding he had gained and with how much his anxiety had been reduced during therapy. In fact, when asked to evaluate the therapeutic process, John expressed a high level of satisfaction in a self-report therapy satisfaction questionnaire. For example, he expressed particular satisfaction with exposure to anxiety-provoking thoughts and becoming aware of the interactions between his thoughts, his thoughts about his thoughts, his emotions and his self-sabotaging behaviour. At 1 month follow-up, John still reported being satisfied with his improvement and feeling confident that he would be able to continue applying what he had learned in therapy.

He was able to understand how his anticipation led itself to fear, which was then confounded by his judgement. 'So I'm going to worry about my wife, I shouldn't have this thought, what a terrible person I am, this will never end'. He was able to halt this type of sequence through curtailing the chaining. The situations he was better able to cope with included situations where his anticipation immediately increased his fear, where he would normally start ruminating about lack of control and ask reassurance from his wife. For example, reading, talking and everyday life were predictable situations where he was fine. However, browsing the computer was a situation where he could suddenly come across an item or a site and he did not know where it would lead. So, here he still felt he needed to be on guard.

Concerning objective measures, the Why Worry questionnaire (Freeston, Rhéaume, k Letarte, Dugas, & Ladouceur, 1994) to understand what motivated his worrying, the Intolerance of Uncertainty scale (Buhr & Dugas, 2002), the Health Anxiety Inventory (Lucock & Morley, 1996), the Beck Anxiety Inventory (Beck & Steer, 1991) and the Multidimensional Perfectionism (Frost, Marten, & Lahart, 1990) scale indicated significant change after treatment, and John reported an increase in life satisfaction as well.

The following is an excerpt from a dialogue between John and the therapist where the therapist became aware of how committed John was to self-monitoring and how a core belief can maintain self-sabotaging behaviour, even in the face of the benefits of not maintaining the behaviour.

Vignette (T=Therapist; John=J) – John and self-monitoring

T: So when you're on the computer, what are you doing?

J: Well, I'm watching my feelings.

T: Watching, that sounds an intense activity? Does it really help?

J: Well, I'm looking out for hints that there may be danger that I'm losing control.

T: And how do you recognize danger?

J: Well, if I detect a new sensation or if I realize something has escaped me, like something I didn't see on the screen.

T: So you found out the body is noisy. Doesn't monitoring itself create sensations?

J: Yes, it's true. I always find something, so I become preoccupied.

T: Again, how does monitoring help you? Or do you find you become more anxious?

J: It doesn't help, I agree. Already I'm panicking because there's so much going on and I could miss it. So, once I start monitoring, it's difficult to stop.

T: So monitoring encourages your anxiety. Does that make sense?

J: Well, it does because even though I'm anxious, I think if I'm just normal, I'm not focused and then I'm not protecting myself and so monitoring seems right.

T: So the more you monitor, the more you need to monitor and the more anxious you are. Yes?

J: Yes, it's true.

T: And if you don't monitor?

J: Well, I feel better, but it's funny, it feels like an emptiness, like I should be doing more.

Case 2 – Ann

Definition of problem

Ann was a 24-year-old married woman with a 1-year-old little boy. She was working part-time at a restaurant. She described herself generally as a worrier but her specific worries involved feeling worried because she felt she lacked coping skills and confidence. As with John, we attempted to answer the question why had she presented now with this problem. Ann started therapy initially for her persistent anxiety about the possibility of climate changes and subsequent natural disasters such as earthquakes, floods, etc. Specifically, she had been heavily influenced by the apparent Mayan prediction concerning the end of the world in December 2012 and was holding on to fears that the end-of-the-world catastrophe would result in dire changes for human life. This prediction was now a dominant preoccupying worry that impaired Ann's ability to function properly on a daily basis. She had a difficult time doing daily chores and making plans for the future, and her rumination would create tension in her marriage. Before she started therapy, she was receiving services from a public social worker and was prescribed an antidepressant (Celexa 10 mg) for her anxiety by her doctor.

The evaluation suggested that Ann had the tendency to generate catastrophic scenarios. The sequential and irrational manner in which Ann formed ideas inappropriately up to the worst-case scenarios left her overwhelmed and feeling personally inadequate to face certain specific events. Therefore, she behaved as if her imagined worst-case scenarios were the reality. An example is given in Figure 6.5.

Exploration

The therapist noted the tendency of Ann to lapse into a narrative when talking about her worries, one event chaining on to another. This chaining was particularly not worthy in her worries but also appeared in her everyday discourse. There was clearly a pattern in the build-up of the narrative of each worry, which always led to an end-point where she was overwhelmed, stranded alone and beyond her resources to cope. The end of the world signified for her the ultimate event of this nature where she would be incapable of saving herself. There were, however, numerous other less preoccupying situations where Ann often felt overwhelmed and incompetent. The therapist detected verbal and non-verbal cues showing that Ann lacked self-confidence and self-esteem. She presented herself as self-effacing, always seemingly on the brink of not coping, in a rush, juggling appointments and rendezvous, and afraid always to be not up to standard. She frequently criticized her performance, reported instances of incompetence and seemed in awe of particularly older people and people she perceived as more intelligent than herself. She would avoid voicing on opinion or commenting in the presence of such company for fear of being judged. The end of her anxiety-provoking narratives often involved finding herself stranded, lost and incompetent in the company of others.

The exploration led to the following theory. Ann had become vulnerable to feeling she was likely to find herself powerless in the face of adversity. Her imagination fuelled narratives where she found herself immersed in such narratives that remained vivid in her mind. Here, what needed to be established was her trigger and how the triggers generated anxiety. Further, there was a chronic lack of appreciation of self that needed to be explored.

Developmental factors

At birth, Ann had been placed in a foster family. She lived with the same foster family until the age of 14. She had a good relationship with her foster parents, who considered her part of the family. However, the foster parents

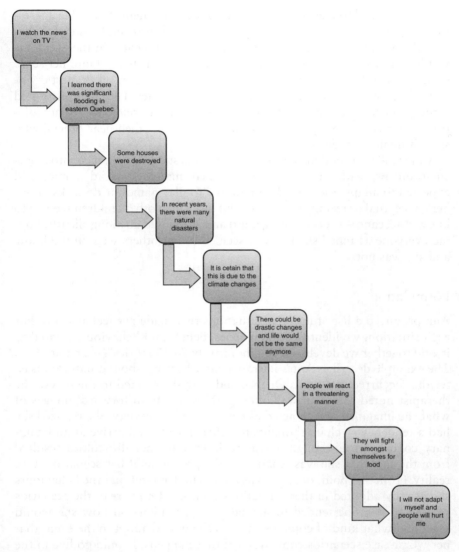

Figure 6.5 This figure described how Ann's narrative sequence become imaginary and played on her anxiety about her personal vulnerability of being stranded and helpless in an end of world scenario.

divorced, which forced Ann to transfer to many other foster families. Ann actually knew her biological parents; however, she chose not to pursue a relationship with them, fearing rejection. Several factors reported by Ann may have contributed to the development of this self-perception as a weak person. She mentioned that the foster mother with whom she lived until the age of 14 tended to overprotect her and to warn her against possible aggression. Furthermore, during adolescence, Ann lived in several foster families and always felt the threat of being sent to a youth centre in the event she would not meet their requirements. One recent event that fed into her sense of self-vulnerability was the fact that Ann had experienced domestic violence, both verbal and physical, with her last partner. The therapist noted throughout Ann's discourse of her childhood constant references to her inferiority, her vulnerability to danger and her 'nerves' when near others, who she felt might be judgemental.

Ann recalled several instances where she was suddenly plunged into a new environment, with an already established interpersonal dynamic, and expected to adapt. She was often required to play games or do tasks above her conceptual or technical development but which other children seemed to know (Meccano – Lego – word games) and she would go along silently, hoping everyone assumed she knew. It seemed to her others were in the know and she was not.

Formulation

Ann produced a list of different situations that made her feel anxious. For each situation, we identified the worries, beliefs and behaviours related to it, and together we developed collaboratively 'Ann's stories' (see Figure 6.5). The example describes Ann's narrative after hearing about a natural disaster that occurred in eastern Quebec and how she reacted to the news. The therapist noted that Ann was often grabbed by 'flash-forward' images of what she imagined, which acted as triggers for her anxiety. She realized she had a tendency to chain thoughts together quickly and arrive at an imaginary conclusion as though it was real. Thereby, her difficulties resulted from the fact that she was reacting in the present as if her scenarios were reality. From this point on, Ann was able to understand that the behaviours she usually adopted in these situations reinforced how 'real' the scenarios seemed to her. She tended to mentally prepare plans on how she would react and what kind of coping strategies she would adopt in the event that her worst-case scenarios come true ('If that happens, I could go live in the forest'), which led inevitably to negative thoughts on coping ('But I don't know to survive in the woods'). Also, Ann avoided conversations with her friends and family as well as watching television documentaries where the principal subjects were the end-of-the-world or natural disasters. But ironically, when aroused, Ann also sought out information and reports on disasters in a selective way that increased her anxiety. Furthermore, her physiological and psychological reactions that occurred (increased heart rate) added somatic information to confirm her feeling or impression that a threatening incident might happen. The therapist wondered about this apparent sabotage behaviour. For example, on her way to a concert in a park near her home town, she had very quickly latched on to an end scenario where she was caught in a crush and suffocating crowd. Her somatic and psychological reaction had led to her plonking herself down on a bench, incapable of moving or breathing, almost as though she were acting out the end-scenario. The end-scenario left her helpless and breathless, overwhelmed and feeling personally incapable of saving herself. These scenes playing on her powerlessness were a constant theme. The therapist reasoned that Ann's anxiety was produced by her narratives, her emotion visibly building as she recounted her stories. The intervention centred on her narrative.

Intervention

A scenario (Figure 6.5) was developed by asking her to visualize herself in a natural disaster situation and to go through the sequence of probable events. The first step of the treatment consisted of helping Ann realize that her scenario came from her imagination.

In order to test out the hypothesis of the power of narrative with Ann, we constructed different alternative stories about events that had unfolded or could unfold in her life. Ann realized that frequently she crossed over into the imagination and it was this 'imaginary bit' that created anxiety. The therapist tested out the role of the imaginary by asking Ann to rehearse stories that continued to be grounded in reality and ending in realistic possibilities. In changing the story, her anxiety subsided. The realistic possibilities were always more nuanced than the imaginary ones and left her feeling more in control. Coupled with the narratives, another element crucial to maintaining Ann's anxiety was her selective fact seeking, whereby she apparently reinforced and maintained her fears. For example, she tended to seek information on the Internet about the end of the world and natural disasters that had occurred and/or that might occur. She would deliberately seek detailed consequences of catastrophes when anxious and dwell on the gory details, so increasing anxiety. Ann agreed to limit her fact searching and eliminate any searches motivated by her anxiety.

Subsequent sessions had the aim of changing Ann's narrative and repositioning her within the sequence of events in order for her to handle the situation realistically. The therapist and client had fun constructing a variety of alternative narratives to her catastrophic scenarios (see Figure 6.6). The other narratives played on her imagination but ended in a neutral or positive manner. Then, Ann visualized herself in the alternative scenario and described how she felt, noted the differences in feeling produced by the scenarios. Ann also practised this technique regularly at home, whenever the scenarios appeared.

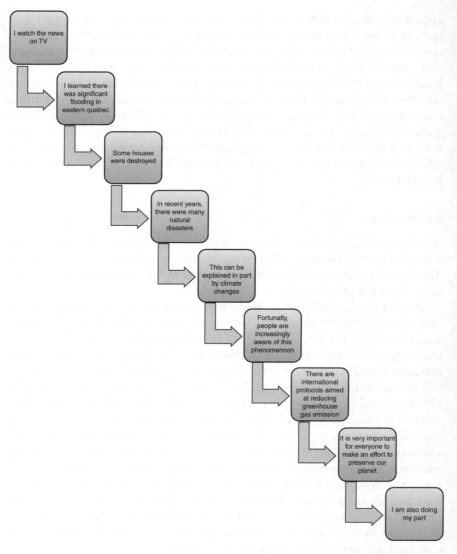

I watch the news on TV

I learned there was significant flooding in eastern quebec

Some houses were destroyed

In recent years, there were many natural disasters

This can be explained in part by climate changes

Fortunatly, people are increasingly aware of this phenomennon

There are international protocols aimed at reducing greenhouse gas emission

It is very important for everyone to make an effort to preserve our planet

I am also doing my part

Figure 6.6   This figure describes how an alternative scenario for a natural disaster was built up using Ann's ability to be immersed in a narrative chain.

Reformulation

The therapist explored with Ann the several personal themes common to her worries. These themes related to threats to herself where she considered herself particularly vulnerable. Listing and connecting up the themes in her personal narratives with the therapist, Ann realized that she often felt at the mercy of others. This self-theme ran through not only her worry narratives but also her pattern of social interactions. Often, she felt inferior to others and that what other people had to say was more important and more informed than her own talk (see dialogue).

Intervention

After developing alternative scenarios for different narratives that made Ann feel anxious, the therapist addressed this perception of self-vulnerability. Indeed, this theme of being at the mercy of others was a common factor present in all of her catastrophic scenarios. Consequently, the self-vulnerable perception reinforced by her ingratiating behaviour filtered reality and had the effect of maintaining anxiety. Therefore, the therapist and Ann worked on this point by exploring behaviour maintaining the self-vulnerable perception and its place and the consequences throughout Ann's history. In order to reposition her self-perception in a more realistic manner, the therapist explored the evidence of her competence in areas where she performed well and with confidence. Together with the therapist, she made a list of qualities and attributes that she possessed that made her feel adequate and capable in these situations. In the same vein, Ann developed a narrative about past and present experiences, in which the therapist identified her strengths and her abilities to deal effectively with various feared situations. The therapist highlighted with Ann her positive caring and coping attributes that she tended to dismiss with 'yes… but…' conditions, 'yes but anyone can do that…' and 'yes but that doesn't mean that I can cope…'. However, using third person technique, the therapist asked, How would you perceive someone with these attributes? What would they be capable of doing? Ann had sufficient competence to cope with very difficult and challenging situations such as raising a child, dealing with an abusive relation and most of all functioning well in her job. Ann had always imagined she had to possess or acquire noble, superior qualities to be able to feel confident. But she discovered confidence came naturally when she unconditionally enumerated the everyday attributes she noticed in herself.

Outcomes and evaluation of therapy

The alternative narratives on Ann's catastrophic scenarios helped reduce her anxiety. She reported that she became aware of how anxiety manifested itself to her and that she was acting in the here and now as if the catastrophic scenarios were the reality. After the therapy, Ann mentioned that she felt more in control when she was confronted with a situation that made her feel anxious. Indeed, Ann reported having a more positive view about the future because she had acquired skills enabling her to deal more effectively with anxiety events. Furthermore, the interventions that addressed her self-vulnerable perception helped her to reposition her self-perception with others and be more assertive in a realistic manner. Ann was now able to see objectively her strengths as well as her limitations. This development was assessed by self-report through examples she brought up of her experiences with new activities. For example, Ann had enrolled in a class related to her work and participated fully in the discussions. Ann also felt strong enough to consider recontacting her biological parents without bothering about others. Her life satisfaction increased and scores on the Why Worries Questionnaire (Freeston et al., 1994) decreased.

The following is a dialogue where the therapist and Ann first make the connection between her anxiety scenarios and her vulnerability as a self-theme. Her realization of the link between her positioning in her anxious narratives and other everyday situations helped her address and change a core self-belief underlying her worries.

Vignette (T = Therapist; Ann = A) – Ann and powerlessness

T: So your stories always end with you being stranded.

A: Yes. I realized that – always the worst case. I always seem to end up with the same dire fear.

T: But I think from what you've said, your powerlessness in these scenes is an extreme form of what you feel elsewhere. Isn't it?

A: What do you mean? That the fear is similar, it's the same fear in different disguises?

T: No, not that you're always afraid. But your feelings about yourself with regard to others.

A: Well, the panic's the worst thing I fear, the scene that most threatens. It's not just physical threat, it's very emotional.

T: So that's important, isn't it? Emotional similarity but in different degrees. Would you say it's similar in other situations? It's the same in other situations... the same but less intense?

A: I mean... I'm... well I do put myself in the same mood in other stressful situations, except the consequences don't spiral off.

T: An interesting point. So, you wear the same attitude and you feel in a familiar position.

A: Well, less intense but I'm still down there... not up to it.

T: You mean you feel inferior in a lot of situations, not just anxious ones.

A: Yes and I'm so used to it, I put up with it.

T: Can you give examples?

A: When I'm with people, my colleagues, my boyfriend's parents, I sometimes have similar feelings of being overwhelmed, like I'm lost, helpless, in the face of their knowledge. Well I consider them in the know.

T: So this position of being, you said, helpless, it repeats itself.

A: Yes. I hadn't fully realized it before. I don't know why. Sometimes the people are very nice too. I guess it's just a habit.

Case 3 – Martin

Definition of problem

Martin was a 38-year-old man, father of two young children. For the past 15 years, he had lived with his partner, the children's mother. He worked in information technology for a major company. Martin confided that he was contemplating relocating and quitting his current job because of interpersonal conflicts; he said this had occurred a few times before, with past employers. He added that the arrival of his second child was difficult for him because it complicated his capacity to organize his life. He explained that unpredictable or unexpected situations could create conflicts in his relationship with his spouse. He noted feeling irritated by people who are unable to plan properly.

Martin presented for psychotherapy because for the previous 2 years, mainly in the evening, he had experienced spells of anguish and anxiety. He presented for his physical symptoms of heart palpitations, tremors, chills, blurred vision, numbness in the hands, tightness in the throat, jaw and neck pain and headaches.

During the interviews, Martin spontaneously described his model of experiencing his stress accumulating in a kind of 'tank' (as in a hydraulic system) that could contain a certain maximum capacity. He now said he thought his physical symptoms resulted when his stress overflowed the system. He felt that the system acted entirely outside of his ability to control it and he reported feeling 'condemned' to suffer from this process for the rest of his life. His objective in seeking therapy was to confirm if he had a medical problem or not.

The therapist's assessment of Martin after preliminary evaluation was the presence of somatic anxiety brought about by a stressful pattern of behaviour, both at home and at work. He had adopted several strategies that he considered aided his stress (overpreparation, avoidance and an abrupt interaction style) but that potentially exacerbated his stress. Martin had opted for a medical explanation because he saw no way out of the problem and because it was the less threatening option. The formulation required further exploration of all these factors plus some experiments to establish which patterns were a maintaining feature.

Exploration

The therapist was able to tease out from Martin a number of other areas in life where he experienced personal and interpersonal stress. These included work, work conversations, meal times, interpersonal interactions, planning and family occasions. One area was work and it was clear that Martin had a low opinion of his co-workers due to his perfectionist personality, calling them all 'twits'. The therapist was able to flush out a sequence to the perfectionist aspects of his personality, such as his fear of making mistakes and his extremely critical attitude towards himself and others, which led him to become more susceptible to anxiety, mainly in the areas of health and interpersonal relationships. To cope with this anxiety, Martin used strategies (e.g. extreme vigilance, muscle tension, reassurance, catastrophic expectations, anticipation, intolerance of uncertainty, rigid rules and expectations with apprehension), which had the paradoxical effect of maintaining his anxiety, preventing him from having confidence in his problem-solving abilities and leading to low self-esteem (Figure 6.7). Therefore, when a work situation threatened his sense of competence in his skills or his self-esteem, his insecurity was triggered and this led him to use self-sabotaging strategies (e.g. verbal attacks, thoughts rumination, pervasive thoughts and vindictive plotting), culminating in interpersonal conflicts, which in turn heightened his anxiety, sometimes leading to full-blown anxiety attacks and a heightened risk of making life-altering impulsive decisions (e.g. quitting his job and moving town). The therapist was a young female, and frequently his critical style spilled over in therapy, which the therapist astutely picked up and reflected back as an experiment to help him reduce stressful conflict and hence anxiety. She made the client aware of how his critical attitude engendered tension in himself (and potentially herself) and affected the interpersonal interaction. These effects produced more tension and reactions in others, so not only confirming his prejudice that others were 'twits' but also bringing a risk of spiralling negativity. Frequently, he would approach people with a question, expecting a duff response, and so almost soliciting it by this premature judgment and phrasing: for example, 'I don't suppose you know about this program? No. I thought not. Is anybody an expert here?' These interactions, while confirming his view of others, also produced in Martin a constant fear of his own failure and not being competent enough in his work. So, for example, he would meticulously plan his actions both time-wise and in detail, so he would never be at a loss of what to do. Any loose time not foreseen and accounted for was a threat to his competence. His anxiety peaked when things were not done on time or just so or he had not strictly pre-planned activities.

The therapist's summary of Martin was as a man plagued by a number of sources of stress that had led to somatic complaints. He seemed to experience stress at work, in the home, with his family, and in interpersonal interactions. When the stress triggered feelings of insecurity and incompetence, stress turned to panic. In order to make himself feel more secure, he had adopted strategies to buffer himself against the uncertain, the unforeseen or ego-threatening through the adoption of a rigid pattern of interactions and planning, which exacerbated conflict and stress. In order to test this causal model, more information was needed on the relation between his perfectionist

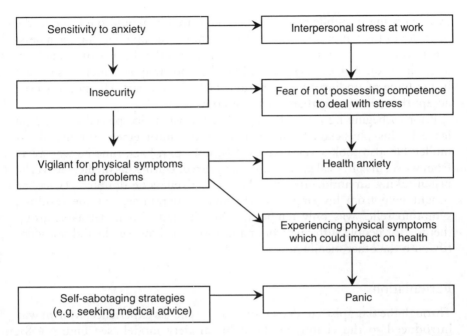

Figure 6.7 Vicious circle of anxiety. This schema illustrates specifically the link between Martin's work, stress, health, anxiety and coping fears and his somatic and cognitive complaints. Self-sabotaging strategies elevated the anxiety into panic.

pattern of planning and his anxiety. Also, it was important to discuss with Martin his potential control over somatic anxiety by stress management (Figure 6.7).

Developmental factors

Martin reported having had a typical and stable childhood with his younger brother, mother and father. He explained that his parents were not stern disciplinarians; he described their style of parenting as 'rather uninvolved'. Martin reported that he had some difficulty adapting at school. In adulthood, at work, he had experienced problems with some of his superiors. He explained that his symptoms had a sudden onset, approximately 1 year after the birth of his second child. He noted having undergone many medical tests over the 2 years, none of which revealed a medical explanation for his experience. Martin was sure he had a medical condition that had been undetected by the doctors. His discourse focused almost entirely on his somatic complaints throughout his life, which also dominated his life decisions. Because of his disabling symptoms, Martin avoided being alone with his children; he also avoided being in public places because he feared he would faint due to the intensity of his symptoms, which arose without warning. During the assessment process, he said that he had always believed that he was suffering from a serious medical illness. He also said that he made frequent Internet searches in the hope of finding an explanation for his symptoms. He did, however, accept that stress exacerbated his symptoms.

Prior to beginning psychotherapy, Martin was twice placed on medical leave by his physician. So he had received reinforcement for his illness model. He also took several days off without pay. Each time he was away from work, his physical symptoms disappeared. During his medical leave, he began taking an antidepressant whose effectiveness he doubted. Twice, he sought help from his employee assistance programme, but the resulting symptom relief was only temporary. Martin had also undertaken group therapy for people suffering from panic disorder; however, he did not identify with the other members.

Formulation

Through the therapist's understanding of the client's experience, Martin was introduced to the vicious circle of his anxiety model (see Figure 6.8), customized to his experience. The first general schema links his perfectionism with his stress and his sensitivity to anxiety plus his health concerns and rigid interpersonal style. Martin appreciated that his different complaints, which he had seen as fragmented, were encompassed in a single model. Once Martin understood and accepted the model, he worked with the therapist to create an exhaustive list of the strategies he had been using to feel secure, which were then placed in an hierarchical order, from the easiest to the hardest to change, according to his own scale of difficulty. These included planning meal times at home, relaxing, relating to his kids and his relations with others at work whom he considered 'twits'. The formulation involved exposing with Martin his interlocking pattern, where perfectionist meticulism led to overplanning and a demanding routine that produced somatic and psychological anxiety in Martin and tension in his relations with others. The therapist and Martin decided to target an aspect of his perfectionism, his overplanning, as a gateway to a more relaxed interpersonal style.

Intervention – Perfectionist planning

Martin elected to begin by working on his perfectionism and hyper-planning strategies rather than on his interpersonal problems because it was more accessible for him. As an experiment, the therapist and Martin agreed that he could be less concerned that meals be served on time at his house. Martin reported that he felt less stressed and that being more flexible was relaxing. Each week, Martin identified which self-sabotaging strategy to try to change for the next therapy session. He was provided a three-column-table home-work (one column for the old, maladaptive strategy, one column for the new, adaptive strategy and one column to note outcome) to encourage him to take time to analyze how he managed his anxiety, to find new strategies most appropriate and apply them and to observe how he felt after. The new strate-gies involved less planning in his routine. For example, he did not 'have to' always eat at the same time and follow the same order at meal times. He real-ized he was less frustrated when he was more flexible. This exercise pleased Martin as it appealed to his perfectionist tendencies. Martin completed the table and report every week so that he could analyze together with the thera-pist the better to support him in this process of change and clarify new strate-gies as needed. He completed and brought back the table every week.

Martin liked the monitoring. The monitoring helped Martin to see that there was a sequence of events, thinking and acting that triggered his panic attacks and other physical symptoms. Contrary to what he had previously believed, the attacks did not come 'out of the blue' and he could therefore have some control over them. In a series of behavioural experiments, Martin approached new situations without excessive planning and preparation. By changing these rigid thoughts and behaviours, he was able to recognize that he was more competent in coping with unexpected or unfamiliar situations than he previously believed, and this had a significant impact on his self-esteem.

Another part of the treatment was the twice-daily practice of active mus-cle relaxation as well as breathing exercises to help reduce his physical symptoms. Martin's mixed hypotheses about him suffering a stress-related illness were tested by training Martin in breathing techniques and progres-sive relaxation. The therapist and Martin agreed that if he practised these regularly and his tensions and somatic signs improved, he would consider a tension–anxiety explanation of his somatic complaints rather than an undi-agnosed medical illness model. Martin did indeed practise the exercises and noted improvements not only in his somatic complaints but also in the intensity of his anxiety response and so was prepared to consider the two linked. Martin challenged his own previous hydraulic model of emotions and himself produced arguments to refute it. He dismantled his former beliefs that his stress 'just built up', that inevitably it would 'spill over' to somatic complaints and that if it built up too much, he would 'explode'.

Intervention – Interpersonal issues

A revelation to the client was how his anxiety was connected to his interper-sonal attitudes. After adoption of alternative planning schedules and reduction of stress, the therapist addressed interpersonal therapy. At the interpersonal level, the therapist mainly worked to reframe Martin's belief that others contributed to his anxiety attacks and physical symptoms and that he was condemned to suffer other's foolishness. The therapist helped him to see through role-play that it was his rigid style of interaction that prevented him from coping with the unexpected and led him to feel angry and tense, which triggered panic attacks. For example, he would pose a question to a colleague, expecting in his tone and expression an inadequate answer. He would subsequently scrutinize the answer to find inadequacies, so souring further interaction or stalk away feeling vindicated. Martin was encouraged to question his prejudices and his rigid attitudes towards others in order to reduce his anger and anxiety in his interpersonal relationships. He gradually became aware of how maladaptive, even aggressive, interpersonal styles can sometimes develop from anxiety.

Martin also felt he could not change the environment where he worked as he was surrounded by twits, or, as he put it, 'condemned to be with twits' and that if he communicated with them, his tension and insecurity would get worse. So he decided he should say nothing, do nothing and not engage at all in conversation or feedback with colleagues but keep his ideas to himself. But these same strategies he adopted to safeguard himself against stress coupled with his self-sabotaging solutions provoked his panic attacks. Again, the therapist devised a behavioural experiment where Martin began gradually to question his colleagues more and express his ideas rather than tolerate his frustration to contain his 'pressure' or 'steam'. In fact, subsequently, he reported reduced tension.

At the midpoint of psychotherapy, when Martin was experiencing almost no physical symptoms, he had a sudden relapse after a dispute with his boss. He had resorted to his abrupt and bottled-up response rather than calmly responding and seeking further information. The therapist helped him process this experience with reference to the 'vicious circle' model and choose more effective coping strategies (Figure 6.8).

So as can be seen from Figure 6.8, the therapist considered his perfectionism played a key role in producing a sensitivity to anxiety. He worried about being up to scratch, competent and efficient, and this worry led inevitably to insecurity, which made him sensitive to anxiety. This sensitivity led to his health anxiety and also to strategies to regulate everyday and interpersonal contact, which ultimately increased stress response somatically and relationally, all this to safeguard his ability to cope. But, of course, these same strategies put in question his ability to cope. So the hypothesized intervention was to lift off sabotaging strategies and introduce constructive ones.

Outcome and evaluation of therapy

After 20 sessions, Martin reported feeling the benefits of the relaxation exercises – less pain in his neck and shoulders – and that he was regaining control over his life and feeling less condemned. He had stopped researching his 'medical' symptoms on the Internet; he had not gone to the emergency and had experienced

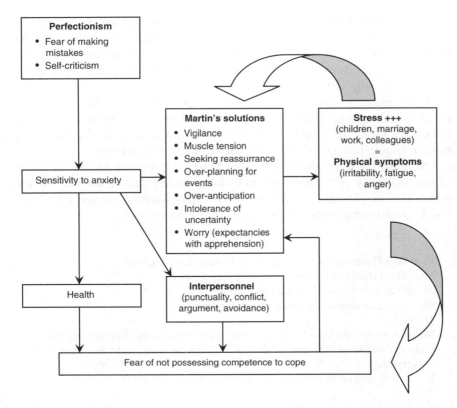

Figure 6.8   Vicious circle of anxiety. This schema describes the principal components of Martin's overall vicious circle, including interpersonal, perfectionist, family, work, health and coping concerns and how they interacted around the fear of not possessing competence.

only minor anxiety attacks, reminding him to keep practising his new, more adaptive mental habits and interpersonal strategies (Figure 6.8). Two months after the end of psychotherapy, Martin reported no physical symptoms related to anxiety save for a mild episode that occurred 3 weeks before our follow-up call. He explained that he had gradually stopped doing his exercises and relaxation because he was feeling fine and was on vacation. When he realized that the symptoms had returned, he recommenced doing his exercises and the symptoms disappeared immediately. For example, if Martin did not prepare in advance what he had to say but let himself be more spontaneous, he felt more relaxed and to his surprise he did not lack things to say but rather appeared less wooden. Martin had prejudged what his boss wanted to say and interpreted it as a reprimand. When examined closely, the boss was only seeking information, and we saw that the reason he asked Martin was because he valued his competence. He said that he now feels better able to take a step back and confront his anxiety rather than suffer the consequences of avoidance. Now, he follows the steps of therapy, when he has a tinge of anxiety; he starts breathing, which releases his tension; he checks to see if he is overplanning, preparing and prejudging and then faces the situation naturally as himself (Figure 6.9).

Martin filled out the Generalized Anxiety Disorder Scale (Wells, 1997) in order to gain a better understanding of the severity of the anxiety as well as the coping strategies used by Martin and his attitudes about the usefulness of worrying in general, all of which decreased after treatment.

The following is a dialogue following Martin's agreement to test the utility of overplanning as a means of controlling anxiety and his report on the outcome. The dialogue reveals to the therapist Martin's awareness of the link between complaints, stress and his perfectionist style.

Vignette (Therapist=T; Martin=M) – Martin and planning
M: Yes, I tried being more flexible. It was difficult
T: What was difficult? Changing routine?
M: Not planning so rigidly, it changed things.
T: How?
M: For years I thought I was right, giving the impression of being competent, sharp, poised. I still find it difficult not to be bang right on time with everything.
T: You think you appeared a 'competent' 'efficient' person?

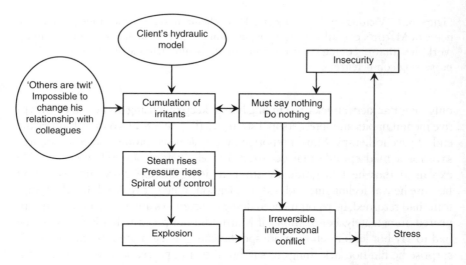

Figure 6.9   This schema describes how Martin's hydraulic model of stress interacted with his rigid view of his relationship with clients to produce a paralyzing tension and apparently intolerable conflict.

M: I thought so, though inside I was tense.

T: Now, how do you think you appeared?

M: I realize I put others on edge, it wasn't necessary.

T: And now, how do you find being natural, just being yourself?

M: I'm less frustrated, less edgy. I've realized I don't have to be so concerned with those things. I'm naturally well organized. I still like to be on time. But I'm more relaxed. I don't plan like I used to. I certainly have less stress complaints.

T: And less complaints about people?

M: Well, relations with the kids are better, they kind of opened up more and we're more friendly, and basically things get done, we eat, wash up, but it is more relaxed. I have less symptoms, medical symptoms. So I guess it was stress.

T: And at work?

M: Ah, now not everything changes at once. It's a work in progress. But I realize I was a bit stiff with people. I still think some of them are 'twits' but I suppose I don't feel it reflects on me. I don't get so rattled about it.

T: So what's your conclusion?

M: I was in a pattern and, well, that the whole business was giving me pains, tension.

T: What exercise brought this home?

M: The breathing and relaxation, the natural way I now act. I felt I was doing good, organizing my life. So I guess being less rigid, relaxing more; changing my routine, especially early in the morning. At my job, with my interactions with people, well there's still work to do. It's not easy, and it's easy to forget when I'm rushed. I sometimes catch myself. So I have to prac-tise. Well, I realize that even things do not have to be done to the minute, they can still work out.

Discussion

All three cases described here followed a case formulation approach. The approach is presented here in the spirit of the guidelines put forward by Ira Turkat, Vic Meyer and Michael Bruch, in sticking closely to the client's experience and concerns rather than relying on a blanket diagnosis. This person-centred approach produces not only an authentic picture that relates to the person in their entirety as a functioning person at work, in the family, and in interpersonal daily life. The approach also steers us away from a rei-fied focus on symptoms, which, in a sense, de-contextualizes the person from their own experience and compartmentalizes the person into bodily, mental and emotional signs disconnected from one another. In the case of Martin, the presenting symptoms were somatic and could have easily led to somatic treatment. Likewise, his interpersonal problems could have been considered a secondary diagnosis.

It is difficult because of the interactive nature of the formulation to isolate in the three cases our adherence strictly to anyone therapeutic approach. Models were tested, revised and further validated collaboratively with the client on the basis of their experience rather than a source manual. There were elements of both the meta-cognitive model of worry and classic exposure in John's intervention but the model also used insight into his contradictions and ambivalences, which were addressed independently and not present in standardized treatment.

Martin was an interesting case since his treatment for anxiety included changing interpersonal and perfectionist planning strategies, which could very easily have been sidelined or considered a separate diagnosis and treated separately. But in our case formulation, these aspects formed a core part of the cycle maintaining Martin's panic and anxiety: one could say an essential part only revealed by mapping the sequence in a collaborative and ecological schema.

Ann represents perhaps the application of a more uniform narrative approach but even here the narrative content was idiosyncratic and thematic. It ultimately related to a vulnerable self-theme revealed not by a top–down prescribed model (i.e. schema-focused approach) or a downward arrow supposedly leading to more global 'deeper' reasons behind an assumption but simply by idiosyncratically relating content of the personal fears to the vulnerability of the person's self.

The case formulation approach emphasizes connecting up in a functional analysis all aspects of everyday functioning, some of which may seem initially irrelevant, even to the client. But the analysis helps to understand how the pattern of interpersonal and anxious behaviours produce not only self-evident somatic and behavioural symptoms but also direct or indirect behavioural and personal consequences remote from original anxiety, such as frustration, anger and impatience. Negative emotions seem produced initially by a seemingly isolated anxiety response that is the client's focus but while respecting this focus, the background context from which it arises must be considered.

Behavioural or cognitive experiments were used when appropriate for testing the supposed impact of thoughts or behaviours. In Ann's case, there was a direct link between her own feelings of social vulnerability and the content of her narratives of her ending up helpless following a disaster. However, using the strengths implicit in Ann's ability to immerse herself in her narrative scenario, the therapist was able to use imagination to modify her anxiety. Whereas a more conventional positive autobiography and reality-testing procedure helped her change assumptions about the judgment of others and her own coping abilities.

In the case of Martin, intervention was necessary at several levels to effect change and the order of interventions was crucial. It is doubtful, for example, if his interpersonal tension could have been reduced without confronting his hydraulic model or that his irritation and stress in his family dynamics could have reduced without dismantling his perfectionist preparation routines. Obviously, the case formulation approach here insisting on listing all problems from no matter which domain and connecting them collaboratively is a key factor in linking up what might appear to be independent problems.

The construction of individualized schema in collaboration with the person and verifying and validating the sequence in discussion with the person confirm the validity of the schema path. Further discussion elicits the 'point of entry' into the vicious circle of anxiety and hence pinpoints the priority to address, which in turn gives a temporal order to the intervention.

The concept of a vicious circle or conflict from which the person cannot escape seems crucial to deciding on levels of intervention and to deciding on the appropriate sequence for the 'point of entry' to break the cycle since frequently the pattern is recursive with one thought about a thought leading to a reaction that generates another thought. Anxiety seems never a simple matter of one reaction but a tortuous chain. Deconstructing anxiety frequently reveals a process rather than a vague state. This reciprocal process linking of thoughts is crucial to understand their progression. For example, in the case of John, the cognitive strategy of accepting and letting aversive thoughts go by itself would have been ineffectual without considering also the moral judgments such thoughts produced due to his perfectionism about 'reacting in the right way' and the subsequent fear that such thoughts could entail loss of control and what this further implied for John. An isolated downward arrow technique may have revealed the meaning of his thoughts about thoughts but not the interaction between his emotions, his testing and avoidance in provoking anxiety.

This schema approach not only furnishes a theory-driven design with fertile ground for subsequently testing hypotheses about causes and consequences. In stimulating and deepening the awareness of the client to the connectedness of their problem, the approach is also likely to elicit any further problems from the client which are necessary for a sufficient formulation.

A further positive point of this case formulation approach was how we were able to use the strengths of each client in devising and applying their own treatment. John's forte clearly lied in his ability to intellectualize and chain together meta-cognitions; so a meta-cognitive approach was successful since it tapped into the same process (his meta-cognition) that caused anxiety. Ann's imagination was clearly instrumental in determining her anxiety, and she possessed a good imagination and storytelling ability. This ability proved useful in finally making her stories more grounded and repositioning her. Martin's perfectionist tendencies allowed him to monitor precisely his own strict planning and rigid expectancies and permitted addressing specific components in his interpersonal tendencies that were producing him anxiety.

References

Barlow, H. B. (Ed.). (2002). *Anxiety and its disorders. The nature and treatment of anxiety and panic* (2nd ed.). New York: The Guilford Press.

Beck, A. T., & Steer, R. A. (1993). *Beck Anxiety Inventory manual.* San Antonio, TX: Psychological Corporation.

Borkovec, T. D., Alcaine, O., & Behar, E. (2004). Avoidance theory of worry and generalized anxiety disorder. In R. G. Heimberg, C. L. Turk, & D. S. Mennin (Eds.), *Generalized anxiety disorder: Advances in research and practice* (pp. 77–108). New York: Guilford Press.

Buhr, K., & Dugas, M. J. (2002). The iintolerance of uncertainty scale: psychometric properties of the English version. *Behavior Research and Therapy, 40,* 931–945.

Cartwright-Hatton, S., & Wells, A. (1997). Beliefs about worry and intrusions: The Meta-Cognitions Questionnaire and its correlates. *Journal of Anxiety Disorders, 11,* 279–296.

Craske, M. (1999). *Anxiety disorders.* Boulder, CO: Westview Press.

Freeston, M. H., Rhéaume, J., Letarte, H., Dugas, M. J., & Ladouceur, R. (1994). Why doo people worry? *Personality and Individual Differences, 17,* 791–802.

Frost, R. O., Marten, P., Lahard, C., & Rosenblate, R. (1990). The dimensions of perfectionism. *Cognitive Research and Therapy, 14,* 449–468.

Hayes, S. C., Strosahl, K. D., & Wilson, K. G. (1999). *Acceptance and commitment therapy: An experiential approach to behaviour change.* New York: Guilford Press.

Ladouceur, R., Freeston, M. H., Rhéaume, J., Dugas, M. J., Gagnon, F., Thibodeau, N., et al. (2000). Strategies used with intrusive thoughts: A comparison of OCD patients with anxious and community controls. *Journal of Abnormal Psychology, 109,* 179–187.

Lucock, M. P., & Morley, S. (1996). The Health Anxiety Questionnaire. *British Journal of Health Psychology, 1,* 137–150.

Mathews, A. M. (1990). Why worry?: The cognitive function of anxiety. *Behaviour Research and Therapy, 28,* 455–468.

O'Connor, K. P., Gareau, D., Gaudette, G., & Robillard, S. (1999, November). Relaxation and the treatment of generalized anxiety disorder. *Presentation at the Association for the Advancement of Behavior Therapy,* Toronto, Ontario, Canada.

Ost, L.-G. (1987). Applied relaxation: Description of a coping technique and review of controlled studies. *Behaviour Research and Therapy, 25,* 397–409.

Watson, D., & Friend, R. (1969). Measurement of social-evaluative anxiety. *Journal of Consulting and Clinical Psychology, 33,* 448–457.

Wells, A. (1999). A metacognitive model and therapy for generalized anxiety disorder. *Clinical Psychology and Psychotherapy, 6,* 86–95.

7

Cognitive-Behavioural Formulation and the Scientist-Practitioner
Working with an Adolescent Boy

David A. Lane and Sarah Corrie

Introduction

Formulation has been identified as a defining competence of skilled psychological practice (Atter, 2009; British Psychological Society, 2005; Corrie & Lane, 2006, 2010; Division of Clinical Psychology, 2011; Health Professions Council, 2009; Johnstone & Dallos, 2006; Lane & Corrie, 2006). Indeed, some would argue that it is the act of formulation that distinguishes the delivery of systematic and rigorous psychological interventions from the kinds of supportive interventions offered by lay helpers (see Butler, 1998).

Since its introduction to clinical psychology regulation in 1969, use of the term now extends to all major disciplines within the psychological professions. However, as noted by Lane and Corrie (2006), '…the use of and process by which formulations are created is contentious' (p. 41). Moreover, the way in which formulation is defined and understood within applied psychology varies from discipline to discipline. For example, within clinical and forensic specialties, strong emphasis is placed on basing formulation on data obtained from the initial assessment, whereas in counselling psychology, this represents a more collaborative process with the formulation unfolding over time. Within educational psychology, priority is given to the knowledge-building process and the structuring of interventions with individuals and systems, whereas for health psychologists, the application of research to formulation of health policy and health promotion is critical. In consequence,

Beyond Diagnosis: Case Formulation in Cognitive Behavioural Therapy, Second Edition.
Edited by Michael Bruch.
© 2015 John Wiley & Sons, Ltd. Published 2015 by John Wiley & Sons, Ltd.

the act of formulation cannot be seen as one specific activity, conducted by all practitioners in the same way, but rather depends on the purpose for which, and context within, a given formulation is to be used.

This chapter offers readers a model of formulation – the Purpose–Perspectives–Process model – that can assist practitioners in devising a systematic and effective procedure which is consistent with a scientist-practitioner approach.[1] We discuss a particular application of this model – DEFINE – as used in the UCL Case Formulation approach. To contextualize this model, we first re-examine the functions that formulation is widely believed to serve and briefly review some of the main controversies surrounding the accuracy and effectiveness of individualized case formulations. We then describe the Purpose–Perspectives–Process model and provide a case illustration[2] using DEFINE to demonstrate how this approach assisted a rigorous, creative and effective approach to working with an adolescent client. The case study is embellished with general guidelines for undertaking this method of formulation, in order to enable the reader to better understand the DEFINE model and to help refine the rigour of their own approach.

The Functions of Formulation: A Review of the Key Debates

In its broadest sense, a formulation can be understood as a psychologically informed explanatory account of the issues, dilemmas or problems with which a client is presenting. This explanatory account forms the basis of a shared framework of understanding that has implications for change, and thus for any intervention subsequently implemented. As a psychological account, a formulation can reasonably be expected to draw upon psychological theory, general scientific principles (such as how to test hypotheses), research findings from the wider literature, prior professional experience and the guidance of peers and senior colleagues (e.g. in the context of supervision).

There are many ways of defining formulation. However, there is a reasonably good degree of consensus about the range of functions that this task can serve. Reasons commonly cited include facilitating a detailed understanding of a client's needs (including both developmental and maintaining factors); refining the search for relevant theoretical concepts; prioritizing client concerns; planning and delivering an appropriate intervention, determining criteria for a successful outcome and working effectively with obstacles to progress (see Corrie & Lane, 2010, for a review).

More specifically, a formulation equips the practitioner with a systematic means of applying relevant psychological knowledge (theoretical constructs, research and other forms of discipline-specific information) to a client's story, problem or dilemma for the benefit of the client and others involved. The information provided by clients and gleaned from various assessment tools is rarely straightforward to interpret. Understanding the client's needs is, therefore, often a process of imposing a sense of meaning on the wealth of complex, often ambiguous and even, at times, contradictory, data obtained. In this context, a formulation can function as a framework for clarifying those questions that are likely to uncover fruitful avenues of enquiry, create thematic links between past events, present circumstances and future hopes and refine the search for any additional information that is needed.

A second function of formulation is to identify which areas of a client's experience or behaviour will be prioritized in any intervention subsequently offered. It is important to recognize that not everything is amenable to change, and therefore, informed decisions must be made about the most appropriate focus of the enquiry and what interventions might be used in the service of any specific goals.

A third function of formulation is to aid empathic understanding, particularly in those cases where the client's behaviour may challenge the practitioner's empathic skills. Consider, e.g. a client's continual 'resistance' to complying with homework tasks. A therapist's response is likely to be more empathic and effective if grounded in a formulation that includes an appreciation of how the client tends to rely on avoidant coping strategies to manage distressing internal events and lacks adaptive alternatives for managing uncomfortable thoughts, feelings and sensations. Sheath (2010) provides an example of how this function of formulation is even more vital when working with clients whose behaviour can evoke strong negative feelings in practitioners and wider society (in this case, clients who sexually offend). Difficulties in terms of insufficient progress, challenges associated with implementing a specific intervention or ruptures in the relationship with the client can be reflected upon in an impartial manner in order to identify potential ways forward.

Along similar lines, having a formulation can help protect against decision-making biases that could impede effective working. The literature on decision-making in professional practice (see Lane & Corrie, 2012) has consistently highlighted a wide range of cognitive errors that permeate our work, often without our awareness. By ensuring that practice-based choices are underpinned by a robust, psychologically informed explanatory account of the relationship between different aspects of a client's experience, it becomes possible to articulate and, where necessary, challenge the thinking that underpins the approach taken. Arriving at a formulation does, therefore, permit a degree of transparency in the decision-making process that supports reflective practice and allows for a critique of any decisions made.

Formulation can also function as a form of professional communication in order to organize professionals around the development of a shared understanding. This then benefits the client through ensuring a consistency of approach. For example, if multiple professionals are involved in a client's care, there is the potential for the client to be subjected to conflicting opinions that hamper effective service provision. A formulation can, therefore, unite many professionals who may be involved in a client's care around the same issues, priorities and goals (Lane, D. A., & Green, F., 1990).

However, formulation also has the potential to become a means of communicating with other professionals about the status of one's knowledge. In her review of the use of the term in clinical psychology, Crellin (1998) describes the influences on how the concept of formulation emerged. Specifically, she highlights how formulation came to represent a form of political leverage through which psychology established its autonomy from psychiatry. For many years, psychology remained within the grip of psychiatric description through the use of symptom matching and diagnostic labelling. As Bruch and Bond (1998) pointed out, clinicians were traditionally expected to define their work with clients in terms of psychiatric classification systems which determined the treatment offered. Influential psychologists at that time (most notably, Eysenck, 1990; Shapiro, 1955, 1957; Shapiro & Nelson, 1955) argued for an approach which emphasized clinical–experimental work (the beginnings of the scientist-practitioner model in the United Kingdom) centred on learning principles, thus challenging these expectations. This was elaborated by Meyer (see Bruch & Bond, 1998) who highlighted that the dilemmas for the clinician are that (a) not all clients sharing the same complaint respond to the procedural requirements of techniques and (b) practitioners are rarely presented with clients with isolated complaints, particularly in mental health settings.

Meyer rejected diagnostic systems as a means of determining choice of treatment and instead advocated individualized formulations that were shared with clients rather than devised by the therapist and then imposed. Further contributions to this approach have followed (see Corrie & Lane, 2010; Kinderman & Lobban, 2000; Kuyken, W., Padesky, C. A., & Dudley, R., 2008; Lane, 1974, 1978, 1990; Lane & Corrie, 2006; Mumma, 1998; Turkat, 1985). Formulation based on diagnostic models was, therefore, counterbalanced by formulations informed by a scientist-practitioner perspective (see Lane & Corrie, 2006).

Although, for reasons of space, we do not elaborate this issue here (the interested reader is referred to Corrie & Lane, 2010), the debate about the role of diagnosis continues, particularly in the current climate where health care delivery faces concurrent demand for both tighter quality control and value for money. Equally, we would argue that the issue of formulation as a political tool is re-emerging in professional dialogues today. As Corrie and Lane (2010: p.8) explain:

> …in an already over-crowded market, the degree of sophistication, complexity and explanatory power of their formulations may become part of how certain professional groups differentiate themselves from others. In this sense, being

able to construct formulations and using these as a basis for communicating with other professionals (1) provides practitioners with a degree of reassurance about their ability to explain clients' concerns and thus, their own competency and (2) provides a vehicle for communicating with other professionals about the veracity and authority of that knowledge.

It follows, then, that the act of formulation can serve multiple functions. Some of these will be explicit and some less so.

Do Formulations 'Work': A Brief Review of the Evidence

Despite the professional rhetoric, it is yet to be empirically determined whether or not having a formulation has any direct impact on therapeutic outcome. Indeed, there is some evidence to suggest that practitioners' faith in formulation as a means of achieving improved outcomes may be somewhat over-optimistic (see, e.g. Schulte, Kunzel, Pepping, & Shulte-Bahrenberg, 1992). Wilson (1996, 1997), e.g. has argued in favour of manual-based, empirically validated interventions on the basis that individually tailored formulations always rely upon professional judgement that can all too easily prove flawed (see also Dawes, 1994; Dawes, Faust, & Meehl, 1989).

Within a cognitive-behavioural approach, a number of attempts have been made to evaluate the inter-rater reliability and predictive validity of formulations (see Barber & Crits-Christoph, 1993; Horowitz & Eells, 1993; Persons, Mooney, & Padesky, 1995). Bieling and Kuyken (2003) have found that while practitioners can agree at the descriptive level about key features of a case, their interpretations of the more explanatory components vary widely. They distinguish top-down and bottom-up criterion for evidence-based conceptualization. The former works from inferences from theory or research applied to the single case. Hence, the theory is used to structure understanding of the client's presenting concerns, shaping both the information sought and the interpretive lens through which the client's narrative comes to be understood. Bottom-up approaches (i.e. those that adopt a data-driven approach to enquiry) work from an attempt to map a reliable and valid case formulation on to the client's presenting difficulties. The practitioner works back to theory as necessary to elaborate upon that understanding.

Based on research into the application of cognitive-behavioural theory, Bieling and Kuyken (2003) propose that accuracy is too varied to provide confidence in any formulation achieved. If we add to this what is known about some of the biases in professional decision-making (Lane & Corrie, 2006, 2012), it is not easy for even highly experienced practitioners to have confidence in the formulations we generate.

Kuyken, Padesky, and Dudley (2009) have responded to these, and other, challenges of cognitive-behavioural therapy formulations by proposing the metaphor of a crucible. As they explain,

> The crucible is where theory, research, and client experiences are integrated to form a new description and understanding of client issues. While grounded in evidence-based theory and research, the conceptualization formed in the crucible is original and unique to the client and reveals pathways to lasting change. (p. 26)

They also propose that one of the reasons why our formulations are not always favourably received by our clients is that they have tended to take the form of therapist-driven accounts presented to the client, rather than being constructed in partnership with them. Their use of the metaphor of a case conceptualization crucible identifies three key features: (1) heat drives chemical reactions in a crucible (the collaborative empiricism between therapist and client provides the heat); (2) like the chemical reaction in a crucible, the formulation develops over time, starting with more descriptive elements and gradually expanding to include predisposing and protective factors and (3) the new substances formed in a crucible are dependent on the characteristics of the chemical compounds put into it.

In her examination of the issue of reliability, Butler (1998) has argued that a direct comparison of the effectiveness of manual-based versus individually tailored approaches may obscure rather than illuminate some of the complexities involved. Specifically, she points out how practitioners use covert formulations, derived from prior theoretical knowledge and experience, that frame how they listen to their clients' concerns form the earliest stages of the therapeutic encounter. Far from being 'less reliable', such an approach may represent an example of practice-based evidence, where evidence derived from knowledge of the client's story and the lessons from our own professional experience form the basis of effective and ethical practice (Corrie, 2003, 2009).

For Butler (1998), the purpose of a formulation is not to arrive at clear-cut answers, but rather to generate multiple hypotheses that can assist choices about the direction of the enquiry. Thus, the benchmark criterion may ultimately be one of usefulness rather than accuracy. Bieling and Kuyken (2003) also observe how issues concerning the reliability and validity of therapists' formulations always contain inconsistencies and that the extent to which the 'quality' of any given formulation directly impacts on outcome (as opposed to exerting a more indirect effect) remains ambiguous. Perhaps this is why Crellin (1998) has argued in favour of a formulation that emerges at the end of therapy, and one that is essentially owned by the client rather than the therapist.

Nonetheless, the debate about the standing of individualized case formulations, and the merits of these relative to disorder-specific models, is not easily dismissed. Moreover, in recent years, the importance of delivering empirically supported interventions has taken on a new meaning in the context of official guidelines, such as those from the National Institute for Health and Clinical Excellence, as well as the UK Government's Improving Access to Psychological Therapies initiative for training and employing an extra 3,600 therapists to deliver evidence-based psychological therapies for depression and anxiety disorders (Department of Health, 2008). Such developments can, if misunderstood, appear to offer straightforward answers about what is indicated for which clients and when.

Drake (2008) has proposed that professionals are increasingly operating in 'a culture of pragmatism' where swift solutions are privileged over more exploratory interventions. In such circumstances, as Josselson (1999) observes, there can be a tendency for practitioners to seek prescriptive guidance on what to do and when. The promise of well-defined procedures that, when systematically applied, can obtain predictable positive results holds an understandable allure for the practitioner confronted with large amounts of clinical information. Nonetheless, many of the challenges encountered in practice cannot be neatly categorized and so do not lend themselves to protocol-based interventions as Meyer long ago argued (Bruch & Bond, 1998). Disorder-specific models and other protocols and frameworks are often very useful. However, in our view, there is no protocol that can eliminate the need for professional judgement and still allow us to practice safely. Effective professional practice demands the capacity to think at multiple levels, hold in mind diverse sources of data and aim for understanding about what contributes to particular concerns whilst simultaneously being able to devise potential solutions. This complexity was acknowledged in the British Psychological Society Guide to Good Practice in Case Formulation (Division of Clinical Psychology 2011).

Having reviewed, albeit briefly, some of the main debates surrounding and development and use of formulation in clinical practice, we make the case for an individualized approach to formulation that retains rigour, holds the practitioner accountable for their clinical decision-making but also allows for the creative application of theoretical constructs and permits a flexibility of approach. A good formulation, as we see it, is not necessarily one that can be demonstrated to be 'correct' in any factual sense, but is rather a framework through which the practitioner can demonstrate the following:

- They were able to identify the issues of central importance.
- They used a specific theoretical model or multiple models in a systematic way to develop their understanding of the client's presenting complaints.

- The formulation enabled the identification of specific hypotheses that lend themselves to subsequent testing.
- The intervention plan was compatible with the theoretical model/s chosen.
- The formulation was linked to the aims of therapy.
- Their formulation influenced the use of particular therapeutic methods or techniques.
- Potential challenges to the therapeutic process were anticipated.

In the next section, we present an approach to formulation that is consistent with the earlier principles and that can be adapted to the needs of any specific enquiry regardless of the theoretical perspective taken. We then provide an illustration of this approach through a case study.

A Generic Framework for Developing Formulations: The Purpose–Perspectives–Process Model

Drawing on the literature reviewed in this chapter, as well as our previous work on both formulation and the scientist-practitioner model (Corrie & Lane, 2010; Lane, 1978, 1998; Lane & Corrie, 2006), we define formulation in broad terms, as the co-construction of a narrative which provides a specific focus for a learning journey. This learning journey takes the client from where they are now to where they want to be, based on a process of negotiating agreed goals. The task of formulation centres on the creation of a shared framework of understanding that has implications for change.

In our work, we have found it helpful to focus on three domains which we would see as a useful guide to constructing helpful formulations with clients. These are the following:

1. The Purpose of your work
2. The Perspectives that inform it
3. The Process you will use to carry it out

This model is presented here, following an illustration of its use in practice. These domains provide a generic framework for thinking about formulation. The DEFINE model we use later is a specific application of those domains.

Purpose

In carrying out any psychological enquiry, it is vital to be clear about its fundamental purpose. The shape that your enquiry subsequently takes will follow on from here. Neither conducting an assessment of, nor devising explanatory hypotheses about, a client's concerns can proceed in any truly informed way until the nature of the enquiry has been agreed by all parties involved. Therefore, the starting point on the shared journey between you and your client begins as you work together to define a clear sense of purpose to the work that lies ahead. This gives rise to the following types of questions:

- What are you setting out to achieve (in terms of results, processes of change, relationship, or type of journey)? How do you explain this – what is your story?
- What is your client defining as their purpose in engaging in this encounter with you, here and now? What do you do to make it possible for the client to tell their story and to feel heard?
- What type of client purpose is best served by your offer or your service context?
- With whom would you not work (whether due to limits of competence or service constraints), and where is the margin of that boundary?
- What is the context for this encounter that makes it meaningful?

According to the requirements of a particular case, establishing the Purpose for which an explanation is required may be a relatively swift and straightforward process or a significant piece of work in its own right. Determining factors will be numerous and varied, ranging from the practitioner's preferred approach, to case management issues and the service in which the work is provided, as well as the number of stakeholders involved and how each party understands the issues of concern and defines their involvement. The combination of factors in each particular case will lead to the privileging of certain types of information over others, shaping beliefs about the choices that practitioner and client have available to them (Honeychurch, 1996). In consequence, the landscape of knowledge and prevailing conditions do not merely reflect the realities in which practitioners provide their services; they also organize them (Gonçalves & Machado, 2000).

Perspectives

As part of developing a shared purpose, it is important for the practitioner to be able to define what they bring to the encounter. This includes their values, beliefs, prior knowledge and preferred therapeutic approach, as well as the models that inform their work (and those of the service in which they see their clients). However, clients also bring perspectives of their own which will inform the work that is undertaken and which must, therefore, be given equal consideration in the enquiry that follows.

Identifying and exploring these perspectives gives rise to questions like the following:

- On what sort of journey are you and your client engaged (e.g. are you working within a therapeutic model that is concerned with treating symptoms to promote recovery from a specific disorder? Or are you working with a therapeutic framework that encourages the facilitation of the client's self-told story? Are you looking to change some aspect of the client's functioning or seeking change in the wider system that surrounds the client?)
- Some journeys prescribe or proscribe certain routes (such as specific techniques and methods). How do you ensure coherence between your perspective and that of your client?
- What are the values, beliefs, knowledge and competences that you each bring to the encounter? How do you ensure that the client is able to explore their values, beliefs, knowledge and competence within the encounter?

Traditionally, those who use psychological interventions have tended to enter the journey towards a shared understanding from one of two positions. The first is the view that they, as the professional, hold the key to the client's dilemma and that this lies in a single theory or model – i.e. a particular perspective. The second is a preference for hearing the story first and then seeking the perspective which best fits.

In the first example, practitioners will look at specific aspects of the client's concerns rather than the client as a whole. Practitioners operating from this position do not need to hear the entire story first. Certain aspects of the client's story will be privileged over others, as a function of practitioners' allegiance to their chosen perspective (such might be the case for those practitioners who listen selectively for examples of unhelpful, biased cognitions). Of course, this does not mean that such practitioners do not seek to ensure that the client feels heard. However, the formulation which follows will be filtered through the particular lens of a specific theoretical or conceptual worldview which identifies a limited number of key events as critical to bringing about change.

For those who favour the second approach, the starting point is one of hearing the story first and then seeking the perspective which best fits. There have always been practitioners who seek multiple explanations. Carkhuff and Berenson (1967), Meyer (see Bruch & Bond, 1998) and Lane (1975), amongst others, aim to hear the story and then consider it through multiple perspectives as they work with the client to construct, deconstruct and reconstruct its meaning. Indeed, as Bruch (1998) pointed out, one of the features of Meyer's work was his willingness to draw upon a wide range of perspectives in addition to his core model. Thus, the formulation that emerges will take varied forms; key events are identified and explanations for their impact derived from a range of approaches that are subsequently woven into a coherent clinical theory specific to the client.

Process

Once the Purpose of the work has been defined, and the Perspectives that underpin it are clear, then it becomes possible to structure a Process for the work that is to follows. Without the Purpose and Perspective defined, the Process becomes the delivery of a series of techniques that are essentially uninformed by psychological principles and knowledge. Although teaching clients specific techniques can be highly beneficial and requires a high degree of competence, we would argue that it is not an example of skilled professional practice. In such an approach, the essence of the client as a unique individual is absent, as is the psychological investigation necessary to determine what is happening in the client's life that leads them to the point of change. In this context, the key question becomes this: What Process (including any method or tool) is necessary to ensure that the Purpose is met within the constraints of the Perspectives available to us?

As scientist-practitioners, we need to be able to move between the idiosyncrasies of the client's story and any relevant evidence-base that might guide the exploration. Thus, the practitioner moves from the particular to the generic and then creates a formulation that satisfies the demand for investigative rigour and individual relevance. Its use assumes that there is an applicable evidence-base that can support the enquiry or that a generic hypothesis-testing model could supply appropriate evidence. As such, the approach to Process follows a research enquiry – a hypothesis-testing process.

This empirical approach to Process in applied practice requires two elements to be present, one generic and the other particular (Lane, 1973). The generic element refers to those aspects of the story which are shared among the community of practitioners that adopt an empirical framework, and which reflect the culture in which members of that community are socialized. The generic requires the enquiry to satisfy applied research criteria, such as reliability and validity. Experiments conducted and conclusions reached are expected to be subjected to measures of confirmation and disconfirmation. Methods adopted, as well as any intervention that proceeds from it, need to be consistent with the relevant literature as well as the available evidence-base. For example, in considering a client presenting with an issue around depression, understanding is required of both the literature on features of influence on the development and maintenance of depression as well as the evidence-base on the effectiveness of different interventions.

The second element, the particular, represents the approach as it is adapted for the specific enquiry to take account of the stakeholders engaged. Thus, the approach is also co-constructed though combining generic and particular stories. To follow on from the earlier example of depression, the particular requires that the client is enabled to tell their story in terms of their unique experience of depression. It requires that the client is engaged as co-researcher in exploring factors which matter to them and others involved. Any formulation which emerges must feel salient to them, and the intervention plan must be one that the client believes to be both desirable and feasible. Outcomes and any evaluation must enable the client to maintain any gains for the future and optimize their life chances resulting from the intervention – i.e. the journey needs to lead to a place which is preferable to where the client started.

In the next section, we provide a case example to illustrate the empirical approach to Process.

A Process Model Derived From the Empirical Approach: DEFINE

Bruch (1998) has referred to the five phases in the DEFINE model as it was applied in case formulation at UCL (see Chapter 2). We believe that these five phases are relevant beyond the confines of this case study and so present them here for the reader to personalize. These phases are contained in the acronym DEFINE (Definition, Exploration, Formulation, INtervention, Evaluation) and are described as follows, using a case study – an adolescent boy whom we refer to as 'Peter' – to illustrate its application.

The Definition phase of DEFINE

In the Definition phase of the DEFINE model, the principal concern is one of arriving at an agreement on the main issue(s) of concern. This enables a journey of change to commence. Critical questions used to aid clarification include the following: How can each party be enabled to tell their story and come to an agreed understanding of the shared concern they are going to work on together? How does each party define the issue that concerns them? What objectives are they seeking to achieve, and what role do they each wish to take in achieving those objectives?

The main task in the Definition phase of the enquiry is to increase awareness of the key issues in order to arrive at a consensus about the question to be tackled. Each party who represents a 'stakeholder' in the process and outcome of the work is encouraged to tell the story from their perspective in order to gain a clear sense of how the parts of the story connect for them, their sense of ownership of the story and the diversity of possibilities present. For example, do they see a possible solution, or are they so committed to their interpretation of events that it allows no deviation from the current perspective? Once the 'stories' from all parties are clarified, it becomes possible to see the linkages between them, the points of divergence and to work towards agreements around shared areas that might form a starting point for the journey. Often clients can agree on the behaviour that concerned them while disagreeing on the reasons (causes) for it. However, if they are open to the possibility of change, they can agree that this might be worth investigating further.

Peter – A case example   Peter, a 14-year-old boy, was referred for behaviour problems consisting of 'violent and impulsive outbursts' and an 'aggressive attitude' in the school setting. There was some conflict between the teaching staff with some wanting him removed from school immediately, and others prepared to consider the possibility of working with him to bring about change. The referral was to the Islington Education Guidance Centre, whose purpose was to support professionals, children and families in resolving behavioural issues in a way that maintained children in school.

The starting point in working with Peter and his teachers was to clarify each participant's story in order to define shared areas of concern that might form the basis of an intervention. In defining the areas of concern, the aim was also to clarify whether the referral was consistent with the purpose that the Islington Education Guidance Centre was designed to serve.

The first task was, therefore, to enable key participants to tell their story and to seek clarity about the issues of concern so that factors of influence could be identified and explored. A definition of the issues as 'violent and impulsive outbursts' and an 'aggressive attitude', e.g. clearly lacks specificity and cannot be explored in any detail. In consequence, it was necessary to discover precisely what Peter was doing that the teachers were defining in this way and what Peter himself also believed that he was doing.

The choices at this stage included interviewing key stakeholders, asking them to clarify the behaviours of concern, using formal questionnaires, direct observation and a review of existing reports on his behaviour collected by teachers. In this case, a starting point was to review the anecdotal reports received by the Head of Year from individual teachers to see what specific behavioural information might be available. This produced a

number of examples that could potentially be used as a starting point. These
were the following:

1.   Peter running around the classroom when requested to stay in his seat
2.   When asked by other pupils to stay quiet, arguing with them or hitting
     them (the 'violent outbursts' initially noted)
3.   Refusing to carry out instructions from some teachers
4.   Leaving school without permission

These examples raised further questions. For example, did Peter always
respond to requests to stay in his seat with running around the classroom,
or did he sometimes comply? And if he did sometimes comply, what differ-
entiated these occasions? Did he consistently refuse some teachers' requests
or refuse all teachers requests some of the time? What factors would prompt
his refusal? What caused him to leave school, and what would constitute a
legitimate request?

Anecdotal material was treated with caution as it cannot, in isolation, be
considered a basis for Definition. Rather, it is one of several sources of
information that needs to be verified through further interview and/or
observation to arrive at a working statement that can form the basis for
reliable observation. Some further examples help illustrate this process of
verification. The following are in relation to Point 1:

- If Peter got up and walked around (rather than ran around) the classroom,
  would this still be an issue of concern?
- How fast did he have to move for this to be labelled as 'running'?
- Was it acceptable for Peter to walk/run when this was not accompanied
  by a request to stay in his seat?
- What exactly does the concern look like so that it could be observed?
  (This was not clear).

Similarly, the example of Peter arguing with or hitting other pupils when
they asked him to remain quiet implied a functional relationship between
the request and the response. However, it was not clear whether this hypothesis had actually been tested or was an assumption of causation by the
teacher. Since this was seen as an example of the violent outbursts, was it
implied that all outbursts had a trigger or were there outbursts without a
specific antecedent? In working within an empirical approach to formulation, there is little point of creating an observation schedule until these issues
are clarified. In Peter's case, it was decided that rather than talk to the
individual teachers, a more efficient starting point would be to discuss
the reports with the Head of Year, since he had previously discussed the
reports with the teachers.

In reviewing the reports with the Head of Year, it became clear that, in his view, each example of behaviour did not matter; it was the general failure to comply with instructions that triggered concern (ranging from anger to despair) for the teachers and was interpreted as 'an aggressive attitude'. The Head of Year also had a view on why this was an issue with some teachers. Specifically, he felt that Peter complied with requests from strong teachers but proved challenging with 'weaker' ones. He had no idea why Peter left school on occasions stating that permission was always required.

At this point, we were presented with a decision point (Lane & Corrie, 2012): Do we frame this as an issue for the teachers (i.e. 'strong/weak') and explore definitions around how they manage the classroom? Or should we explore this as an issue for Peter in terms of what he would define as the behaviours of concern? (Note that we could not, at this stage, assume the accuracy of the Head of Year's assumptions that Peter chose to ignore some teachers rather than others.)

In trying to decide the route to take, the history of the issue can provide clues. For example, if this was a relatively recent issue, it would be possible to check if changes in those teaching Peter corresponded with the emergence of the problematic behaviour. If, however, this is a long-standing issue, how far back in time does it go back – e.g., to a previous school? There is also a political dimension – how would teachers respond to the idea that the problem behaviour is a matter of weak/strong teachers rather than being an issue with a difficult child? This is a very sensitive matter in schools. Although the Head of Year might state this privately in a conversation, it might not be an avenue of exploration that can be approached directly.

In school-based referrals, there is usually a great deal of background information available. In this case, there was evidence to suggest problems throughout Peter's school career, although there was also information to suggest that the problems had definitely worsened in the last year, at least from a teacher's perspective. There were also reports on the family background indicating that Peter's father was in prison and that the family were facing financial difficulty. Moreover, there had been a change of teacher as Peter had changed years and had also made some choices in terms of subjects to pursue for GCSE. He was judged to be a weak student who might get D or E grades with effort. Given that the issues seemed to have become more of a problem in the year leading up to the referral, it was decided to seek to define the issues from Peter's point of view at this point.

Peter's story   It is important that the interview is set up in a way that does not compromise the ability to hear the client's story. The arrangements for the interview were established with the Head of Year who agreed it would be appropriate to ask Peter to see someone from outside the school who could take an independent view of the current situation and listen carefully to his story. On meeting Peter, it was confirmed that this was indeed how the meeting had been set up. Nevertheless, he remained cautious and wanted to understand the consequences of any refusal by him to discuss specific issues. Assuring the client that the interviewer (DL) was genuinely interested in hearing his point of view was a starting point, but Peter first wanted to learn something about the person to whom he would be revealing his story. Once he was satisfied with the answers he had been given, he began to tell his story about life in school.

For Peter, life in school was both difficult and contradictory. He felt that he was struggling in a number of subjects and believed that help was not available. In his view, there was no point in talking to the teachers as they did not listen and insisted upon following their instructions regardless of whether or not it was possible to do so. Moreover, some teachers were not respected by pupils, whereas others were feared, and some were liked. A key issue for Peter was that of respect, and it was important, in his view, to gain respect from other pupils. This for him was primarily through making sure they '…looked up to him' (i.e. were afraid of him), and if someone crossed him or tried to tell him what to do, they had to be subdued to avoid the risk of loss of respect. Peter recognized that he misbehaved in class. However, he said this was mainly when he was confused about a topic and when it was not possible to ask for help, as help was unlikely to be forthcoming and would result in loss of respect from peers. When asked about leaving school without permission, he said he had only done this on two occasions. In each case, this had occurred when he was, so 'wound up I would have hit someone if I didn't get out'. For him, leaving was a better way to manage the situation than hitting someone.

Towards defining the issue of concern   What was apparent from the conversations was that if asked just to describe the behaviour (without interpretation), there was reasonable agreement between Peter and the staff about what had happened. The difficulty arose when each party added their interpretations of the behaviour, which implied specific motivation for the actions observed, as there was substantial disagreement.

This is a very common problem when discussing children's behaviour with teaching staff – both add justifications to the description making it difficult for them to separate what they believe to be a cause from what they might be able to objectively observe as the behaviour of concern. Our first task, therefore, was to define the behaviour of concern in such a way that each party could agree on what needed to be observed. We would later have to agree objectives for each party before finally specifying the behaviour we were going to analyse.

There are a number of ways to do this. For example, it is possible to do further interviews to tease out the behaviours. Another possibility would be to set up an observation schedule and ask staff and the pupil to complete it. It would also be possible to use a teaching assistant to observe or use standardized questionnaires (see Lane, 1990, for a full review of options). In this case, as there were different views amongst the teaching staff, it was decided that a member of the Guidance Centre would observe Peter in a sample of lessons. It was agreed that failing to follow instructions would be the behaviour noted. Additionally, any example of Peter hitting or threatening to hit another child would also be recorded. He was given a report book in which at the end of the lesson, the teacher had to briefly describe any incident and Peter also had to note it. At the end of the day, the teachers and Peter were interviewed about the incident. Recording it at the time helped them to revisit it later in the day. We thus have triangulated sources of data with the teacher, child and observer recording instances of the target behaviour. In addition, the observer undertook a General Setting Analysis (Lane, 1978, 1990). In a General Setting Analysis, the situations in which the behaviour occurs are compared with situations in which it does not occur in order to identify possible factors that increase or decrease the likelihood of occurrence.

The data revealed no incidence of the behaviours in two sample lessons. In the other lessons sampled, there were three examples of not following instructions, one example of threatening another child in one sample, and one example of not following instructions in the second sample. The reports were compared in the triangulation process. These were then examined in the light of the General Setting Analysis. The results were then discussed with the Head of Year in order to obtain his view.

Findings from the Definition stage   What emerged from this phase of the enquiry was that there were examples in all lessons of Peter following instructions. The teachers only noted not following instructions when he had started to interrupt other children, or when he moved about the room and was instructed to stop but did not do so. Peter's view was that he 'got messed up' when he could not do the work set and the teacher failed to offer help when asked. He stated that he, '…warned other kids when they made comments about his struggle that disrespected him so they had to be sorted'.

Noting that he also seemed 'messed up' in other lessons but did not move or otherwise cause difficulties in some lessons, Peter stated that in these cases, he would stop the behaviour when the teacher concerned looked at him because '…you do not mess with that teacher'. In another class, he stated that the teacher was always clear that he could follow the work set and that she helped when asked. The General Setting Analysis provided observations to support Peter's view. He also added (which was not part of the observation) that sometimes he '…got so mad' that he had to leave school to calm himself down; otherwise, he would hit someone. The observer also noted that a fairly consistent outcome of the behavioural sequence in class was that he avoided the piece of work he was supposed to be completing.

The Head of Year was surprised to learn of the reasons why Peter left school without permission. He was not surprised by the differences in response between lessons (in terms of observed behaviour) but was unaware of Peter's justifications for those patterns. The Head of Year's view was that whatever the supposed justification, Peter had to follow instructions. His objective was for the child to comply with instructions. Peter stated that he wanted to have help when he needed it. In agreeing goals for the work, we agreed to further exploration to see if we could clarify the factors of influence on asking for help and following instructions with a possible view to addressing some of them. So we moved on to the Exploration phase of DEFINE.

The Exploration phase of DEFINE

In Exploration, the principal concern is one of identifying those factors that make the appearance of the behaviour more or less likely, and which give meaning to the stories presented. This entails a process of testing the explanatory accounts that each party holds as to why the issue of concern has occurred. In our case example, what emerged were multiple beliefs that shaped each party's response. To move forward, the task was one of encouraging each party to present their explanatory account as a testable hypothesis. It is important to note that no presumption about the relationship is assumed; rather these are identified solely as possible areas for exploration. Hence, we are checking for explanatory accounts that are justified by an evidence-base while maintaining a commitment to the particular accounts of the client and others involved. The lay explanations, the research literature and our own studies were all available to guide the areas for exploration.

Three areas often feature in both the lay and research accounts as worthy of exploration are as follows:

1. What factors predispose the likelihood of a given behaviour occurring (this could include constitutional, developmental, historical and trait factors; personal, interpersonal and systemic factors)? The lay account might include the idea that some children are born bad, have bad genes or a bad upbringing or that certain forms or ways of organizing teaching are not appropriate. The key is to define these in ways that can be tested.
2. What factors in the setting make the appearance of the behaviour more likely (e.g. consideration of settings in which a behaviour does and does

not occur and any differences in those settings)? The lay account might include the idea that some classrooms/schools are better organized than others (e.g. that the child pays attention and works well where the teacher carefully explains the task and tracks completion, and positively reinforces efforts to tackle the task or deals with frustrations. Where these elements are not present, the disruptive behaviour becomes more likely).

3.   What factors precipitate and perpetuate the occurrence of the behaviour in question? (e.g. generating a clear definition of the behaviour being considered including its autonomic, cognitive and behavioural components; the factors that immediately preceded the appearance of the behaviour in question; the immediate consequences of any behaviour and the extent to which the client's story was reinforced or challenged by the outcome. These could include personal, interpersonal and systemic factors.) The lay account might include the idea that the child struggles in English classes because he is a poor reader, gets frustrated with the task and 'blows up'. An alternative approach is to explore the totality of the conditions that make the emergence of the behaviour more likely, thus emphasizing the context in which the behaviour occurred rather than specific precipitating and perpetuating factors (reproduced from Corrie & Lane, 2010).

Through exploring the earlier points, it is possible to find common ground – what we might term, a 'shared concern' – between lay and professional accounts. The process becomes one of increasingly refined observations to explore the extent to which different parties' accounts achieve a degree of coherence, to test the hypotheses that those accounts suggested and to determine likely causal factors.

A certain amount of data based on triangulation observations and discussions about the meaning of those observations to the parties involved was already available. Those data provided possible areas for exploration but did not constitute hypotheses that could be tested. As such, it was important to create hypotheses which could then be subjected to testing. Here, there questions are critical:

1.   What factors predispose the likelihood of a given behaviour occurring?
2.   What setting factors made the appearance of the behaviour more likely?
3.   What factors precipitate and perpetuate the occurrence of the behaviour in question?

Peter's story   In school contexts, there is often a lot of information on children available in files. These were discussed with the Head of Year and organized by him with a sample of teachers to explore possible predisposing factors. A discussion was also held with Peter to discuss his view of the history of issues arising.

Two distinct narratives emerged in the conversations with staff. For some teachers, this was a child with a difficult family background who showed considerable disrespect towards authority, who did not listen and who rejected attempts to help him with his difficulties. For these teachers, the belief was that Peter needed to be placed in a special unit that would be better suited to his needs. For others, Peter was a boy who could be disrespectful and had poor relationships with his peers. However, if he were managed firmly, he would respond positively and valued help as long as it was done in private. These teachers observed that he struggled in class and found it difficult to accept help in front of his peers. They believed that if properly managed, Peter could be maintained in school. There were ongoing records of problematic behaviours through his secondary school career although his primary school reports were more positive. The family were seen as non-cooperative with the school having failed to respond to letters or requests for meetings. His father was currently serving a term of imprisonment and had apparently served previous custodial sentences.

There was social work engagement with the family, and it was the social worker who sought and gained permission from the mother to this current investigation (although the mother made clear she did not want to be involved). The social worker believed that Peter was coping well in a family where the burden for managing in the father's absence fell largely on his shoulders. His mother who had a disability relied on Peter, and he accepted a high level of responsibility for the younger children in the family. He was seen as strict but caring towards his siblings and supportive of his mother and, in the social worker's view, angry towards his father.

Peter was not prepared to talk about his home situation during the current investigation. He saw this as separate from issues in school. However, from talking about issues he experienced with teachers and children, a number of features emerged. A central theme was that of respect. It was very important to him that he received respect from other children (life could be dangerous in his view if you did not have that), and it was obtained by making sure others were afraid of you. He also talked about those teachers whom he respected and those whom he did not. Those whom he saw as strong ('...no one would mess with them') were respected (i.e. people were afraid of them). A separate but related theme was respect for those who listened and helped you with your work (i.e. those by whom he felt respected) compared with those who did not listen of help (those by whom he felt disrespected).

At this stage, we had some detailed information that could form the basis of hypothesis generation which could be tested through further interviews or observations. While we had the original observations triangulated from the classroom observations, they were not set up to test hypotheses but rather to help to define the issues. This can raise issues of reliability and validity when information collected for one purpose is then used for another. In the Exploration phase of DEFINE, we are testing hypotheses so need to be robust in the approach taken. One area that had not emerged was consideration of the consequences of the behaviours observed – what happens as a result of Peter's threats and of his not following instructions? There are several suggestions as to antecedents; at this stage, there was a reasonable idea of the behaviours concerned, but little information about the consequences of those behaviours. We also had some understanding of the beliefs that informed Peter's behaviour, but whether these represented a coherent narrative or simply a series of post hoc justifications was not yet known.

We can also at this point consider what perspectives might be used to explore the pattern that is emerging. From a cognitive-behavioural perspective, we would be interested in the ABC pattern to explore factors that precipitate and perpetuate the behaviours. There was reason to believe exploring Peter's beliefs could provide a useful insight into the meaning the behaviour had for the different parties.

Based on the initial data gathering, it was decided that an ABC analysis together with some exploration of the relevant beliefs in play would provide a potential framework for formulating an understanding. However, the possibility of an alternative was kept under consideration.

It was decided to start with repeated observations in sample classes (different ones to the first occasion) and then a discussion with Peter going through the observations and asking him what was happening from his perspective. He was aware that was intended and agreed to meet at lunch time and the end of the school day when the observations were relatively recent. The observation was set up to note those occasions when he followed instructions and those when he did not, and any general setting differences between them as well as an ABC analysis of those incidents. The distinction was made between generic following of instructions directed to the class and particular instructions directed at him. For the ABC, an observation was made of the sequence of events from an instruction being given to a period of 3 min thereafter. Those observations were then shared with Peter.

A number of features were clear from the observations. First, Peter was more likely to follow instructions when engaged in the work. Second, he was less likely to follow instructions when he was showing signs of difficulty in completing work or when his attempts to get help were ignored. Third, it was clear that if he got into trouble with teachers for failing to follow instructions, the consequence was that he avoided doing the difficult work – teachers were distracted from the primary task of getting him to do the work towards dealing with the non-compliance.

In the conversation that followed, Peter raised a number of issues. He noted that if another child made a negative comment when Peter had difficulties with work, this to Peter was an example of disrespect that he had to act against. Making others afraid of you meant that they respected you. Similarly some teachers were strong, made you afraid and they were respected. He had no respect for teachers who did not help you with your work and who were not strong. He stated that his father was respected by others who were afraid of him. This to some extent protected his family as he felt he lived in a community where you were at risk of attack.

He was asked if there were people whom he respected who did not make others afraid. He thought about this and stated that he respected the Head of Year as someone who did listen and whom others (children and staff) respected. It was also apparent that he entered some classrooms with a mindset which was non-cooperative based on the history of his relationships with that staff member.

At this point, a decision was made to attempt a formulation with him and his Head of Year to construct a coherent account that could explain factors that predisposed, precipitated and perpetuated the behaviours. Out of that, we then attempted the construction of a potential new story to find a way forward.

The Formulation phase of DEFINE

In the Formulation phase of DEFINE, the emphasis is on arriving at explanations that make sense to those involved and which could form the basis of a journey going forward. Again three areas were involved, incorporating generic (the relevant research evidence) and particular accounts (gathered in the setting). These are as follows:

1. The reliability and validity of the data that might be used to arrive at meaningful accounts (NB: the accuracy of the evidence-base matters not just its utility).
2. The different stakeholders had to be prepared to deconstruct their existing accounts and reconstruct a new account which provided a different view enabling change to happen. Those accounts could be personal, interpersonal or systemic.
3. Intervention hypotheses had to be agreed between the parties so that new objectives could be formed. The targets for change might include any area of activity including personal, interpersonal or systemic elements.

The critical question underpinning the development of the new account was 'What new shared account (story) of the behaviour is meaningful to us now, and how can we use that to create a different future?' The formulation had to reflect the story as it was and as it could become as well as the means (people, resources, activities) to arrive at a new, preferred outcome. The process was one of construction, deconstruction and reconstruction based on the agreed hypothesis testing that had taken place. It also had to conform to the characteristics of a good story (Corrie & Lane, 2010) in terms of engagement and positive orientation to be most useful.

The first issue was to decide whether the data were sufficiently reliable and valid to use as a basis for formulation, or whether additional data were needed. Given the triangulation of the data across sources and the classification between the observers, Head of Year and Peter himself, as well as the sampling of data across classes and comparisons between situations in which difficulties did and did not occur, it was decided that there was sufficient justification to proceed. The formulation created was thus as follows:

> Peter is a 14 year old boy who has been in trouble with his school for failure to comply with instructions, leaving school without permission and fighting with other children. He is seen as a child who should be removed from school by some staff but others are prepared to work with him – as long as he changes his behaviour. Peter takes the view that it is important to be respected and this equates to others being afraid of you. He states he does not follow instructions from teachers who do not listen or who are not respected. This is supported by the observation data. When faced with difficult work and unable to get help from the teachers he stops working and will not follow further instructions from teachers. When he has difficulties with work if other children make comments he threatens them to ensure they know that they have to be respectful of him. Very occasionally he gets so angry with other children that he leaves the class to avoid hitting them. His behaviour (threats to children) is reinforced by their submission to him which confirms to him that they are now respecting him. His avoidance of work is reinforced by the fact that teachers then stop asking him to do it. He thereby avoids the negative feelings he gets (which undermine his own self-respect) when struggling with work. His Head of Year accepts this account of the situation and wants to see him learn to comply with instructions. Without this he will not be able to retain him in school.

In discussion between them, both Peter and the Head of Year accepted this as an accurate account of the current situation.

In attempting to deconstruct the story to create an alternative narrative which enables movement forward, we discussed the issue of respect and in particular Peter's view of the Head of Year as someone who was respected but of whom others were not afraid. This led to an exploration of how it might be possible to behave in such a way that a person might be respected without making others afraid. Neither party could specify the behaviours involved, so it was agreed that Peter would observe and make notes on the

Head of Year's behaviour in classes that they shared. He was to focus particularly on interactions between the teacher and the other children including how the teacher gave instructions and how the children responded.

The INtervention phase of DEFINE

In the INtervention phase, the main focus is creating an agreed plan for change and monitoring its impact. Three aspects are central here, namely, that the following:

1. The areas for action are clearly specified and agreed by all parties.
2. A contract for change is established.
3. The agreed programme is implemented and monitored. The theme is one of increasingly refined and monitored practice in order to create the new story that has been re-authored in the formulation.

Working with Peter – the INtervention phase   It was decided to begin this phase with Peter monitoring his Head of Year's interactions, recording these and then discussing them with him. The aim was to identify strategies that drew on those observations that Peter could use when interacting with others.

This was attempted over a 2-week period, and Peter collected a considerable amount of data which were then discussed with the teacher (Head of Year). From this, Peter concluded that the Head of Year's strength came not from people being afraid but because everyone knew the boundaries of what was acceptable, and that the teacher listened carefully to needs expressed, i.e. he tried to support children but also made clear when they would have to follow instructions even if they disagreed. He noted following conversation with the Head of Year that private conversations often happened after the event where the teacher explained his reasoning.

They then discussed how Peter might modify his behaviour to get a better response. The conclusions he drew from this were that even teachers who do listen sometimes have to instruct and that it is better to talk to them privately afterwards, than to confront them at the time. Peter also recognized that sometimes boundaries might be helpful parameters (rather than impositions) from an authority figure. He then agreed with the Head of Year an intervention plan with strategies for named teachers. In some cases, he recognized that if he did not get a hearing, he would leave the matter and take it up with them privately. The Head of Year negotiated a temporary arrangement whereby teachers agreed to meet with Peter briefly and privately to discuss concerns.

Peter was impressed although doubtful that this would happen. The Head of Year stressed that this was a temporary arrangement in order to get compliance from other teachers and from Peter. This intervention was implemented for 1 month and then evaluated.

The Evaluation phase of DEFINE

In the Evaluation phase, the central focus is one of identifying the factors that contributed to change and considering the options that these afford. This comprises evaluating areas of change, optimizing gains and establishing future objectives. It also enables the practitioner to reflect upon and learn from the journey in order that future client interventions can benefit.

In this case example, it was important to justify the quality of interventions and also to check that the framework of practice used was meeting the need. However, for Peter, this was also a learning journey. Reflecting on that journey enabled him to refine his own skills and consider how he might use them again in future, thus supporting the generalization of his new skills.

Working with Peter – the Evaluation phase   Peter found that the number of confrontations with teachers and peers was reduced to near zero in the trial month. He felt that he had been treated with considerable respect by the teachers, and his peers stopped confronting him although no specific intervention was introduced for this. The Head of Year reported positively on the response of teachers to Peter's new approach. However, there was concern about what would happen subsequently. Peter and the Head of Year negotiated that for a period of 3 months he would continue to try the new pattern, but if he needed to talk, he would do so with the Head of Year and would also discuss matters with other teachers. This was evaluated every 2 weeks, which indicated that while there was an occasional incident, these were resolved through the joint conversations. Peter continued to observe patterns in interactions and make judgements and had occasional conversations to address issues arising.

Some Further Thoughts on the DEFINE Model and General Conclusions

In our work, we have found it helpful to focus on three domains which we would see as a useful guide to constructing helpful formulations with clients. These are as follows:

1.   The Purpose of your work
2.   The Perspectives that inform it
3.   The Process you will use to carry it out

As stated previously, these domains provide a generic framework for thinking about formulation. The DEFINE model described in this chapter and illustrated with a case example represents one specific application of those domains.

The DEFINE model illustrates how it is possible to undertake formulation as an empirical process whilst honouring the different stories that each party is bringing to the work that needs to take place. One theme concerns the stakeholders in the story and how they define the journey together at the outset (definition). The story then explores explanations (exploration) they use for their current predicament including both lay and professional accounts. The diverse explanations are then brought together in the form of an account that gives meaning to the journey so far and the one which is about to be undertaken (formulation). The story then takes the characters forward to an alternative future including how they are going to get there (intervention). It concludes by bringing together the ending, wrapping up the learning and looking forward to a different future (evaluation).

We have also sought to provide the reader with an overview of some of the key issues and debates relating to the task of formulation in professional practice. Despite the complexities, it is our position that formulation is always central to psychological practice and part of our ethical and professional responsibility to our clients. However, as noted by Corrie and Lane (2010), it may not always be the case that we have to formulate every aspect of the client's experience in order to identify a helpful way forward. Nonetheless, we would argue that it is essential to develop a systematic approach through which each of us can explain how we identify, understand and respond to the key issues of concern. At the heart of this approach must lie an ability to explain how we draw upon and utilize psychological principles and knowledge to guide our approach and change course during the process of a client enquiry when this proves necessary. Formulation is never a neutral application of the evidence leading to the best possible intervention for the client. Rather it is an account that is created to meet specific needs, for identified stakeholders, at a specific point in time.

The Purpose–Perspectives–Process model offers one approach to formulation to working actively with these issues. We offer it in the hope that it helps readers reflect upon their own, usual way of working and will allow them to devise new, more creative and ultimately more effective ways of addressing the diversity of their clients' concerns.

Notes

1. This chapter draws upon ideas discussed in the first edition of this book (see Lane, 1998) as well as more recent work developed by Corrie & Lane (2010). The interested reader is referred to Corrie & Lane (2010) for a more detailed description of the approach outlined in this chapter.

2. Although the case study is based on work carried out with an actual client, in order to protect confidentiality, some potentially identifying features have been omitted or changed.

References

Atter, N. (2009). Interim supplementary guidance for chartered psychologists seeking approval and acting as Approved Clinicians. *Forensic Update*, 98, 7.

Barber, J. P., & Crits-Christoph, P. (1993). Advances in measures of psychodynamic formulations. *Journal of Consulting and Clinical Psychology*, 61(4), 574–585.

Bieling, P., & Kuyken, W. (2003). Is cognitive case formulation science or science fiction? *Clinical Psychology: Science and Practice*, 10(1), 52–69.

British Psychological Society. (2005). *Subject benchmarks for applied psychology*. Leicester, UK: British Psychological Society.

Bruch, M. (1998). The UCL case formulation model: Clinical applications and procedures. In Bruch, M. & Bond, F. W. (Eds.), *Beyond diagnosis. Case formulation approaches in CBT*. Chichester, UK: Wiley.

Bruch, M., & Bond, F. W. (1998). *Beyond diagnosis. Case formulation approaches in CBT*. Chichester, UK: Wiley.

Butler, G. (1998). Clinical formulation. In A. S. Bellack & M. Hersen (Eds.), *Comprehensive clinical psychology* (Vol. 6, pp. 1–24). Oxford, UK: Pergamon.

Carkhuff, R. R., & Berenson, B. G. (1967). *Beyond counselling and therapy*. New York: Holt, Rinehart & Winston.

Corrie, S. (2003). Keynote paper: Information, innovation and the quest for legitimate knowledge. *Counselling Psychology Review*, 18(3), 5–13.

Corrie, S. (2009). What is evidence? In R. Woolfe, S. Strawbridge, B. Douglas, & W. Dryden (Eds.), *Handbook of counselling psychology* (3rd ed., pp. 44–61). London: Sage.

Corrie, S., & Lane, D. A. (2006). Constructing stories about client's needs: Developing skills in formulation. In R. Bor & M. Watts (Eds.), *The trainee handbook. A guide for counselling and psychotherapy trainees* (2nd ed., pp. 68–90). London: Sage.

Corrie, S., & Lane, D. A. (2010). *Constructing stories, telling tales: A guide to practice in applied psychology*. London: Karnac.

Crellin, C. (1998). Origins and social contexts of the term 'formulation' in psychological case-reports. *Clinical Psychology Forum*, 112, 18–28.

Dawes, R. M. (1994). *House of cards. Psychology and psychotherapy built on myth*. New York: The Free Press.

Dawes, R. M., Faust, D., & Meehl, P. E. (1989). Clinical versus actuarial judgement. *Science*, 243, 1668–1674.

Department of Health. (2008). *IAPT: Improving access to psychological therapies*. http://www.iapt.nhs.uk. Accessed on August 22, 2012.

Division of Clinical Psychology. (2011). *Good practice guidelines on the use of psychological formulation*. Leicester, UK: British Psychological Society.

Drake, D. B. (2008). Finding our way home: Coaching's search for identity in a new era. *Coaching: An International Journal of Theory, Research and Practice*, 1(1), 15–26.

Eysenck, H. J. (1990). *Rebel with a cause. The autobiography of Hans Eysenck.* London: W. H. Allen.

Gonçalves, O. F., & Machado, P. P. P. (2000). Emotions, narrative and change. *European Journal of Psychotherapy, Counselling & Health*, 3(3), 349–360.

Health Professions Council. (2009). *Standards of proficiency: Practitioner psychologists.* London: Health Professions Council.

Honeychurch, K. G. (1996). Researching dissident subjectivities: Queering the grounds of theory and practice. *Harvard Educational Review*, 66, 339–355.

Horowitz, M. J., & Eells, T. D. (1993). Case formulations using role-relationship model configurations: A reliability study. *Psychotherapy Research*, 3, 57–68.

Johnstone, L., & Dallos, R. (2006). *Formulation in psychology and psychotherapy. Making sense of people's problems.* Hove, UK: Routledge.

Josselson, R. (1999). Introduction. In R. Josselson & A. Lieblich (Eds.), *Making meaning of narratives* (Vol. 6, pp. ix–xiii). Thousand Oaks, CA: Sage.

Kinderman, P., & Lobban, F. (2000). Evolving formulations: Sharing complex information with clients. *Behavioural and Cognitive Psychotherapy*, 28(3), 307–310.

Kuyken, W., Padesky, C. A., & Dudley, R. (2008). The science and practice of case conceptualization. *Behavioural and Cognitive Psychotherapy*, 26(6), 757–768.

Kuyken, W., Padesky, C. A., & Dudley, R. (2009). *Collaborative case conceptualization: Working effectively with clients in cognitive-behavioral therapy.* New York: Guilford Press.

Lane, D. A. (1973). Pathology of communication: A pitfall in community health. *Community Health*, 5(3), 157–162.

Lane, D. A. (1974). *The behavioural analysis of complex cases.* Islington, UK: Islington Educational Guidance Centre.

Lane, D. A. (1975). *The guidance centre: A new approach to childhood difficulties.* London: The Kings Fund Centre.

Lane, D. A. (1978). *The impossible child.* London: Inner London Education Authority.

Lane, D. A. (1990). *The impossible child. Stoke-on-Trent* (2nd ed.). London: Trentham Books.

Lane, D. A. (1998). Context focused analysis: An experimentally derived model for working with complex problems with children, adolescents and systems. In M. Bruch & F. W. Bond (Eds.), *Beyond diagnosis. Case formulation approaches in CBT* (pp. 103–139). Chichester, UK: Wiley.

Lane, D. A., & Corrie, S. (2006). *The modern scientist-practitioner. A guide to practice in psychology.* Hove, UK: Routledge.

Lane, D. A., & Corrie, S. (2012). *Making successful decisions in counselling and pyschotherapy. A practical guide.* Maidenhead, UK: Open University Press.

Lane, D. A., & Green, F. (1990). Partnership with pupils. In M. Scherer, I. Gersch, & L. Fry (Eds.), *Meeting disruptive behaviour: Assessment, intervention, partnership* (pp. 252–266). Basingstoke, UK: Macmillan.

Mumma, G. H. (1998). Improving cognitive case formulations and treatment planning in clinical practice and research. *Journal of Cognitive Psychotherapy*, 12(3), 251–274.

Persons, J. B., Mooney, K. A., & Padesky, C. A. (1995). Interrater reliability of cognitive-behavioural case formulations: A replication. *Cognitive Therapy and Research, 19*(1), 21–34.

Schulte, D., Kunzel, R., Pepping, G., & Shulte-Bahrenberg, T. (1992). Tailor-made versus standardized therapy of phobic patients. *Advances in Behaviour Research and Therapy, 14*, 67–92.

Shapiro, M. B. (1955). Training of clinical psychologists at the Institute of Psychiatry. *Bulletin of the British Psychological Society, 8*, 1–6.

Shapiro, M. B. (1957). Experimental methods in the psychological description of the individual psychiatric patient. *International Journal of Social Psychiatry, 111*, 89–102.

Shapiro, M. B., & Nelson, E. H. (1955). An investigation of an abnormality of cognitive function in a cooperative young psychotic: An example of the application of the experimental method to the single case. *Journal of Clinical Psychology, 11*, 344–351.

Sheath, M. (2010). Case formulation: The dilemmas posed by child sex offenders. In S. Corrie & D. A. Lane (Eds.), *Constructing stories, telling tales: A guide to formulation in applied psychology* (pp. 149–172). London: Karnac.

Turkat, I. D. (1985). *Behavioural case formulation.* New York: Springer.

Wilson, G. T. (1996). Manual based treatments: The clinical application of research findings. *Behaviour Research and Therapy, 34*(4), 295–314.

Wilson, G. T. (1997). Treatment manuals in clinical practice. *Behaviour Research and Therapy, 35*(3), 205–210.

8

Cognitive-behavioural Case Formulation in the Treatment of a Complex Case of Social Anxiety Disorder and Substance Misuse

Samia Ezzamel, Marcantonio M. Spada and Ana V. Nikčević

Introduction

Social anxiety disorder is characterized by an excessive fear of social interactions and performance situations (American Psychiatric Association, 2000). With large and sustained treatment benefits, individual cognitive-behavioural therapy (CBT) should be routinely offered to all adults presenting with such a problem. The National Collaborating Centre for Mental Health (NCCMH) recommends that this follows either one of the specified models for the treatment of social anxiety.

Whilst such disorder-specific treatment protocols are empirically supported, they do not accommodate for co-occurring conditions (Bruch, 2014). This is of particular importance given that social anxiety disorder often presents alongside other psychological disorders, most notably depression (Fehm, Beesdo, Jacobi, & Fiedler, 2008), generalized anxiety disorder (GAD) and alcohol misuse (Thomas, Randall, Book, & Randall, 2008), with social anxiety disorder almost always preceding alcohol misuse (Kushner, Sher, & Beitman, 1990).

Beyond Diagnosis: Case Formulation in Cognitive Behavioural Therapy, Second Edition. Edited by Michael Bruch.
© 2015 John Wiley & Sons, Ltd. Published 2015 by John Wiley & Sons, Ltd.

This chapter details a complex case of social anxiety disorder, which occurred alongside alcohol and benzodiazepine misuse, depression and hallucinogen persisting perception disorder (HPPD). HPPD develops primarily as a consequence of lysergic diethylamide acid (LSD) use and is characterized by 'the re-experiencing, when the individual is sober, of the perceptual disturbances that were experienced while the individual was intoxicated with the hallucinogen' (APA, 2013: p. 531). These experiences, also referred to as 'flashbacks', may manifest as perceptual disturbances in geometric forms, peripheral field images, flashes of colour, intensified colours, trailing images and halos around objects (APA, 2013). It is estimated that HPPD develops in approximately 4.2% of people who use hallucinogens (APA, 2013).

Despite calls for research, literature regarding the treatment of HPPD is mainly anecdotal and pharmacologically focused (Halpern & Pope, 2003). Clinical cases discussed in the literature include the use of behavioural approaches (systematic desensitization and relaxation techniques) (Matefy, 1973) and cognitive approaches which frame the 'flashbacks' as post-traumatic stress disorder (Stott, 2009). Stott (2009) found that reliving and narrative interventions yielded little therapeutic effect; however, by focusing on the key appraisals maintaining the condition, treatment gains resulted. As such, it appears that, rather than the content of the 'flashbacks', the individual's appraisal of their occurrence could be the driving force in maintaining the disorder. Apart from these case examples, the literature regarding the treatment of HPPD is sparse.

Considering the complexity of this case and possible interaction of the presenting difficulties, an idiographic case formulation approach to treatment was chosen. This was based on the case formulation approach developed at University College London (Bruch, 2014).

The Client

Steve,[1] a 35-year-old Caucasian male, was referred for CBT during his 18-week programme that he was completing at a residential drugs and alcohol rehabilitation setting in Essex, United Kingdom. He started using LSD as a teenager and developed HPPD following a particular intoxication at the age of 15. To manage the residual 'visuals' (perceptual disturbances), he took Clonazepam, a potent benzodiazepine that he purchased over the Internet, for 10 years.

Although he had always felt that he was a 'shy child', Steve's social anxiety increased when he developed HPPD. He subsequently started to drink excessively. His alcohol and Clonazepam use further escalated following the separation from his long-term girlfriend.

Phase 1: Definition of Problems

Given the apparent complexities of the interaction between social anxiety, substance use, HPPD and depression that emerged through the initial assessment session, the need for innovation in exploring and possibly interlinking these problems was evident. This is why a case formulation approach was adopted.

The case formulation process began by asking the client to describe, in his own words, the difficulties he was experiencing. He was encouraged to explain how he saw his problems, not how others (e.g. family, friends and professionals) perceived them. Specific problem statements were sought because they form the foundation upon which the client's goals of treatment can be operationalized.

Steve identified his presenting problems as 'visuals' and 'social awkwardness'. When asked to describe the visuals, Steve reported:

> *I've had visuals since a trip on acid when I was 15. Things are constantly moving and distorted. Swirls are coming out of the wall behind you right now, and I can see a sort of halo around your head. I hear echoes of conversations from yesterday. I feel like I'm in my own world, separate to everyone else.*

Steve identified that his sense of 'social awkwardness' developed when he started to experience the visuals and described feeling 'distanced, dissociated, like I'm constantly trying to make sense of the visuals'. This led him to believe that he did not 'have anything to contribute to discussions' and consequently that he would be better off avoiding social situations.

This discussion led to the initial hypothesis that inflexibility of switching attention away from the visuals underlay both of these problems. This hypothesis was tested through imaginary exposure to a social situation, with Steve describing his thoughts and emotions aloud. Steve described how he would try to focus his attention away from the visuals when in social situations by counting items in multiples of five, and that this in itself proved that he was not focusing on the conversation, which led him to focus more attentional resources on his difficulties with maintaining focus on the discussion.

Preliminary treatment goals

During the initial sessions, Steve identified his treatment goals as follows:

1. 'To reduce the visuals'.
2. 'To be less socially awkward'. Steve described how, if he were less 'socially awkward', he would be able to focus his attention on a conversation and would feel less 'frozen', which would enable him to contribute to the discussion.

Initial hypothesis

From this initial problem definition, it was hypothesized that inflexibility of attention was common to both the social anxiety and maintenance of the perceptual disturbances, and that avoidance and the use of safety behaviours (such as counting in multiples of 5) contributed to the maintenance of Steve's social anxiety. It was also hypothesized that rumination about his sense of 'social awkwardness' and perceptual disturbances contributed to Steve's low mood. This initial hypothesis was discussed with Steve, and the following specific problem areas collaboratively defined:

1. 'Excessive concerns about social situations'
2. 'Avoidance or struggling in social situations'
3. 'Rumination'
4. 'Use of alcohol and Clonazepam'

Phase 2: Exploration of problems

Further exploration of the presenting problems through Socratic questioning (Padesky, 1993) facilitated gaining an understanding of Steve's experiences of the visuals and related sense of social awkwardness through a collaborative, guided discovery. This was of particular importance given the low prevalence and lack of literature regarding HPPD. An alternative hypothesis, regarding the potential of the visuals to 'override' cognitive processing rather than them being modulated as a result of attentional flexibility, was eliminated by asking Steve to describe the visuals in one particular situation. It emerged that the visuals could vary in intensity depending on levels of engagement in tasks. Through this exploration, metacognitive beliefs (Wells, 2000) about the dangers and uncontrollability of the visuals were also identified, and the role of focusing attention on the visuals in maintaining them began to emerge. Steve's metacognitive beliefs centred primarily on the danger and uncontrollability of the visuals, e.g. 'I'll be stuck with the visuals, no matter what I do' and 'my brain has shut down and I'm going mad'. Positive metacognitive beliefs about the benefits of using alcohol and Clonazepam (Spada, Caselli, & Wells, 2013; Spada, Proctor, Caselli, & Strodl, 2013) were also identified. These included 'If I drink, then I'll be able to think more clearly' and 'If I use Clonazepam, then I'll be able to focus'.

The exploration phase also entailed the identification of specific safety behaviours that Steve utilized in social situations. These included counting in multiples of five, nodding, trying to constantly smile and attempting to hide shaking in order to be perceived as comfortable. Steve described how he would view himself as a social object, a concept characterized by the individual's assumptions that others can observe the manifestation of physiological symptoms of anxiety being experienced, such as hands shaking (Clark & Beck, 2010). The following is an extract of Steve's description of himself as a social object:

> *Others can look at me and see what's going through my mind. I become aware of my lips, I start biting my lips. All of a sudden I become so super-conscious of my lips and how I'm contorting them into all sorts of funny positions. My jaw doesn't sit right, it's taking my lips in all funny ways. They feel strange. Rubbery. I can't take my attention away from thinking how I must appear to others.*

Following social situations, Steve would engage in a detailed analysis of how he felt he had behaved in the situation. This rumination was fuelled by metacognitive beliefs about its benefits, including 'if I ruminate, I'll figure out what I need to do to come across as more comfortable next time'.

Developmental history

By exploring historical events from the individual's life, an aetiological perspective of vulnerability to, and development of, presenting problems over time can be gained (Wells, 1997). This understanding is associated with an increased likelihood of successful change (Kirk, 2011) and was facilitated through completion of a timeline of Steve's life and his psychological difficulties (Figure 8.1).

Steve first noticed that he was becoming anxious around others following the death of his father, when Steve was 11. With family friends referring to him and his brother as 'the men of the house', Steve initially felt a sense of 'macho-ness' and responsibility for his mother. However, as conflict increased at home and his brother developed depression, Steve yearned to escape from the situation. By taking LSD, he 'could shut it all out'.

Concurrently, Steve found that LSD helped him to 'play the joker' at school, a role that he adopted as he felt 'unable to hold deep and meaningful conversations'. He used it weekly until the 'bad trip' (intoxication), at the age of 15. Steve described how, in contrast to other trips, the hallucinations did not fade gradually over the following week, but remained at the same intensity, with him feeling that he was 'constantly' re-experiencing the hallucinations. This led Steve to feel 'changed' and 'socially awkward', as he felt that he was 'stuck' in the hallucinations. Consequently, his social anxiety 'increased 10-fold', impacted by the belief that his ongoing experiences of hallucinations would negatively affect how he came across in social situations. To manage this, Steve

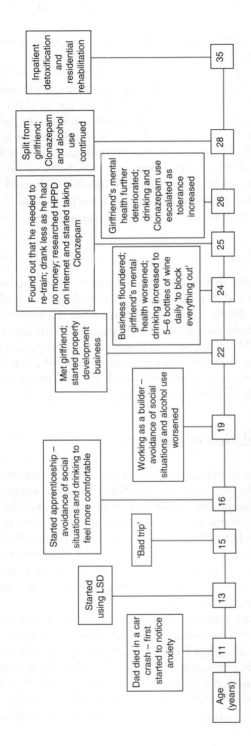

Figure 8.1 Timeline of Steve's life.

would avoid social situations or drink in order to feel more comfortable around others.

Steve's drinking spiralled during a prolonged period of increased stress: his girlfriend experienced mental health difficulties, his business floundered and he learned that he would need to retrain for modern qualifications. Noticing his perceptual disturbances increasing in intensity, Steve researched HPPD on Internet forums and read that taking Clonazepam could aid in reducing his visuals. He bought this online and took it daily for 10 years as he felt it weakened the visuals. Alongside this, Steve would drink to feel more comfortable in social situations. When his girlfriend suddenly left, Steve attributed this to being 'socially awkward' and 'no longer needed'. Consequently, his alcohol and Clonazepam use escalated.

Functional analyses

A functional analysis enables the mechanism of a specific behaviour to be understood in terms of its triggers, responses, maintaining and problem consequences (Spada, 2006). Functional analyses for the problem areas identified in Phase 1 were completed using Spada's (2010) functional analysis matrix (e.g. see Tables 8.1 and 8.2). Based on the notion that behaviour is a continuous process, problem consequences in each functional analysis were identified as stimuli for other behaviours thereby allowing for the interlinking of problems (Bruch, 2014; Spada, 2010).

Phase 3: Formulation of problems

Rather than a fixed explanation about a specific problem as offered in disorder-specific protocols, a case formulation draws on cognitive and behavioural principles and practice to offer an idiographic hypothesis about how the individual's problems developed, how they have been maintained and how they are interrelated (Bruch, 2014; Meyer & Turkat, 1979). Considering its hypothetical nature, the formulation was triangulated through clinical supervision in order to gain others' perspectives on the appropriateness of the presented hypotheses and possible alternative explanations and thereby reduce therapist bias (Bruch, 2014).

A genetic element indicated by the prevalence of anxiety disorders in Steve's family may have increased his vulnerability to developing social anxiety (Beatty, Heisel, Hall, Levine, & LaFrance, 2002). Additionally, processes of vicarious learning through observing his relatives' anxiety and subsequent responses may have led to negative expectancies of social encounters (Bandura, 2005; Davey, 1997). Following his father's death, a combination of an increased sense of responsibility for his family and the difficult dynamics

Table 8.1 Functional Analysis of Struggling in Social Situations.

	Stimuli	Primary responses	Secondary responses	Maintaining consequences	Problem consequences
Environmental	During a social situation				
Cognitive		'Because of the visuals, I'm coming across as blank and socially awkward'			
	'People think that I'm stupid and socially awkward'	'My visuals are taking over my mind'		Temporary distraction from original negative automatic thoughts	Proliferation of negative automatic thoughts as more time is spent focusing on self and isolating self
	'My visuals stop me from being able to focus on conversations'	'If I count items in multiples of five, then I'll be able to focus'		Reinforcement of beliefs about the benefits of using safety behaviours ('it's because I used the safety behaviours that I didn't look stupid')	Increased self-focused attention which makes visuals seem to be more intense
		'If I smile and nod, people might not see me as socially awkward'			

(Continued)

Table 8.1 (Continued)

	Stimuli	Primary responses	Secondary responses	Maintaining consequences	Problem consequences
Physiological	Dry mouth, sweaty palms			Reduction of physiological sensations in the moment	Increased physiological sensations when faced with future situations
Behavioural			Nod, smile and count in multiples of five		Avoidance of social situations and use of alcohol to manage anxiety
Emotional	Anxiety			Reduction of anxiety in the moment	Increased anxiety due to avoidance Sense of hopelessness

Table 8.2 Functional Analysis of Excessive Concerns Following Social Encounters.

	Stimuli	Primary responses	Secondary responses	Maintaining consequences	Problem consequences
Environmental	Following a social encounter				
Cognitive		'I can't trust my mind' 'Am I thinking about what I think others would think?'		Rumination 'feels' like problem solving	Proliferation of negative automatic thoughts as more time is spent focusing on self and isolating self Increased self-focused attention
	'I came across as awkward and socially inept'	'Everybody else has moved on from their withdrawals except me; I'll never be able to recover'		Temporary distraction from original negative automatic thoughts	
	'Did that really happen?'	'If I analyse how I behaved, I'll be able to change what I do next time and maybe I'll seem less awkward' 'I'll never be able to come across as normal without Clonazepam'			Increased feeling of being unable to trust own judgement

(Continued)

Table 8.2 (*Continued*)

	Stimuli	Primary responses	Secondary responses	Maintaining consequences	Problem consequences
Physiological	Dry mouth, sweaty palms			Reduction of physiological sensations in the moment	Increased physiological sensations when faced with future situations
Behavioural	In room alone		Rumination about the situation Replaying the situation over and over Focusing more on the things that made me feel awkward		Avoidance of social situations
Emotional	Low mood			Improvement of mood in the moment	Low mood worsens Feelings of being overwhelmed with what needs to change

that developed at home may have contributed to a self-perception of incapability and a desire to 'escape' from this situation and related emotions. In response to this, Steve began to use LSD. However, the resulting HPPD led him to feel extremely self-conscious and socially awkward. Steve consequently associated social situations with anxiety through classical conditioning and experienced anticipatory anxiety prior to social encounters. Through avoidance, Steve gained an initial sense of relief (negative reinforcement), which aided the maintenance of the avoidance behaviour.

Worrying about social encounters developed over time through believing that worry would prepare him for unwanted eventualities (Wells, 2009). However, worry came at the cost of heightened anticipatory anxiety and focus on threat (Bar-Haim, Lamy, Pergamin, Bakermans-Kranenburg, & van Ijzendoorn, 2007). Such bias brought a reduction of attentional resources for the situation, increased negative self-appraisal and led to negative anticipation of future events (Clark & Wells, 1995; Rapee & Heimberg, 1997).

In social situations, Steve's attention would become increasingly self-focused. This would be predominantly centred on his perceptual disturbances. He would also worry about others' perceptions of him. This is consistent with information-processing literature (Hirsch & Clark, 2004) and the cognitive model of social phobia, which assumes the inward shifting of attention and detailed self-monitoring in response to social threat (Clark & Wells, 1995). Through viewing himself as a social object, excessively negative self-images would proliferate (Hackmann, Suraway, & Clark, 1998), heightening awareness of anxiety, preventing processing of the situation and others' responses (Wells & Clark, 1995) and consequently reinforcing the perception of incompetence. Safety behaviours would serve to temporarily relieve anxiety but exacerbate it in the longer term by maintaining judgemental biases and negative feedback (Taylor & Alden, 2010; Wells et al., 1995).

Following a social encounter, Steve would undertake a detailed analysis fuelled by positive beliefs that ruminating would help to solve the problem. Again, attention would be biased, emphasizing negative self-perceptions and an excessively negative recollection of the event (Clark & Wells, 1995). This would feed into anticipatory anxiety and worry about future encounters (Hofmann, 2007).

Concurrently, Steve would engage in worry about the visual disturbances, attempting to suppress these through the use of Clonazepam. However, this maintained his beliefs about the uncontrollability of his worry and the visuals, as he transferred the control from himself to external factors (Wells, 2009) and was unable to suppress either of these processes. Along with post-event rumination, this would lead to feelings of hopelessness and depression, and subsequent use of alcohol to regulate his mood.

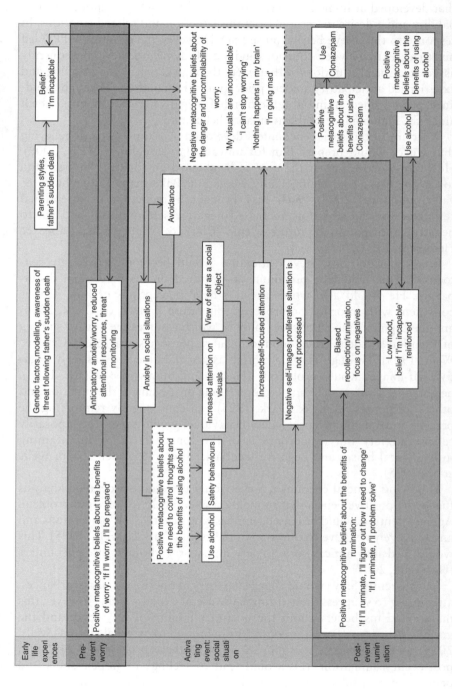

Figure 8.2   Idiographic case formulation.

The formulation thus identified the potential role of genetics and vicarious learning in contributing to Steve's vulnerability to developing social anxiety and of the visuals in triggering the development of this anxiety. In response to this anxiety, Steve avoided socializing, employed safety behaviours and his attention would become focused on himself and the visuals. Although these measures served to reduce anxiety in the short term, they led to the maintenance of judgemental biases and negative self-perception. Metacognitive beliefs aided the maintenance of rumination and worry in relation to social situations, and in the use of alcohol and Clonazepam to reduce the anxiety and visuals respectively. However, these processes also contributed to the deterioration of Steve's mood, anticipatory anxiety and substance use. A diagrammatic representation of the Steve's case formulation is presented in Figure 8.2.

From this formulation, it was hypothesized that, by modifying the positive metacognitive beliefs that Steve held regarding worry, rumination and substance use, these behaviours could be replaced with more adaptive strategies, and in turn, Steve's levels of anxiety and low mood improved. Modification of negative metacognitive beliefs regarding the uncontrollability and danger of Steve's worry and visuals could also aid in reducing Steve's anxiety regarding these processes. Additionally, it was hypothesized that graded exposure to social situations and abandonment of safety behaviours would aid in gaining disconfirmatory evidence about Steve's predictions and, over time, would lead to reduced social anxiety. Considering the hypothesized role of self-focused attention in maintaining the anxiety and visuals, it was hypothesized that increasing flexibility of attention could facilitate reduction in Steve's attention on himself as being awkward and on the visuals and thus reduce his anxiety and his perception of the visuals as being uncontrollable.

Phase 4: Intervention

Development of a treatment plan

Reformulation of presenting problems and treatment goals   With a greater understanding of the role of attention and avoidance in maintaining his problems, Steve reformulated his problems and treatment goals (see Table 8.3).

Treatment programme and supporting rationale   The formulation aided in planning the methods and sequence of treatment (Bruch, 2014). As Steve expressed ambivalence about abstaining from alcohol and Clonazepam, motivational interviewing techniques would be used to enhance Steve's

Table 8.3   Reformulated Presenting Problems and Treatment Goals.

Presenting problems	Treatment goals
'Worrying and ruminating about social situations'	'To reduce rumination and worry about social situations'
'Avoidance or keeping safe in social situations'	'To engage more in social situations irrespective of how anxiety-provoking they are and to drop safety behaviours'
'Use of alcohol and Clonazepam'	'To reduce the use of alcohol and Clonazepam'
'Focusing on the visuals'	'To reduce attention focus on the visuals'

desire and confidence in his ability to change (Miller & Rollnick, 2012), particularly in preparation for discharge from rehabilitation, which was scheduled for his eighth week of therapy. A brief intervention, motivational interviewing, improves substance misuse outcomes (Smedslund et al., 2011) and has demonstrated large effect sizes in improving engagement in treatment (Hettema, Steele, & Miller, 2005). Subsequently, the role of metacognitive beliefs about alcohol use in cognitive and emotional self-regulation would be challenged, as these are key contributors to alcohol misuse (Spada, Caselli, et al., 2013). Assuming a similar mechanism regarding the metacognitive beliefs held about Clonazepam, these too would be targeted in this way.

Although *in vivo* exposure has consistently proven most effective in treating social anxiety disorder (Federoff & Taylor, 2001), perseverative thinking in the form of rumination and worry can hinder engagement and impact on outcomes (Price & Anderson, 2011), and therefore would need to be targeted prior to exposure-based intervention. To reduce Steve's post-event rumination, metacognitive therapy interventions would be introduced to develop alternative ways of relating to thoughts by modifying positive and negative metacognitive beliefs and perseverative thinking (Wells, 2009), particularly in relation to the danger and uncontrollability of rumination and worry. Results from an open, uncontrolled trial of metacognitive therapy for GAD demonstrated statistically significant treatment gains, in which large effect sizes on measures for anxiety, depression, meta-worry and trait anxiety were maintained at 12-month follow-up (Wells & King, 2006). A subsequent randomized comparative study of metacognitive therapy versus applied relaxation for GAD demonstrated the superiority of metacognitive therapy in significantly improving trait anxiety and worry, with recovery rates of 60 and 80% respectively maintained at 12-month follow-up (Wells et al., 2010). When independently analysed, these results were higher than aggregated recovery rates from cognitive therapy, CBT and applied relaxation (Fisher, 2006).

To interrupt the rigid and excessive self-focused attention, which is understood as a driving force in rumination and worry (Wells, 2009), and which appeared to be particularly evident during Steve's engagement in social situations, the attention training technique (ATT) would be used. A pool of evidence demonstrates the effectiveness of this metacognitive therapy technique in treating anxiety and depression (Papageorgiou & Wells, 2000), and superiority over cognitive therapy in reducing both self-focused attention and fear of negative evaluation in social anxiety disorder (Donald, Abbott, & Smith, 2014).

Due to the lack of research into the treatment for HPPD, the case formulation played a key role in developing a treatment hypothesis for working on the visuals. More recently, ATT has been introduced into the treatment of auditory hallucinations, based on the premise that self-focused attention moderates hallucinations (Ensum & Morrison, 2003), and the assertion that ATT facilitates flexible control over cognitions (Wells, 2007). Preliminary evidence from case reports indicates its utility in reducing self-focused attention, attentional biases and ruminative processes associated with auditory hallucinations (Valmaggia, Bouman, & Schuurman, 2007). Assuming a similar basis for the perceptual disturbances, ATT could aid in reducing Steve's attentional bias and related worry, rumination and sense of hopelessness. This would be trialled using pre- and post-practice ratings of self-focused attention and eliciting feedback from Steve regarding the intensity of the perceptual disturbances in order to evaluate this hypothesis and the effectiveness of this intervention, in line with the scientist-practitioner approach advocated in case formulation (Bruch, 2014).

These techniques of externally focused attention training and modification of rumination and worry are concordant with clinical practice guidelines for the treatment of social anxiety disorder. Additionally, NCCMH recommends graded *in vivo* exposure to avoided situations. This enables processing of incompatible information, thereby disintegrating fear structures and in turn reducing hypervigilance and attentional biases (Foa & Kozak, 1986). As Steve was residing at a rehabilitation unit at the beginning of his course of CBT and had limited time out of the unit, graded exposure would be challenging to implement, as by now Steve felt comfortable with the group of residents that he was in treatment with and the feared situations were based outside of the rehabilitation unit. In view of this, a therapy extension of three telephone CBT sessions was granted by the setting's management team to enable graded exposure work to be done.

The preparatory work for the graded exposure intervention (construction of a graded hierarchy and identification of safety behaviours) would therefore be done prior to discharge from rehabilitation and the exposure tasks planned for and reviewed during the three telephone sessions. A graded exposure hierarchy is integral to *in vivo* exposure as it pinpoints relevant situations to target, facilitates a stepped approach and provides an idiosyncratic outcome measure (Katerelos, Hawley, Antony, & McCabe, 2008). As safety behaviours maintain anxiety, identification and abandonment of these are crucial to the effectiveness of exposure (Taylor & Alden, 2010).

Building on the attentional flexibility developed through ATT, situational attentional refocusing (SAR) would also be introduced as this supports *in vivo* exposure by encouraging the individual to switch from focusing on internal experiences to external cues that disconfirm threat-related predictions (Wells, 2000). A preliminary study has shown that SAR increases the effectiveness of exposure with regard to within-session anxiety and beliefs about negative consequences (Wells & Papageorgiou, 1998). Although there is ongoing debate about the utility of cognitive restructuring, a review of meta-analyses suggests that it may enhance exposure-based interventions in social anxiety disorder (Rodebaugh, Holaway, & Heimberg, 2004), with greater effect sizes at 6-month follow-up for post-exposure restructuring of predicted consequences and dysfunctional cognitions in comparison to exposure alone (Hofmann, 2004). Therefore, SAR and cognitive restructuring would be combined with the graded exposure tasks. To evaluate the effectiveness of this combination of *in vivo* exposure, SAR and cognitive restructuring, a cognitive-behavioural graded exposure hierarchy would be used to monitor changes in the strength of belief of key cognitions and subjective units of discomfort (SUDs). The use of behavioural experiments involving exposure to feared social situations prior to discharge from rehabilitation would also serve in socializing Steve to *in vivo* exposure and cognitive restructuring, providing an indicator of Steve's willingness to engage in such interventions and aiding in socializing him to the intervention.

Implementation of treatment

The intervention methods and planned sequence of these are summarized in Table 8.4.

Motivational interviewing and challenging metacognitive beliefs about alcohol and Clonazepam use (sessions 2–8) There was particular emphasis on motivational interviewing during the initial sessions, as Steve indicated that he believed that he would need to use alcohol and Clonazepam following discharge from rehabilitation in order to manage his social anxiety and visuals. This aimed to increase discrepancy between Steve's current and ideal situation to thereby enhance his motivation to change through the use of open-ended questions and regular reflective responses by the therapist to highlight discrepancies (Miller & Rollnick, 2012). Techniques to evoke 'change talk' and build Steve's confidence in

Table 8.4 Summary of the Course of Therapy.

Session number→ / Intervention↓	1	2	3	4	5	6	7	8	9	10	11
Assessment, problem exploration and case formulation	▓	▓	▓	▓							
Motivational interviewing and challenging metacognitive beliefs about alcohol and Clonazepam use	▓	▓	▓	▓	▓	▓	▓	▓			
Metacognitive therapy for rumination and worry, and perceptual disturbances						▓	▓	▓	▓	▓	▓
Graded exposure and cognitive restructuring							▓	▓	▓	▓	▓
Evaluation and creation of therapy blueprint									▓	▓	▓

his ability and commitment to change were utilized, including a decisional balance matrix to explore Steve's ambivalence and highlight reasons for change (Miller & Rollnick, 2012).

This process facilitated the identification of metacognitive beliefs held about alcohol and Clonazepam use. Negative metacognitive beliefs, which are instrumental in maintaining maladaptive behaviour, were challenged first by questioning the evidence about uncontrollability of use. Positive metacognitive beliefs, which are instrumental in the initiation of maladaptive behaviour, were then questioned by exploring whether alcohol and Clonazepam truly produced the expected outcomes (Spada, Proctor, et al., 2013).

Metacognitive therapy for worry, rumination and perceptual disturbances (sessions 6–11) The metacognitive therapy intervention drew on techniques outlined by Wells (2009). Specifically, techniques were chosen that targeted thought control strategies, challenged the dangers and uncontrollability of rumination and worry, and increased flexibility of thinking.

The suppression-counter suppression experiment demonstrated to Steve the futility of trying to control his thoughts and experiences, and the free association task illustrated detached mindfulness, in which thoughts are viewed as passing events in the mind, as an alternative perspective (Wells, 2009). Rumination and worry postponement, aimed at challenging beliefs about the uncontrollability of these processes, were practised daily (Wells, 2009); Steve found this helpful in reducing these behaviours.

By relating it to detached mindfulness, a rationale for ATT was given, and it was trialled during a session, using a script that targets selective attention, rapid attention switching and divided attention in turn (Wells, 2009). Pre- and post-practice levels of self-focused attention demonstrated the utility of the intervention. Steve practised ATT daily using a guided recording, recording his pre- and post-practice ratings of self-focused attention over a period of 7 weeks. Steve attributed the reduced change from pre- to post-practice ratings to having become 'used' to the lower self-focused attention. He was also spending time deciding upon ratings, during which his self-focused attention increased again. Steve was therefore instructed to determine ratings immediately after practising.

The continued reduction in differences between pre- and post-treatment ratings and immediate increases following a break in ATT practice indicated a practice effect, which was supported by Steve's observations of 'getting used to it' and 'zoning out'. To increase its difficulty and further develop his attention flexibility, practice was undertaken in noisier environments. Steve reported finding it easier to switch his attention from his perceptual disturbances and worries.

Graded exposure and cognitive restructuring (sessions 7–11)   The three telephone sessions were distributed over 6 weeks, with increasing time between sessions, as this can support maintenance of therapy outcomes (Mathew, Whitford, Kenny, & Denson, 2010). Explaining the rationale of graded exposure was of paramount importance, as this enhances self-efficacy and confidence in undertaking tasks, perceived helpfulness of treatment and frequency of interpersonal exposures at 1-month follow-up (Ahmed & Westra, 2009).

To tailor the intervention to Steve's needs, a graded hierarchy of feared social situations, based on percentage ratings of SUDs, was constructed (Katerelos et al., 2008). Although grading of tasks was aimed for, Steve was required to engage in activities with associated SUDs ratings of 80–85% during his first week following discharge. Ungraded exposure has proven highly unsuccessful (White & Barlow, 2002); therefore, anxiety-provoking events during his remaining stay served as behavioural experiments in preparation for this. Rather than achieving habituation, these behavioural experiments tested the cognitions and predicted outcomes associated with the feared situations (Bennett-Levy et al., 2004).

A cognitive-behavioural exposure hierarchy aided in predicting and reviewing SUDs and associated cognitions for each task. Identified safety behaviours were abandoned to facilitate between-session habituation (Taylor & Alden, 2010), and SAR used in conjunction to reduce Steve's self-focused attention and support reappraisal of threat-related risks (Wells & Papageorgiou, 1998). Tasks were continued until SUDs reduced to less than 30/100 in order to provide disconfirmatory evidence of predictions and achieve within-session habituation (Antony & Swinson, 2000). Exercises were repeated until a 50% reduction of initial SUDs, indicating between-session habituation, was reached (Clark & Beck, 2010). By reflecting on disconfirmatory evidence, anticipated social consequences and dysfunctional cognitions were restructured.

Phase 5: Evaluation

Standardized outcome measures were administered at assessment, midway through therapy, discharge and 6-month follow-up (see Table 8.5).

The reduction in scores on the Beck Depression Inventory (Beck, Steer, & Garbin, 1988) and the Beck Anxiety Inventory (Beck & Steer, 1990) indicates improved mood and anxiety. On the Penn State Worry Questionnaire (Meyer, Miller, Metzger, & Borkovec, 1990), Steve's scored reduced from 60 to 40, taking him below the 45-point threshold for GAD (Behar, Alcaine, Zuellig, & Borkovec, 2003). In line with the aim of ATT, the increase in the scores on the Attentional Control Scale (Derryberry & Reed, 2002) indicates stronger beliefs about control over attention. Concordant with the reduction in worry, anxiety and depression symptoms, this suggests a reduction in the activation of the cognitive attentional syndrome (Fergus, Bardeen, & Orcutt, 2012; Wells, 2009).

Steve identified that his goals had been mostly or fully achieved; this demonstrates progress in areas specific to Steve's problems (Kirk, 2011). Idiosyncratic measures of improvement, obtained from the cognitive-behavioural exposure hierarchy and verbal feedback, were concordant with these improvements. Steve spoke of how he now recognized that he was often worrying about aspects that were not significant, describing how he would postpone the worrying and shift his attention to other tasks. When describing his visuals, Steve stated: 'They used to feel so consuming, but now I can move my attention to focus on identifying all the noises in the environment and that's it – when the attention isn't focused on them, they're not there anymore, and when they come back, my attention can move to focus on something else instead and then they go away again'.

Table 8.5 Changes in Standardized Outcome Measure Scores across the Course of Therapy.

Measure	Assessment	Session 6	Discharge	Six-month follow-up
Beck Anxiety Inventory (BAI; Beck & Steer, 1990)	40/63	40/63	29/63	7/63
Beck Depression Inventory (BDI; Beck et al., 1988)	39/63	40/63	22/63	12/63
Penn State Worry Questionnaire (PSWQ; Meyer et al., 1990)	60/80	67/80	38/80	40/80
Attentional Control Scale (ACS; Derryberry & Reed, 2002)	25/80	23/80	36/80	47/80

During the final telephone session, Steve reported that he had been attending aftercare groups for the past 3 weeks and was using public transport to travel to these groups, activities that he had previously avoided due to his social anxiety.

Additionally, Steve's maintenance of abstinence of alcohol and Clonazepam use at 6-month follow-up further support the improvements in standardized measures and demonstrate treatment gains. This is particularly promising given that approximately 72% of individuals who attend a residential rehabilitation are considered to have 'successfully' completed treatment and have overcome their substance dependence (National Treatment Agency for Substance Misuse, 2012).

Conclusions

Through an idiographic approach that focused on understanding the mechanisms maintaining Steve's identified problems and conceptualizing their interrelation, this case study demonstrated the utility of a case formulation approach for complex presentations. This collaborative understanding guided the case formulation, which in turn led to a tailor-made intervention incorporating metacognitive techniques, *in vivo* exposure and motivational interviewing. It also explored the utility of functional analyses as both a problem-exploration tool and technique in rumination-focused interventions.

Whilst published evidence into psychotherapeutic approaches in HPPD is scarce, this case study indicates the effectiveness of CBT, in particular ATT, in reducing Steve's perceptual disturbances and associated anxiety. The improvements expressed by Steve with regard to a greater sense of control over his worry and visuals as a result of feeling more able to shift his attention indicate sustained treatment benefits. These are further supported by maintenance of abstinence from alcohol and Clonazepam and continued improvements in standardized outcome measure results at 6-month follow-up post-discharge. On reflection, measures of general life adjustment would have been beneficial for establishing the impact of therapy on factors wider than the identified problems; however, the residential nature of the treatment setting meant that a 'real-life' baseline could not have been established.

Given the complexity of Steve's presenting problems, the case formulation approach enabled these problems to be understood in relation to each other and provided a means of developing an intervention hypothesis that targeted both common mechanisms underlying multiple problems and mechanisms maintaining individual problems. This was found to be particularly beneficial in the conceptualization of the visuals, an area that required innovation and an idiographic approach. In addition to guiding the sequencing of interventions, this approach enabled the effective treatment of multiple problems in a time-limited setting.

Note

1. Pseudonyms have been used throughout this case study, and identifying information changed or removed, in order to preserve the client's anonymity and confidentiality.

References

Ahmed, M., & Westra, H. A. (2009). Impact of a treatment rationale on expectancy and engagement in cognitive behavioural therapy for social anxiety. *Cognitive Therapy and Research, 33*, 314–322.

American Psychiatric Association. (2000). *Diagnostic and statistical manual of mental disorders* (4th ed.). Arlington, VA: American Psychiatric Publishing.

American Psychiatric Association. (2013). *Diagnostic and statistical manual of mental disorders* (5th ed.). Arlington, VA: American Psychiatric Publishing.

Antony, M. M., & Swinson, R. P. (2000). *Phobic disorders and panic in adults: A guide to assessment and treatment*. Washington, DC: American Psychological Association.

Bandura, A. (2005). The evolution of social cognitive theory. In K. G. Smith & M. A. Hitts (Eds.), *Great minds in management* (pp. 9–35). Oxford, UK: Oxford University Press.

Bar-Haim, Y., Lamy, D., Pergamin, L., Bakermans-Kranenburg, M. J., & van Ijzendoorn, M. H. (2007). Threat-related attentional bias in anxious and non-anxious individuals: A meta-analytic study. *Psychological Bulletin, 133*, 1–24.

Beatty, M. J., Heisel, A. D., Hall, A. E., Levine, T. R., & LaFrance, B. H. (2002). What can we learn from the study of twins about genetic and environmental influences on interpersonal affiliation, aggressiveness, and social anxiety?: A meta-analytic study. *Communication Monographs, 69,* 1–18.

Beck, A. T., & Steer, R. A. (1990). *Manual for the Beck anxiety inventory.* San Antonio, TX: Psychological Corporation.

Beck, A. T., Steer, R. A., & Garbin, M. G. (1988). Psychometric properties of the Beck Depression Inventory: Twenty-five years of evaluation. *Clinical Psychology Review, 8,* 77–100.

Behar, E., Alcaine, O., Zuellig, A. R., & Borkovec, T. D. (2003). Screening for generalised anxiety disorder using the Penn State Worry Questionnaire: A receiver operating characteristic analysis. *Journal of Behaviour Therapy and Experimental Psychiatry, 34,* 25–43.

Bennett-Levy, J., Westbrook, D., Fennell, M., Cooper, M., Rouf, K., & Hackmann, A. (2004). Behavioural experiments: Historical and conceptual underpinnings. In J. Bennett-Levy, G. Butler, M. Fennell, A. Hackman, M. Mueller, & D. Westbrook (Eds.), *Oxford guide to behavioural experiments in cognitive therapy* (pp. 1–20). Oxford, UK: Oxford University Press.

Bruch, M. (2014). The UCL case formulation model: Clinical process and procedures. In M. Bruch (Ed.), *Beyond diagnosis: Case formulation approaches in CBT.* Chichester, UK: John Wiley & Sons.

Clark, D. A., & Beck, A. T. (2010). *Cognitive therapy of anxiety disorders: Science and practice.* New York: The Guildford Press.

Clark, D. M., & Wells, A. (1995). A cognitive model of social phobia. In R. Heimberg, M. Liebowitz, D. A. Hope, & F. R. Schneier (Eds.), *Social phobia: Diagnosis, assessment and treatment* (pp. 69–93). New York: The Guildford Press.

Davey, G. C. L. (1997). A conditioning model of phobias. In G.C.L. Davey (Ed.), *Phobias: A handbook of theory, research and treatment* (pp. 301–322). Chichester, UK: John Wiley & Sons.

Derryberry, D., & Reed, M. A. (2002). Anxiety-related attentional biases and their regulation by attentional control. *Journal of Abnormal Psychology, 111,* 225–236.

Donald, J., Abbott, M. J., & Smith, E. (2014). Comparison of attention training and cognitive therapy in the treatment of social phobia: A preliminary investigation. *Behavioural and Cognitive Psychotherapy, 42,* 74–91.

Ensum, I., & Morrison, A. P. (2003). The effects of focus of attention on attributional bias in patients experiencing auditory hallucinations. *Behaviour Research and Therapy, 41,* 895–907.

Federoff, I. C., & Taylor, S. T. (2001). Psychological and pharmacological treatments of social phobia: A meta-analysis. *Journal of Clinical Psychopharmacology, 21,* 311–324.

Fehm, L., Beesdo, K., Jacobi, F., & Fiedler, A. (2008). Social anxiety disorder above and below the diagnostic threshold: Prevalence, comorbidity and impairment in the general population. *Social Psychiatry and Psychiatric Epidemiology, 43,* 257–265.

Fergus, T. A., Bardeen, J. R., & Orcutt, H. K. (2012). Attentional control moderates the relationship between activation of the cognitive attentional syndrome and symptoms of psychopathology. *Personality and Individual Differences, 53,* 213–217.

Fisher, P. L. (2006). The efficacy of psychological treatments for generalised anxiety disorder. In G. C. L. Davey & A. Wells (Eds.), *Worry and its psychological disorders: Theory, assessment and treatment* (pp. 359–377). Chichester, UK: Wiley.

Foa, E. B., & Kozak, M. J. (1986). Emotional processing of fear: Exposure to corrective information. *Psychological Bulletin, 99,* 20–35.

Hackmann, A., Suraway, C., & Clark, C. M. (1998). Seeing yourself through others' eyes: A study of spontaneously occurring images in social phobia. *Behavioural and Cognitive Psychotherapy, 26,* 3–12.

Halpern, J. H., & Pope, H. G. (2003). Hallucinogen persisting perception disorder: What do we know after 50 years? *Drug and Alcohol Dependence, 69,* 109–119.

Hettema, J. E., Steele, J., & Miller, W. R. (2005). Motivational interviewing. *Annual Review of Clinical Psychology, 1,* 91–111.

Hirsch, C. R., & Clark, D. M. (2004). Information-processing bias in social phobia. *Clinical Psychology Review, 24,* 799–825.

Hofmann, S. G. (2004). Cognitive mediation of treatment change. *Journal of Consulting and Clinical Psychology, 72,* 392–399.

Hofmann, S. G. (2007). Cognitive factors that maintain social anxiety disorder: A comprehensive model and its treatment implications. *Cognitive Behaviour Therapy, 36,* 193–209.

Katerelos, M., Hawley, L. L., Antony, M. M., & McCabe, R. E. (2008). The exposure hierarchy as a measure of progress and efficacy in the treatment of social anxiety disorder. *Behaviour Modification, 32,* 504–518.

Kirk, J. (2011). Cognitive-behavioural assessment. In K. Hawton, P. M. Salkovskis, J. Kirk, & D. M. Clark (Eds.), *Cognitive behaviour therapy for psychiatric problems: A practical guide* (pp. 13–51). Oxford, UK: Oxford University Press.

Kushner, M. G., Sher, K. J., & Beitman, B. D. (1990). The relation between alcohol problems and the anxiety disorders. *American Journal of Psychiatry, 147,* 685–695.

Matefy, R. E. (1973). Behavior therapy to extinguish spontaneous recurrences of LSD effects: A case study. *Journal of Nervous and Mental Disease, 156,* 226–231.

Mathew, K. L., Whitford, H. S., Kenny, M. A., & Denson, L. A. (2010). The long-term effects of mindfulness-based cognitive therapy as a relapse prevention treatment for major depressive disorder. *Behavioural and Cognitive Psychotherapy, 38,* 561–576.

Meyer, T. J., Miller, M. L., Metzger, R. L., & Borkovec, T. D. (1990). Development and validation of the Penn State Worry Questionnaire. *Behaviour Research and Therapy, 28,* 487–495.

Meyer, V., & Turkat, I. D. (1979). Behavioural analysis of clinical cases. *Journal of Behavioural Assessment, 1,* 259–270.

Miller, W. R., & Rollnick, S. (2012). *Motivational interviewing: Facilitating change* (3rd ed.). New York: The Guildford Press.

National Collaborating Centre for Mental Health. (2013). *Social anxiety disorder: Recognition, assessment and treatment. National Clinical Guideline Number 159* [Full guideline, final draft]. Leicester, UK: The British Psychological Society and the Royal College of Psychiatrists.

National Treatment Agency for Substance Misuse. (2012). *The role of residential rehab in an integrated treatment system.* London: National Treatment Agency for Substance Misuse.

Padesky, C. A. (1993). *Socratic questioning: Changing minds or guided discovery?* Paper presented at the European Congress of Behavioural and Cognitive Psychotherapies. London.

Papageorgiou, C., & Wells, A. (2000). Treatment of recurrent major depression with attention training. *Cognitive and Behavioural Practice, 7*, 407–413.

Price, M., & Anderson, P. L. (2011). The impact of cognitive behavioural therapy on post event processing among those with social anxiety disorder. *Behaviour Research and Therapy, 49*, 132–137.

Rapee, R. N., & Heimberg, R. G. (1997). A cognitive-behavioural model of anxiety in social phobia. *Behaviour Research and Therapy, 35*, 741–756.

Rodebaugh, T. L., Holaway, R. M., & Heimberg, R. G. (2004). The treatment of social anxiety disorder. *Clinical Psychology Review, 24*, 883–908.

Smedslund, G., Berg, R. C., Hammerstrøm, K. T., Steiro, A., Leiknes, K. A., Dahl, H. M., & Karlsen, K. (2011). Motivational interviewing for Substance Abuse. *Cochrane Database of Systematic Reviews, 5*, CD008063.

Spada, M. M. (2006). Cognitive-behavioural case formulation in the treatment of alcohol problems. In A. V. Nikčević, A. Kuczmierczyk, & M. H. Bruch (Eds.), *Formulation and treatment in clinical health psychology* (pp. 19–41). London: Routledge.

Spada, M. M. (2010). *Cognitive behavioural therapy for problem drinking: A practitioner's guide.* London; Routledge.

Spada, M. M., Caselli, G., & Wells, A. (2013a). A triphasic metacognitive formulation of problem drinking. *Clinical Psychology & Psychotherapy, 20*, 494–500.

Spada, M. M., Proctor, D., Caselli, G., & Strodl, E. (2013b). Metacognition in substance misuse. In P. Miller (Ed.), *Principles of addiction: Comprehensive addictive behaviors and disorders* (Vo. 1). Oxford, UK: Elsevier.

Stott, R. (2009). Tripping into trauma: cognitive-behavioural treatment for a traumatic stress reaction following recreational drug use. In N. Grey (Ed.), *A casebook of cognitive therapy for traumatic stress reactions* (pp. 49–60). Hove, UK: Routledge.

Taylor, C. T., & Alden, L. E. (2010). Safety behaviours and judgemental biases in social anxiety disorder. *Behaviour Research and Therapy, 48*, 226–237.

Thomas, S. E., Randall, P. K., Book, S. W., & Randall, C. L. (2008). A complex relationship between co-occurring social anxiety and alcohol use disorders: What effect does treating social anxiety have on drinking? *Alcoholism: Clinical and Experimental Research, 32*, 77–84.

Valmaggia, L. R., Bouman, T. K., & Schuurman, L. (2007). Attention training with auditory hallucinations: A case study. *Cognitive and Behavioural Practice, 14*, 127–133.

Wells, A. (1997). *Cognitive therapy of anxiety disorders: A practice manual and conceptual guide.* Chichester, UK: John Wiley & Sons.

Wells, A. (2000). *Emotional disorders and metacognition: Innovative cognitive therapy.* Chichester, UK: John Wiley & Sons.

Wells, A. (2007). The attention training technique: Theory, effects and a metacognitive hypothesis on auditory hallucinations. *Cognitive and Behavioural Practice*, *14*, 134–138.

Wells, A. (2009). *Metacognitive therapy for anxiety and depression*. New York: The Guildford Press.

Wells, A., & Clark, D. M. (1997). Social phobia: A cognitive approach. In G. C. L. Davey (Ed.), *Phobias: A handbook of theory, research and treatment* (pp. 3–26). Chichester, UK: John Wiley & Sons.

Wells, A., Clark, D. M., Salkovskis, P., Ludgate, J., Hackmann, A., & Gelder, M. (1995). Social phobia: The role of in-situation safety behaviours in maintaining anxiety and negative beliefs. *Behaviour Therapy*, *26*, 153–161.

Wells, A., & King, P. (2006). Metacognitive therapy for generalised anxiety disorder: An open trial. *Journal of Behaviour Therapy and Experimental Psychiatry*, *37*, 206–212.

Wells, A., & Papageorgiou, C. (1998). Social phobia: Effects of external attention focus on anxiety, negative beliefs and perspective taking. *Behaviour Therapy*, *29*, 357–370.

Wells, A., Welford, M., King, P., Papageorgiou, C., Wisley, J., & Mendal, E. (2010). A pilot randomised trial of metacognitive therapy vs. applied relaxation in the treatment of adults with generalised anxiety disorder. *Behaviour Research and Therapy*, *41*, 429–434.

White, K. S., & Barlow, D. H. (2002). Panic disorder and agoraphobia. In D. H. Barlow (Ed.), *Anxiety and its disorders: The nature and treatment of anxiety and panic* (2nd ed., pp. 328–379). New York: The Guildford Press.

APPENDIX

INVITED CASE TRANSCRIPT
THE INITIAL CLINICAL HYPOTHESIS

IRA DANIEL TURKAT

The Center at Manatee Springs and University of Florida College of Medicine,
Gainesville, FL, USA

Summary — The interviewing skills of many behaviour therapists are inadequate, and several reasons are noted for this. The present manuscript focuses on construction and use of an initial clinical hypothesis. A strategy for generating the initial hypothesis is discussed and illustrated by means of transcripts from an initial interview with a complex clinical case. A method for teaching skills in initial clinical hypothesis generation is presented as well.

The initial interview has a critical role in the practice of behaviour therapy. Unfortunately, its conduct often 'leaves much to be desired' (Wolpe, 1982: p. xi). Time and again, I have observed initial interviews that produce much information but provide little understanding of the patient's psychopathology. There are several reasons for this. First, despite what we would like to think, training programs in behaviour therapy are often below par (Wolpe, 1982: p. xi; 1986). Second, few published accounts of the reasoning that goes on during the course of an interview are available. Third, much behavioural teaching is too technique-oriented, generating a simple-minded approach to the interview. I have found it especially disturbing to watch a beginning student being

Requests for reprints should be addressed to: Ira Daniel Turkat, The Center at Manatee Springs, 5627 Ninth Street East, Bradenton, FL 34203, USA.

Beyond Diagnosis: Case Formulation in Cognitive Behavioural Therapy, Second Edition.
Edited by Michael Bruch.
© 2015 John Wiley & Sons, Ltd. Published 2015 by John Wiley & Sons, Ltd.

trained by a technology-oriented behaviour therapist. The student, having spent four or five sessions collecting information, runs out of questions for the patient and then asks the supervisor, 'Now, what should I do?' The reply is to begin implementing ('pet') techniques matched to patient complaints in the guise of 'target behaviours'. Thus, not only does the student fail to learn a problem-oriented approach but also gets the erroneous impression that etiological information has no value in intervention design.

The proper goal of the interview is to develop a behavioural formulation. It is this that guides intervention. In the course of developing a behavioural formulation, the clinician plays the role of detective: generating hypothesis and evaluating them (Meyer & Turkat, 1979). The hypothesis-testing process begins *immediately*. Without a hypothesis to test, the interview is largely wasteful (Wolpe & Turkat, 1985).

In the present chapter, I will illustrate how an *initial* hypothesis was developed for a complex clinical case. It is important to keep in mind, however, that the initial hypothesis may be wrong. When valid data contradict the initial hypothesis, it must be abandoned, and a new hypothesis developed and evaluated. This is what is meant to be a 'hypothesis-testing approach'.

The present illustration focuses on the development of initial clinical hypothesis and how the course of interview was dictated by it. Illustrations of interviewing from beginning to end can be found elsewhere (e.g. Turkat, 1986; Wolpe, 1982), as can other discussions of initial clinical hypothesis generation (e.g. Wolpe & Turkat, 1985).

Case Material

The present case was seen in a major medical centre in the southeast United States. The patient was an insulin-dependent diabetic who was referred because he was having difficulty giving himself insulin injections. The nursing staff had indicated that when Charles (a pseudonym) needed to inject himself with insulin, he became angry, and this interfered with self-administration. At the time of the interview, Charles was in the second semester of his freshman year at a major university.

DR: What's going on with you?
PT: Trying to go to school, I guess.
DR: Are you doing that okay, or having a rough time with it?
PT: Its pretty rough. I'm only taking 13 hours, everybody else is taking 15 and 16.
DR: Why only 13?
PT: Just to see if I could take it or not.
DR: Notice any difficulties in taking what you have now?
PT: At times, like when they force me to have lack of sleep.

Commentary. At this point, data from three sources can be utilized to begin construction of an initial clinical hypothesis: (a) the referral information, (b) the patient's report and (c) the patient's behaviour. While the amount of information is relatively limited (e.g. <30 sec of interview data), the clinician is already attempting to develop an initial hypothesis to guide subsequent questioning. Several points should be considered in regard to this process. First, the hypothesis must account for *all* of the data presented. Second, it should provide a set of predictions. Finally, it is a source of inferences. Hence, from the very beginning of the interview, the clinician is *forced to think*, instead of merely collecting information.

Returning to Charles, the referral data tell us that he is emotionally aroused by self-injection of insulin to the point of interference with this life-sustaining action. It is noteworthy that the patient is experiencing anger. Anxiety reactions to self-injections are common, but anger responses are not. Thus, a critical question is, 'Why is this person experiencing anger in this situation?' Anger is an emotional response which occurs typically when a principle, rule or expectation (of perceived value) is violated. If so, then it follows that *something about self-administration of insulin is perceived as an important rule violation* for Charles. One could speculate as to what this rule/principle violation may be, and use of other available data may simplify our search.

The second source of data is the patient's verbal report quoted earlier. In response to the open-ended question, 'What's going on with you?'.

Charles indicated that he was '*trying to go to school*'. This suggests an effort or *struggle*. Accordingly, the next question was aimed to confirm if this was a struggle or not. Charles not only confirmed that this was a struggle, he indicated that he was taking a course load less than everyone else. One might expect a reduced course load if Charles felt overwhelmed, but his response was, 'Just to see if I could take it or not'. This statement smacks of *rule defiance*. The choice of a reduced course load was not due to feelings of stress or inadequacy according to Charles, but rather to *test his independence*. Finally, when asked if there were any problems associated with this reduced load, Charles indicated affirmatively: 'When *they force me* to have lack of sleep'. This statement implies that things are being done to him that are *against his will*. This, from just a few seconds of interview data, we get a picture of any angry young man who seems very concerned about his independence, others' infringement upon him and his ability to defy others' rules or norms.

Pulling together the information gathered from the referral and initial interview exchange, we see a connection. Self-injection of insulin is imposed upon him and, hence, is associated with anger. Discussion of Charles's course load reveals a similar concern about others infringing upon him, proving his independence from others (i.e. taking 13 credit hours) and generally viewing others as 'forcing him' to do or not to do certain things. In short, Charles resents restrictions being placed upon him and is determined to fight against such restrictions.

This 'fight' becomes even more apparent when the third source of data is considered: Charles's behaviour in the interview. This can be characterized as rigid, combative and 'tough'. Thus, we have a fellow who is concerned about appearing strong, independent and resentful of restrictions being placed upon him.

Why would someone be *excessively* motivated to appear strong, independent and resentful of being controlled? It would make sense that such a person may be quite *fearful of seeming weak or dependent*. Thus, the initial clinical hypothesis here is that Charles has an inordinate fear of appearing weak or dependent. What does this hypothesis offer us? First, it accounts for the data presented to this point. Second, it provides predictions which can be tested.

The initial hypothesis suggests that Charles is angry about insulin injections because they make him appear weak. He takes a reduced course load because it 'proves' that he is not weak, but independent. His overconcern with appearing weak or dependent leads him to view things generally in a combative manner (e.g. '*trying* to go to school', '*they force* me to have lack of sleep'). He acts 'tough' in the interview to 'prove his independence'.

Adoption of the initial clinical hypothesis offers some of the following predictions:

1. Charles will not permit himself to appear weak or dependent. Thus, in the interview, e.g. he will not disclose much, particularly if it involves emotional expression other than anger. He will stay fact related.

2. Charles will not have many, if any, close friends. Clearly, close friendships are incompatible with always being 'tough' and being unable to let one's defences down.

3. Charles will be uncomfortable in any situation where there is a possibility of him appearing weak or dependent. Thus, e.g. Charles will experience discomfort in situations where his lack of knowledge about a particular topic may be revealed to others (e.g. speaking in class).

4. Charles will have social problems because of his tendency to view things in a combative, weak/strong manner. It is likely, e.g. that he misinterprets others' actions at times, which causes a variety of difficulties.

5. Charles probably came from a family of 'strong', independent, emotionally constricted, parents.

6. Treatment which does not involve modification of the fear of appearing weak or dependent will most likely fail. Thus, e.g. desensitization aimed only at taking injections would be misdirected.

With these thoughts in mind, we return to the interview with Charles.

DR: Like cram all night?

PT: I try not to do that. I live in the dorm and I can't go to sleep, I just don't get any sleep.

DR: Everybody partying, has this been a problem?

PT: Yes.

DR: Do you do that occasionally?

PT: Sure.

DR: But not every night?

PT: No, not even every weekend.

DR: How often do you think you should be?

PT: Not at all.

DR: Why?

PT: Because of my understanding of the effects of alcohol.

DR: Do they do any other kinds of partying? Smoke dope, things like that?

PT: Yes, they do.

DR: Is that something you would like to do or have done?

PT: Not do it.

DR: Alright, now let's focus on school for a minute. What things have been difficult? One you have to stay up all night, and that could be due to demands of school work, the demands of living in a dorm. What other kinds of problems with school?

PT: Nothing really.

DR: No problems? Fine.

DR: Besides school, how are things going otherwise?

PT: Pretty fair, I guess. Besides the fact that I'm the only one who doesn't drink socially.

DR: Are you happy?

PT: Sometimes

DR: Have you been depressed at all?

PT: Yes.

DR: How often does this happen?

PT: It just depends.

DR: Do you remember the last time you felt depressed?

PT: I try and forget about those.

DR: It's important for us to talk about it to see if we can understand it.

PT: Okay.

DR: Let me first explain a little bit about what I'm trying to do. What I'm trying to do now is get an idea of what's going on with you. And, if there are problems that you're having, try and see what they are, and perhaps, why they developed, and then see if there is something we can do about it. Okay? And if so, I'll tell you just what I think. I'll tell you if there is something we can do, and if there is no problem, I'll tell you that, and if I think there is, I'll tell you that. So, I'm just trying to get an idea of whether or not you need to do something about it. And if you do, what the options might be and how one might go about doing that. I'm not here just to say that you're crazy or mentally ill or anything like that, because you're obviously not. Now, I'll ask tons of questions.

Commentary. At this point, Charles's defensiveness is evident, and so the therapist switches the topic to 'neutral background information' (e.g. 'Where are you from?', 'What brought you to this university?'). He then returns to see if, in fact, Charles will be able to discuss his problems (the 'weak' side of him).

PT: That's what fraternity rush is like too.

DR: I have never been compared to that. Okay, feel free to make any comments or statements you like, and ask me any questions.

PT: Okay.

DR: First of all, I try and get as detailed responses as I can. That will help me understand better. And so, if you feel I'm prying about something and don't want to go into it, tell me. Obviously it will help if we can get things right on the table. Now, we were talking about depression. When was the last time you felt depressed? Tell me about it.

PT: I don't recall that.

Commentary. In the vast majority of cases, most respond positively to this 'speech' by the therapist and begin to open up. However, the hypothesized major problem Charles is experiencing seems to be exerting its influence. A switch in tactic is indicated.

DR: When was the last time you had a bad bout of anger?

PT: A day ago.

DR: What happened?

PT: I tried to give myself a shot and it hurt. It makes me very mad. I just don't like it at all.

DR: Okay, so you tried giving yourself a shot and it hurt, and you became angry. About what?

PT: I guess about the fact that I even have to do it. The fact that I even have to put up

with it and forced to do something that everybody else does not have to do.

Commentary. This is quite consistent with the initial hypothesis. An attempt to test the prediction that the patient has difficulty 'appearing weak' is evaluated by assessing his reaction to first learning that he has diabetes.

DR: When were you first diagnosed as diabetic?

PT: The 26th of March.

DR: About a year ago.

PT: (nods in agreement)

DR: Before you were diagnosed, any problems?

PT: What?

DR: With life in general.

PT: Sure. I had bad times. Everybody has bad times, but I pretty much enjoyed everything.

DR: Had friends?

PT: Yes.

DR: Close friends?

PT: The ones that I wanted, yes.

DR: Girlfriends?

PT: Yes.

DR: Getting on okay with Dad?

PT: Very good.

DR: Mom?

PT: Well, we never get along.

DR: Okay. Before you became diabetic, life was fine?

PT: No, you can't say that it was fine. Situations stay the same. I changed.

DR: I'll get back to those situations in a minute. Okay, you went down and were having these symptoms. Did you tell your father you were having these symptoms?

PT: Yes, he was the physician?

DR: He is your physician?

PT: Yes.

DR: Did he notice these things or did you notice them and tell him about it?

PT: I did and called him from school one day.

DR: What did he say? 'Come on over, I want to check you out?'

PT: He just said, 'Come on down'.

DR: Did he take some blood?

PT: No, just a urine specimen.

DR: Then what happened? Tell me in exact detail from that incident, what happened.

PT: I left school and went down to the hospital and I got my urine checked. Came home and at five o'clock, they called me and told me to come back 'cause I had sugar in my urine, and I had to go back and get a blood test.

DR: Okay...

PT: They stuck me in the finger and found out that the blood sugar was about 380, 385 or something about like that.

DR: What did that mean to you when they said on the phone that there was some sugar in your urine?

PT: It meant a lot, I knew what it was. I went to school with a diabetic.

DR: What happened when they told you on the phone? What type of reaction did you have?

PT: They didn't tell me personally, but when it was related to me, my father told me.

DR: I mean when they said it was some sugar in your urine on the phone.

PT: My father told me. They, at the hospital called him, they didn't tell me.

DR: I understand, but how did *you* react?

PT: I knew what I was going for, to get a blood sample. And I knew that there was sugar in the urine, but he told me and it wasn't over the phone it was face to face.

Commentary. Clearly, Charles continues to focus on a description of events and, despite direct questions, persists in avoiding discussion of how he personally reacted. The circumstances regarding Dad's approach to informing Charles that he has diabetes are pursued.

DR: Where were you?

PT: At my house.

DR: At your house, your father came home?

PT: Right.

DR: Was it unusual for him to come home at this time?

PT: No.

DR: He came home and what did he do? Just go on as usual, 'Son, come here we need to talk' or what?

PT: No, he just told me, there was some sugar in my urine.

DR: Kind of matter of fact.

PT: Just like, you know, I had the test earlier in the day and I wanted to know the results and he told me.

DR: Did he seem upset?

PT: No, but he is a physician.

DR: Was he rather cold?

PT: No.

DR: Stern?

PT: I suppose, he's just that way.

DR: Not very emotional or expressive?

PT: Right.

DR: Okay, so he told you and your reaction was...

PT: I just got in the car and left. I guess I didn't let it sink in.

DR: Do you remember anything?

PT: No, not until after I had my blood test.

DR: Now, when they told you they had to take your blood at that time ...

PT: I was more angry at that time about having to have my blood taken.

DR: Angry?

PT: I get very angry when somebody tells me I have to be cut up or stuck.

DR: How about if people tell you, you have to do other things that you don't want to do? It doesn't necessarily have to be cut or stuck.

PT: Pretty much. I just don't like to be told what to do. I feel that I'm independent and somehow I feel that that infringes upon my independence.

DR: Okay. Now, so if someone tells you you have to be stuck, or you have to take a shot, that will cause anger?

PT: Right, if they're serious, yes.

DR: Now, let's say I was serious and said you have to stand on your head in the corner.

PT: I would ask you why.

DR: Let's just say I said: 'just because I'm in charge here and you have to do it'.

PT: I would probably question your authority.

DR: Let's assume that you couldn't question my authority, that I was the ultimate authority. Your grades at school were dependent upon it.

PT: I would probably rebel.

DR: By doing what?

PT: Whatever would make you maddest, probably.

DR: By saying, 'I'm not going to do it'?

PT: If I thought that would be the way, or if I thought trying to do it and falling down would make you madder, whatever.

DR: Why is it so upsetting to be told what to do?

PT: I really have no idea, besides the fact that I like to be independent like I said and it just feels that it's taking away my right to make decisions.

Commentary. Charles's problem with threats to his independence is quite clear. Other predictions are evaluated.

DR: Okay, Right now, at this University, do you have any friends here?

PT: When I came here, I knew not a soul and that's another reason I came here, because I didn't want to keep the same friends. All my graduating class went to State.

DR: Why?

PT: I didn't want to keep the same friends all my life, I just wanted to meet more people.

DR: Anyone here that you have become fairly close with?

PT: Some of the people.
DR: Guys?
PT: Guys and girls.
DR: Anyone you are really close with?
PT: Yes.

Commentary. This statement appears to contraindicate the initial clinical hypothesis; its validity is assessed.

DR: One, two, three?
PT: Two.
DR: What's their names? First names.
PT: Glen and Laura.
DR: Okay. Now, are you closer with Glen or are you closer with Laura?
PT: Depends on what you want to talk about.
DR: Okay, you're feeling inadequate. Can you talk to either one about that? Let's say you felt really inadequate.
PT: At what?
DR: At just life. You just feel like you are totally screwing up. That you're a failure, that you haven't done anything right.
PT: We usually can talk about a chem test or something like that.

Commentary. The degree of closeness seems consistent with the initial clinical hypothesis.

Subsequent questioning revealed that Charles was experiencing anxiety on tests in which he did not know the material well and in public speaking situations, because 'I don't have oratorical skills'; again, the possibility of appearing inept, weak or dependent.

DR: Okay. Other situations that make you nervous?
PT: I'm trying. Nothing stands out.
DR: Nothing else?
PT: (patient confirms)
DR: Attractive females?
PT: Make me nervous? They might, but I tend to cover it up.
DR: Now, do you have a girlfriend here?
PT: No, I just date different people.
DR: Do you date often?
PT: What do you consider often, not every night?
DR: Once a week?
PT: Probably
DR: Same girls or different?
PT: Same girl crowd.
DR: Now are these more or less friends?
PT: Just friends.
DR: Nobody you have any kind of love relationship with?
PT: No.
DR: Okay. By the way, are you religious in any way?
PT: Yes.
DR: What is your religion?
PT: Bapt: ist.
DR: Very religious?
PT: What do you mean by very religious?
DR: Strong religious feelings?
PT: Yes.
DR: In high school, did you have a girlfriend?
PT: For a while.
DR: How long was that?
PT: A year.
DR: What was the relationship like?
PT: Awkward.
DR: How do you mean?
PT: I was Baptist, she was Catholic.

DR: So what was awkward about it?

PT: Besides the fact that my mother was a daughter of a Baptist preacher and she doesn't seem to see eye to eye with any Catholic. I call her prejudiced, she doesn't like it, but she is.

DR: Any girl that you've ever been in love with?

PT: I suppose. I mean for a while you go head over heels for somebody and then you realize, hey I don't want any part of it.

DR: Who comes to mind when I say that, 'a girl you loved'?

PT: I suppose my first love when I was an eighth grader or whatever.

DR: And what happened?

PT: She was a junior.

DR: She was a junior in high school.

PT: Right.

DR: So you had a crush on her?

PT: Right.

DR: And that wasn't going to work out?

PT: No.

DR: Did she look at you as a boyfriend?

PT: Oh, no.

DR: What did she look at you as?

PT: I guess as a little pet or play toy.

DR: Did she ever get any idea that you were in love with her?

PT: I don't know.

DR: When you say love, what do you mean by that?

PT: Somebody that I can respect and have a good time with. Just doesn't try to pressure me to do anything.

Commentary. Several predictions seem confirmed. Of particular interest is the patient's definition of love, which contains the clause, '…doesn't try to pressure me to do anything'.

Towards the end of the initial interview, it was explained to Charles that it appeared he had problems worthy of treatment, which were discussed generally in this meeting. The mechanics of setting up future appointments were discussed. The meeting ended as follows:

DR: Any other questions or comments before we split up for now? You've got stuff to think about.

PT: I don't know if I will or not, that's the thing.

DR: I don't know if you will either. I suspect you will.

Discussion

The earlier excerpts from the initial interview with a complex clinical case highlight the approach to and implications of developing an initial clinical hypothesis. As can be seen, careful observation and consideration of even extremely limited clinical information enable an initial hypothesis to be constructed. The hypothesis guides later questioning in the interview. If eventually shown to be valid, it will have direct implications for treatment. If shown to be incorrect, it will force the clinician to search for a more useful hypothesis. Thus, in many respects, the viability of an initial hypothesis is secondary to the importance of developing one. Of course, the earlier on one can find a useful hypothesis, the more productive the interview will be.

Teaching students how to develop initial hypotheses is an important priority for supervisors in behaviour therapy. One of my favourite exercises in so doing is to play a videotape of an initial interview for no more than 1 min and then have the student describe exhaustively all that has been observed. Considerable prompting is often necessary, as students miss much information. After several replays, almost all the presenting data can be written on a blackboard. At that point, having the student attempt to construct an initial hypothesis is undertaken. He or she 'tests' it by seeing if the hypothesis accounts for all the data or not. If it does not, it is abandoned. If it does, the student is promoted to make several predictions, based on the presumed validity of the hypothesis. At this point, the videotape is turned on, and the remainder of the interview is observed. If the student has made accurate predictions, a powerful lesson has been learned.

References

Meyer, V., & Turkat I. D. (1979). Behavioral analysis of clinical cases. *Journal of Behavioural Assessment,* *1*, 259–270.

Turkat, I. D. (1986). The behavioral interview. In A. R. Ciminero, K. S. Calhoun, & H. E. Adams (Eds.), *Handbook of behavioral assessment* (2nd ed.). New York: John Wiley & Sons.

Wolpe, J. (1982). *The practice of behavior therapy* (3rd ed.). New York: Pergamon Press.

Wolpe, J. (1986). Individualization: The categorical imperative of behavior therapy practice. *Journal of Behavior Therapy and Experimental Psychiatry, 17,* 145–153.

Wolpe, J., & Turkat, I. D. (1985). Behavioral formulation of clinical cases. In I. D. Turkat (Ed.), *Behavioral case formulation.* New York: Plenum.

Index

Beyond Diagnosis: Case Formulation in Cognitive Behavioural Therapy, Second Edition.
Edited by Michael Bruch.
© 2015 John Wiley & Sons, Ltd. Published 2015 by John Wiley & Sons, Ltd.